The Education of the
MEXICAN NATION

The Education of the

MEXICAN NATION

George F. Kneller

OCTAGON BOOKS

A DIVISION OF FARRAR, STRAUS AND GIROUX

New York   1973

Reprinted 1973
by special arrangement with Columbia University Press

OCTAGON BOOKS
A DIVISION OF FARRAR, STRAUS & GIROUX, INC.
19 Union Square West
New York, N. Y. 10003

Library of Congress Cataloging in Publication Data

Kneller, George Frederick.
    The education of the Mexican nation.

        Bibliography: p.
        1. Education—Mexico.   I. Title.
LA422.K6   1973   370'.972   73-1817
ISBN 0-374-94595-0

Printed in USA by
Thomson-Shore, Inc.
Dexter, Michigan

To

MRS. EARL C. PADGETT

in deepest appreciation

Preface

THIS VOLUME is the outgrowth of investigations covering a period of six years, during which time the author made several trips to Mexico for a total of more than eighteen months. On two of these occasions he conducted thirty graduate students, teachers, and specialists on educational trips, traversing five thousand miles of varied terrain. More than one hundred schools and cultural institutions were visited, and innumerable conferences were held with educational officials and others.

The entire manuscript was read and criticized by Dr. Cameron Duncan Ebaugh, senior specialist, American Republics Section, U. S. Office of Education, Washington, D. C., and Professors Ernest J. Hall and Francisco L. Gaona, of Yale University, all of whom brought to the investigation a lifetime of experience in the field. The work also benefited from the critical appraisal and helpful suggestions of Dr. Pablo Martínez del Río, professor of history and anthropology at the National Autonomous University of Mexico, Señora Paula Vela de Mallén, instructor in the secondary schools and the National Preparatory School, Mexico City, Jorge Espino Vela, M.D., Mexico City, and the Reverend Miguel Bernad, S.J. The editorial and proofreading labors of John Derby, Arthur Dowd, and Ormonde de Kay, Jr., sympathetically rendered, materially helped to clarify the phraseology and expression. Worthy of especial mention is the loyal and talented service of Miss Patricia Lock, who assisted greatly in the areas of research and organization.

Grateful acknowledgment is made to these persons and to many other individuals and agencies in Mexico, public and private, for their services generously given.

GEORGE F. KNELLER

Yale University
New Haven, Conn.
April, 1950

Contents

Tables

Charts

I. The Land and the People

We are certain that the only culture that can survive is one which springs, without deformation, from the roots of our own community.—Jaime Torres Bodet, Minister of Education, 1944; Director General of UNESCO, 1949–.

We possess a culture to defend, partly acquired from the West, partly inherited from our worthy native tradition, partly constructed by ourselves; we have constitutional standards and laws achieved through the effort and suffering of our people; and all this will be the most precious heritage of our children.—Manuel Gual Vidal, Minister of Education, 1947.

THE MEXICO of popular literature is a fable and a dream; the real Mexico is obscured by sentimental descriptions of its beauty or by biased, irresponsible censure. From the first glowing prospectuses submitted by Columbus and Cortés to the royalty of Spain, one exaggeration has been heaped on another to produce a fictitious national existence derived chiefly from the mind of the writer. Even reports based on first-hand experience have not cleared away the accumulation of false beliefs; instead, they have inspired superficial travel tales that ignore the vital problems of a nation alive and at work. Popular interpreters of Mexico indulge in descriptions of the people as poetic, picturesque, paradoxical, chaotic, anachronistic, and (most hackneyed of all) of the country as "the land of contrast." These writers have given way to lush hyperbole about curious exoticisms, inebriate celebrations, and eerie events which occur only infrequently and are not part of the country's daily life. Manuel Gamio, world-famous anthropologist, suggests that these accounts are usually of the made-to-order type, "for which writers are well paid." He adds: "Much American ignorance is to be blamed on deliberately biased and malicious press reports, emitted by unconditional and persistent enemies of Mexico. . . . On the other hand, friends of the country . . . write of Mexico as a veritable promised land, a paradise . . . and of Mexicans as simple, amiable creatures."[1] The reader is left with the impression that the average Mexican devotes his entire life to siestas and fiestas and passes his time in a round of colorful, carefree pageantry for the delectation of the tourist. Features such as these exist, of course, but they are not characteristic of the hard reality of Mexican life.

On a more serious level, students are given distorted or one-sided impressions of Mexico's tradition. Mexico has its tradition, to be sure, but the problems of its people are anthropological, sociological, and psychological rather than purely philosophic or aesthetic. Even so accomplished a study as F. S. C. Northrop's recent *The Meeting of East and West* assumes that Mexican life is determined mostly by philosophy and aesthetics. Nowhere does Northrop mention mass psychological upsurge or refer to the indomitable influence exerted by native peoples. Instead, he ascribes the "vital contemporary development" in Mexican culture to "aesthetic intuition," "mystical passion," "anti-positivism," "Thomism," and, most puzzling of all, to a "rebirth of interest in Mexico's philosophy and literary tradition as it is rooted in European forms." Neglecting such basic factors as poor soil, inadequate resources, and the natural handicaps to transportation, too many observers conclude that the Mexicans must be incurably lazy or incorrigibly stupid not to exploit the riches which legend places at their feet.

There is yet another deeper source of misunderstanding. Foreign commentators frequently misinterpret facts by judging them from an alien point of view. Referring specifically to education, George Sánchez sagely warns against assessing Mexican achievement in terms of values obtaining in the United States: "Some of the cultural factors which influenced education in the United States were not operative in Mexico . . . still other factors varied in significance in the two settings."[2] Notwithstanding pressure from foreign

---

[1] Gamio, "The United States and Mexico," in *Aspects of Mexican Civilization*, p. 157.

[2] Sánchez, *The Development of Higher Education in Mexico*, pp. 1-2: "What is often overlooked is that the process also involved a fundamental reorienting of the European pattern. It changed the Indian but not without altering the Spaniard."

capitals, Mexico has evolved her own peculiar ethos and lives her own life. An interpretation of Mexican life and behavior is unsound if it restricts itself to alien influences without stressing what happened when these influences came into contact with the Mexican way of life.

Mexico's problems are little different from those which in reputedly more advanced nations still cry out for solution: health, sanitation, low standards of living, class consciousness, inflation, shady politics, mass inertia, and a host of others. Her sons and daughters cherish the same aspirations, the same desire for a place in the sun as do the peoples of other lands. Illiterate many Mexicans may be, but they are no longer inarticulate; and they combat their illiteracy with a zeal as yet not fully appreciated abroad. They love beauty and art and excel in these fields, but they do not expect to live by them. Their institutions of learning foster pure scholarship in the traditional manner, but that is becoming less and less their major concern.

Today, Mexico's common people seek greater participation in the management of their country and of their personal lives. This mass movement, characteristic mostly of the last decade or two, is revolutionizing the country in more than the political sense. Its effects penetrate all phases of national life and are a major cause for concern to the classes that have enjoyed a monopoly of privilege. Everywhere in the country there is repudiation of the wretched lot that has been the Indian's inheritance; Mexicans are resolved that the younger generation shall not suffer as much deprivation as did their parents. Resentful of abuse from exploiting overlords, who have too often betrayed and frustrated them, Mexico's peoples are driving toward fuller individual recognition and more active citizenship.

"SCHOOLS, LAND, WATER!"

The first obstacle to human enterprise in Mexico is topography itself. Mother Nature, lavish in the matter of initial boons, perversely renders the development of potential resources very difficult.—Manuel Gamio.

The United States, with its level, rich soil, all about the same for cultivating purposes from New England to Georgia and to the Middle West; a land open to the flow of civilization; the tool fit for one place, being simply moved along in increased rate of production. Compare that with Mexico where the climate and the soil and the kind of tillage change from north to south, from east to west, and within only a few miles around any given spot.
—José Vasconcelos, Minister of Education, 1926.

Always the same disproportion between production and consumption . . . when drought kills the crops, the peon hears the same thing everywhere— there is no work.—Gregorio López y Fuentes *(El Indio).*

A general survey of Mexico's physical resources leaves one conscious of the heavy weight of age and neglect: huge areas of parched land are untouched and useless, springing to life only after a drenching rain. Mexico is a rugged, untamed, hauntingly picturesque panorama of lilac-hued mountain clusters, interspersed with awesome, breath-taking ravines and escarpments. Its topography is characteristic of Central America, where climate is affected more by elevation than by latitude. Perennial snow covers Mexico's towering peaks and volcanoes; below lie valleys lush with tropical vegetation. Detrimentally scant in some regions, rainfall is overabundant in others. To the north, vast desert lands, hot and dry, like the coastlands and the tapering territory to the south, exhibit all the characteristics of the torrid zone. In contrast, the Central Plateau, with an average elevation of five to eight thousand feet, provides the delightfully springlike weather that is especially attractive to tourists. There are but two seasons: the rainy, from June to October, and the dry.[3]

Such topographical and climatic peculiarities hamper communication and transportation. In vain visiting scientists and engineers have sought to recreate for Mexico what in their own country has been so easy of achievement. Mexico's topography has also tended to retard the rate of social progress, which to the undiscerning appears inexcusably slow. Before the building of the Pan-American highway, for example, many neighboring communities were literally isolated from one another except for limited and expensive

[3] Recommended as a good general treatment on Mexico is *The Annals of the American Academy of Political and Social Sciences* (Philadelphia), CCVIII (March, 1940).

boat service. Yet, as Stuart Chase has observed, topographical complexities have saved Mexico from becoming too soon westernized, mechanized, Americanized—in short, have preserved her national character. A solution to one of Mexico's problems is found in her present rapid progress in air transportation, which recent visitors have commended in terms most pleasant to Mexican ears. Climate may vary widely over the broad topography of Mexico, but in any given place it is relatively stable and predictable, a factor of considerable importance for the field of education. Schools are not subject to the fuel shortages, the bady ventilated classrooms, and the thermostatic changes encountered in more violent climates. Open-air classes abound in every school area. Outdoor swimming pools, play fields, and courts employ to great advantage the healing qualities of a vigorous sun in building and preserving the health of children. In addition, Mexico's scenic countryside, visible through school windows, makes commonplace the wall decorations and pictures found in most of the world's classrooms.

In the past century Mexico suffered severe territorial losses. Spanish occupation and exploration in the sixteenth and seventeenth centuries had incorporated sufficient regions to the north to create a Mexico twice her present size; but as a result of hostilities with the United States in 1836 and 1847, Mexico was forced to yield territory now forming the states of Texas, California, New Mexico, Arizona, Colorado, Utah, Nevada, and part of Wyoming. Today, with an area of 763,994 square miles, Mexico is about one-fourth as large as the United States. Of the other American republics, only Brazil and Argentina are larger.

The land left to Mexico is comparatively deficient in agricultural productivity. Millions of acres of virgin soil remain untouched, so undependable is the yield; while millions more, worked by antiquated machinery and methods, bring forth scant returns. Only one-fourth of the country is profitably farmed, and only one-fifth of the cultivable land is irrigated. A primary cause for concern is the low production of corn, Mexico's chief food. To date, the annual yield amounts to no more than one-sixth that of the average crop of Iowa; consequently, unreasonably large quantities of this staple have to be imported. The high price of corn tortillas (pancakes) is daily street-corner talk, the implications of which seldom bode good for those who choose to exploit the land in disregard of national need.

To meet the deficiency in arable land, agrarian reforms have sought to transfer farm properties from commercial users to subsistence farmers. In the nineteenth century, official recognition of the people's desire for land took the form of Colonization Laws (1823) enacted to move marginal populations to uninhabited regions. Later, the Abolition of Entails (1856) forcibly removed vast tracts of arable land from control of the Catholic church. But individual ownership only complicated matters by destroying the customary communal organization of Indian villages.

The Mexican Revolution again brought land distribution to the fore, and in 1917 the national government assumed unprecedented constitutional power over agrarian organization. Under Article 27 of the Constitution, the state now has the right to intervene in the distribution of all public wealth, especially land. Communities maintain the right to appropriate land needed for their subsistence, even if it has to be taken from large private properties. "In every case," states the law, "the small holding, which is considered a useful institution of the country, will be respected."

During the Cárdenas Administration (1934-39), nearly twice as much land was redistributed as had been during the preceding two decades following the Constitution of 1917. By 1941 fifty million acres of government-confiscated properties had been parceled out to a million and a half families under the *ejido* system—a method of holding a unit of land in common, the title being retained by the state in behalf of the community, and the peasants paying "rent" out of their crops.

But Avila Camacho's government (1940-46) saw little hope for agrarian progress except through individual enterprise, so that in 1941 he awarded thousands of small farms outright to deserving peasants. Even this generous gesture failed to produce the expected returns. Critics of the program emphasized that the *ejido* system was rooted in Indian tradition; they maintained that collective development of the *ejido* was the only way to assure adequate crops, since it allowed the tenant to use community machinery and tools and thus introduced great savings in production.

Under these circumstances agricultural education has been hard pressed not only to make up for inadequate resources but also to carry on amid confused organization, wide-spread apathy, the depressed initiative of rural inhabitants, and the impact of controversial social reforms. Educators have attempted to give training in the best use of land by systematic instruction in modern techniques, wise management, and the most skillful employment of available resources.[4]

Rich oil and metal deposits, many of which have not yet been tapped, are conducive to profitable effort in mining. Forty percent of the world's annual supply of silver is produced in Mexico, and gold to the annual value of thirty million dollars. The petroleum output, nationally administered following governmental expropriation from foreigners in 1938, is now sufficient for export purposes. The fact that many mines are foreign-sponsored has aroused considerable criticism, but Mexican capital has been unenterprising and hesitant, so that consistent development has been possible only by relying on foreign money and foreign technicians. As a result of war needs, large scale experiments in the cultivation of rubber were initiated under the sponsorship and technical supervision of the United States.

About 85 percent of Mexico's export-import trade is with the United States. The consequent economic dependence offends supporters of national self-sufficiency, who dislike subjecting their business life to the mercurial changes of their northern neighbor. But American financial aid has been indispensable in furthering

[4] Torres Bodet, *Educación mexicana*, p. 31. Sánchez, "Education," *Annals of the American Academy of Political and Social Sciences*, CCVIII (March, 1940), 145: ". . . this identification of land and its problems with Mexican culture must be recognized as an important factor in the development of the Mexican social philosophy of education." Bishop Francis C. Kelley is gloomy about prospects of ever improving the situation, since "the root of the Mexican land trouble lies deep in the soul of the Indian man. . . . He will not leave home alone. Either hunger must drive him or home conditions must be reproduced elsewhere for him. It is questionable if he would accept ownership at the price of breaking the bond that binds him to his *compadres*."—*Blood-drenched Altars*, p. 355.

agricultural, industrial, and commercial enterprise and in the construction of much-needed public works.

Mexico remains a rural country. Only five cities boast a population of more than 100,000, and less than one-third of the people live in urban centers. The largest city is the capital, Mexico City, with slightly more than two million inhabitants. No other municipality approaches it in size. Guadalajara is second, with approximately 300,000, followed by Monterrey (275,000), and Puebla (180,000).

Manufacturing plays a minor role in Mexican economy, due chiefly to the lack of iron, coal, and power resources. Emphasis, therefore, has to be placed on schools for an essentially rural rather than industrial nation.

Indian community life and farming still form the backbone of the country's economy. Traditional Indian handicraft in pottery, ceramics, weaving, and leather work, industriously brought to town on the steady heads and strong backs of the natives, or by the indispensable ubiquitous burro, color the market places of the smallest community. Contemporary Mexican rural life is a precious world apart; a living museum of pre-Cortesian Mexico; a history-laden treasure. This treasure school programs aim to protect and preserve.

PATTERNS OF CULTURE

In order to understand many of the most serious problems of our nation, one must realize that Mexico has been the crucible in which two races and two cultures have been fused, and that from this fusion a new element has come into being: something that is Mexican, a personal something which did not exist in the world and which gradually has taken on substance.—Alfonso Caso, Director, National Institute of Anthropology and History.

Independent and even conflicting manners of culture have developed in our land and sometimes have become enrooted in it; but suddenly they are driven away, or they disappear through decay, before they are able to evolve into a higher civilization.—Manuel Gamio.

Education is a means for preserving the cultural treasures of a community, and a really productive educational doctrine cannot be engendered if it is not supported by the peculiarities of the society in which it actuates, and which it wishes to serve and improve.—Octavio Véjar Vázquez, Minister of Education, 1942.

Mexico's cultural origins date back to a period of two hundred years before the Christian era. For centuries previous to the Spanish conquest, the numerous tribes of both valley and high plateau (Toltec, Mixtec, Zapotec, Tarasca, Maya, Aztec and others) struggled for supremacy. Each tribe, notably different from its neighbors in both outlook and accomplishment, succeeded for a time in occupying a dominant position and imposing its customs on the others.[5]

The history of pre-Hispanic Mexico is largely that of the Aztec tribal groups, "crafty barbarians from the North," who, some three hundred years before the arrival of the Spaniards, descended on what is now termed the Central Plateau of Mexico. Given to violent customs, yet preaching humility; temperate and abstinent, yet endowed with a bloody faith; they enslaved their enemies and sacrificed their hearts on the hungry altar of their god of war. The existing Toltec Empire was crushed and the Aztecs in turn attained a comparatively advanced, though controversial, form of culture.[6]

By the time of the Spanish conquest, the Aztecs, despite the lack of a written language, had progressed surprisingly. Their arts and

[5] The most complete modern account of Mexico's cultures is Basauri's *La población indígena de México.* See also Spinden, *Ancient Civilizations of Middle and Central America,* pp. 35, 99, 130-40; and Redfield, *The Folk Culture of Yucatán.* The most recent treatments of the Mayas are Morley, *The Ancient Maya,* and Hagen, *Maya Explorer.* López y Fuentes, in his *El Indio,* pp. 80-81, presents an amusingly biased though illuminating contrast: "What is there in common between the Otomí, who struggle against the cold, drinking pulque, and sleeping in ashes, who live in sheds roofed with maguey waste and eat reptiles and bugs, and the Totonac, of clean customs and brilliant past? What affinity do you find between the taciturn Tepehua and the pig-headed, quarrelsome Huicholo? The inhabitants of this very region, descended from a strong branch, the Nahoa, do they even know the name of the *ranchería,* inhabited by others like themselves on the other side of the sierra?" *Cf.* Larroyo, *Historia comparada de la educación en México,* pp. 44-49.

[6] Burbank, *Mexican Frieze:* "The Indian warriors were trained not to kill, but to take prisoners, so that sacrifice took the place of slaughter in war." *Cf.* Vaillant, *The Aztecs of Mexico,* a heavily documented monograph. Marian Wilcox, article in the *Americana,* II, 691-92, is more cautious than most commentators in her appraisal of Aztec cultural accomplishment, calling it a "mixture of lowest barbarism and the beginnings of civilization." The universally recognized authority is Alfonso Caso, who gives a balanced estimate in "The Indigenous Cultures of Central Mexico," in *Mexico's Role in International Intellectual Cooperation,* pp. 6-7.

crafts were highly developed and stamped with a unique character which persists in the work of modern Mexican artists and artisans. Their economy was of the collective, communal type, in that the land was ruled by the tribe and the craftsmen were organized into guilds. Barter constituted the chief medium of trade; the cacao bean was the only fixed form of currency. Government was of the loose, city-state order; each tribe maintained its own identity, but paid tribute to Tenochtitlán, the capital city (now Mexico City). The Aztecs demonstrated a considerable understanding of child development. Natural inclination was respected, and training was adjusted to the various age levels. Education in the crafts was mandatory. The program was rigid; the method, perceptive; the content, rich in ceremonials and folklore. Only the noble and military classes were educated in actual school buildings; for the rest of the population education was entirely a family affair.[7]

Like present-day Aztecs, the other surviving Indian tribes preserve intact their ceremonials and their attitude toward the crafts. In Yucatán experiments are under way to provide types of education most appropriate for the Maya-speaking population. A model village has been erected in the forested hinterland, in which instruction in Maya folkways and traditions is actually prerequisite to a study of the ways of Western civilization.[8] Another outgrowth of this cultural movement was the creation in 1933 of the Institute of Linguistic Research, which carries on investigations in all fields of indigenous life and supports regional academies for the study of the Nahua, Otomí, Tarasca, and Maya languages.

Education in Mexico is thus becoming Indian-conscious. Mexi-

    [7] John Jesse Dossick: "Education among the Ancient Aztecs," MS, terms Aztec education "religious authoritarianism": ". . . the influence of the priesthood was undoubtedly considerable. It was . . . within their power to mold the minds of the future leaders and followers of each successive generation." Cf. *Estudio acerca de la educación fundamental en México*, Mexico, Ministry of Education, Mexico City, 1947, pp. 18-20. See also Sahagún (16th century Franciscan), *History of Ancient Mexico*, pp. 168 ff. An account of youth education commences pp. 196 ff.

    [8] Redfield, "The Indian in Mexico," *Annals of the American Academy of Political and Social Sciences*, CCVIII (March 1940), 136-40. On the Mayas Francisco Larroyo has this to say: "Maya social institutions did not emphasize war as did the Aztec. Thus the Mayas were intelligent, astute and keen; generous, polite, and hospitable. . . . The life of the Maya was subject to three ends: service to people, religion, and family. . . . The love of work, a sense of honor, sexual continence and a mutual respect were to be the fundamental qualities of man's relationship with woman."—*Historia comparada de la educación en México*, pp. 49, 58-59.

cans have finally learned that though in time Indian customs will inevitably succumb to new influences and their languages become defunct for practical purposes, the country's first inhabitants, the Indians, reflect the uniqueness and originality of the terrain. Like it or not, Indian populations are as enduring as their volcanoes. The renaissance of the Indian soul, the exaltation of the Indian's finer characteristics, and a quickening response to his arts must inevitably constitute the marrow of educational plans and progress.

As with all intrusive cultures, Spanish influence, in particular that of the church, proved beneficial in some ways and injurious in others. Never before had history witnessed the fusing on so grand a scale of two peoples as diverse in character as the Indians and the Spaniards. The accomplishment of the church fathers in effecting this fusion is for many commentators nothing short of a miracle. Irma Wilson aptly conceives it as "an epic of intrepid spirits who labored to realize their part of the program of the Spanish crown, and absorb those peoples within the fold of the Church." Theirs was a "transcendental achievement."[9] The conservative Mexican literary historian Carlos González Peña agrees that not only the program but also the men who carried it out were exceptional: "They combined the ideal of poverty with a kindliness that won the confidence and affection of the conquered; perseverance, with a culture that enabled them to be both apostles and teachers; heroism, with spiritual and physical vigor."[10] With greater assurance, Francis Borgia Steck, writing from the Catholic University of America, asserts that Spain desired to create a "strong, economically progressive and prosperous, morally sound and high-minded citizenry." He offers as proof the education of Indians "on an equal footing with the immigrants from Spain and with the creoles and mestizos born in the colonies." The fact that the church assumed control over educational and cultural development was nothing particularly new or impressive, since the church, "trusted and supported by the civil government, was called upon to direct affairs in the New as well as the Old World."[11]

[9] Irma Wilson, *Mexico; a Century of Educational Thought*, p. 15.
[10] González Peña, *History of Mexican Literature*, p. 4.
[11] Steck, *Education in Spanish North America during the Sixteenth Century*, p. 1. Steck summons others to his defense, among whom are historians Herbert Priestley and Charles Lummis.

Spain's attitude is presented by Epifanio González Jiménez, who in the title of his book purports to reveal "the truth" about Spain in America. Accusing the Indians of being "lazy," "indolent," and in general an "intractable, worthless lot," he bestows high praise on his native land for carrying the torch of civilization to the dark and dangerous recesses of a barbarous country.[12] A similar position is taken by Bishop Francis Clement Kelley, who, though more benevolent toward the Indian, writes with ardent conviction that "Spain's success in Mexico and South America is one of the greatest wonders of history." He claims that it was not Spain but Mexico that failed: "The Spaniard left a civilization. It is the Mexican who is destroying it." For Kelley the opening of the New World by Spain was actually "nothing short of a second creation."[13] Wilfred Parsons, S.J., likewise laments the end of Spanish control: "When Spain left Mexico, it left behind a great culture and what we mean by civilization that was as great as any country will have to show. . . . We still have a long way to go before we will have created all the beauty that was, and is, Mexico's." In fact, adds Father Parsons, it is wrong to consider Mexico before 1800 a colony of Spain; it was simply "a New Spain . . . with all the culture and tradition that that implied . . . even the Inquisition was there . . . for the purpose of protecting the Indian against the rapacity and exploiting tendencies of the Spanish merchants. Polemic writers deny that, but historians have proved it."[14]

Other commentators are of a different mind. Alfonso Caso, for example, renowned anthropologist and Minister of Public Properties, draws on evidence produced by recent excavations. In their zeal to impose a new religion, a new language, new social forms, destruction, says Caso, was not enough; Indian arts were actually forbidden by the Spaniards for many generations:

[12] González Jiménez, *La verdad de España en América*, pp. 27-28 ff. A fellow countryman, Fernando de los Ríos, former ambassador to the United States and professor of law at the University of Madrid, writes fervently of Spain's liberal gifts to the New World in "Action of Spain in America," in *Concerning Latin American Culture*, p. 72 especially.

[13] Kelley, *Blood-drenched Altars*, pp. 14, 19. In any case, asserts Kelley, "if there were bad priests in Mexico, their case must be held for a Judgment higher than man can give."

[14] Wilfred Parsons, *Mexican Martyrdom*, pp. 3, 115.

The conquest destroyed the nobility and the indigenous priesthood, and these two classes of society were the custodians of the science, history, tradition and philosophy of aboriginal culture. Nothing remained of the artistic manifestations which amazed the conquerors: architecture, sculpture, gold and silver work, and the rare art of feather mosaics. They were entirely extirpated, or languished, until they disappeared in the Colonial period.

J. H. Plenn, clinching the argument, apostrophizes: "Souls and land were conquered simultaneously."[15]

The Spaniard did not, however, succeed in totally uprooting indigenous cultures and substituting his own. As Frances Toor, professor of folklore at the National University, has so wisely stated, "The Indian does not imitate; he transforms." The invader succeeded best when he learned the ways of the Indian and sought modification rather than annihilation. There was much to be learned, so the Spaniard finally realized, from his red brother; and much to acquire in material goods. Alfonso Caso reminds us that without Indian gold Spain would not in all probability have entertained ideas of world conquest. "Ransom, plunder and tribute created a veritable river of gold and silver which continued its metallic flow to Spain."

Less stressed, though of equal importance, has been the Indian attitude toward the invader. Perplexed and amused at first by the white man's greed for ornaments and worldly possessions, the native soon became disdainful of it and considered outrageous the Spaniard's habit of measuring even spiritual acquisitions on a scale of material values.[16] Manuel Barranco comments: "The poor Indians were astonished to see these 'sons of the Sun' go insane in their desire for the yellow metal, to them unimportant."[17] But the red man's resistance was weak; for generous gifts of livestock, tools, beasts of burden, and other items to make life more comfortable were only too gratefully received.

[15] Caso, "What Has the American Indian Contributed to World Economy?" *Butrava*, February, 1942, p. 1. Plenn, *Mexico Marches*, p. 194.

[16] James, "Spanish American Literature and Art," in *Concerning Latin American Culture*, p. 196. Mrs. James, of the Pan American Union, succinctly observes that while the Church was officially subservient to the conquistadores, "the bearers of the cross devoted themselves to the more fundamental aspects of a true conquest."

[17] Barranco, *Mexico: Its Educational Problems*, p. 4.

Then, too, the Indians had been conditioned to the role of a conquered nation. From earliest times they had been trained to worship the gods of their conquerors, so that it was not difficult for Spanish missionaries to substitute the Christian God for the long list of deities already found in the Indian's religious ritual. Wisely, though not without constraint, the colonial clergy adapted European religious observances to the pattern of tribal pagan feasts and divine celebrations. Saints replaced pagan gods. Our Lady of Guadalupe, whose shrine is so well known nowadays to Mexico's visitors, ascended the throne of Tepantzin, mother of all heathen gods: and December twelfth became the Virgin's feast day, coincident with the annual pagan harvest celebration.

An assessment of Spanish influence is outside the province of this work, except as that influence is a part of educational history. The issue has been subject to considerable argument, colored in recent times by socialistic thinking and antireligious sentiment.[18] It is clear, however, that the weight of Spanish power thrust the Indian into a subordinate social, economic, and cultural position from which he has not yet completely emerged. The Spanish occupation of Mexico up to 1821 was characterized by exploitation of the native population, by the spread of Spanish culture in the New World, and by the sincere determination of the Catholic church to convert the Indians. Obviously, Mexico could not have remained "undiscovered" by Europeans, and their influence brought a remote civilization into the fold of general world progress. José

---

[18] An academic estimate is available in Ricard's *La "Conquête spirituelle" du Mexique.* This doctoral dissertation of formidable proportions doubts that the invasion was really a "spiritual conquest" and tends to stress the difficulties of the church in New Spain rather than to evaluate critically its activities in the light of four hundred years of human progress. In his conclusions (p. 317) Ricard submits that despite "extremely rigorous" methods employed by the church, the Indians renounced their idols only *"en apparence"*; they continued at night and in secret to worship their gods and to offer sacrifices to them when they had only recently been converted to the Catholic faith. A rare and illuminating appraisal of Spanish culture is provided by Gamio, "Incorporating the Indian," in *Aspects of Mexican Civilization*, pp. 106-7: "Spain did not have, and could not have, the qualities of a colonizing nation . . . a fundamental cause today of the deficient development of Indo-Hispanic peoples. The Spanish people did not exist at the time, either nationally or sociologically, for the inhabitants of the Iberian peninsula were not held together by racial, linguistic, or traditional bonds." Gamio contends that Spain needed nationalization—national identification.

Manuel Puig Casauranc, Minister of Education under President Calles (1926), reminds us in any case that Indian servitude did not begin with the Spanish invasion: "The weight of oppression was thousands of years old."[19]

Mexican official educational programs accept the Spanish invasion (and indeed all "foreign" invasions) as an accomplished fact and endeavor to repair the damage that was done to the good in Indian cultural forms. The Division of Anthropology of the Ministry of Education remains as aloof from the argument as possible and busies itself with unearthing what is endemically Mexican and contributing to the cultural foundations of a unified Mexico.

Mexican civilization today is, therefore, a fusion of many and varied Indian types; it is a composite, as yet by no means fully developed, of the relatively low cultures of isolated groups which have been pocketed for centuries in inaccessible localities. To this has been added contributions from Spain, France, and, more recently, North America. Mexico must be understood, not as a single integrated culture, but as a combination of relatively distinct cultures, each opposing considerable inertia to fervent movements for national unity. Upon this precarious foundation Mexico's education must be built, utilizing to the fullest the diverse and varied materials that contribute to the fabric of her many native cultures.

NATIONAL MAKE-UP AND CHARACTER

The symbolic aspect of Mexican territory seems to be reflected in its people, whose lives parallel the conflict of mountains, the protest of fiery volcanoes,

[19] Quoted in Larroyo, *Historia comparada de la educación en México*, p. 302. Note, however, Miguel Covarrubias' wise words of caution on assuming that native populations would not have progressed of their own accord: "It is easy to imagine the levels of culture that these most civilized of ancient Americans might have reached if they had been allowed to retain their traditions, art, and philosophy; perhaps a civilization comparable to that of China might have continued to flourish in America."—*Mexico South: the Isthmus of Tehuantepec*, p. 404. An attempt at a synthesis is to be found in Silvio Zavala's capable "Síntesis de la historia del pueblo mexicano," in *México y la cultura;* see p. 9 especially. Fernando de los Ríos, in "Action of Spain in America," p. 77, brilliantly concludes: "Spain founded on this continent with a spiritual, introversive conception of culture a society in which the static and conservative forces prevailed over the dynamic social elements; yet it was a restless society . . . hungry for perfection . . . that had not yet found its own authentic way."

the sudden violent torrents which tear trees from their roots and destroy entire villages . . . A country of complicated social phenomena.—Manuel Gamio.

Now it must be a hard man indeed whose head and heart are not set afire when it is given to him to contemplate the squalor, the poverty, the abject physical and mental degradation of so many of our people, our infant mortality rate . . . almost unsurpassed in the whole world, our still uneducated workers besotting themselves in cheap drinking places, our still hungry peasants living in their wretched hovels in atrocious promiscuity with their animals, when they are lucky enough to possess them.—Pablo Martínez del Río, Dean, Faculty of Philosophy and Letters, University of Mexico, 1944.

The population of Mexico is now estimated to be about twenty-two million, or approximately one-sixth that of the United States. The only other American republic with a larger population is Brazil. At 43.3 per thousand, Mexico's birthrate is about twice as high as that of the United States. But her death rate offsets this; infant mortality figures are several times greater than those of her northern neighbor. In the last few years an average of 200,000 children per year, or about one-tenth of the total population, failed to reach their ninth birthday.

On distribution by race, it is difficult to get accurate data, since in making their national census in 1930 Mexican authorities were influenced by a prevailing desire to abandon classification by race. As the anthropologist Robert Redfield states, not only was counting full-blooded Indians a practical impossibility, but racial differences are no longer of first significance in Mexico: "The disposition is to think of one submerged class composed of Indians and mixed-bloods together."[20] The following figures were, however, recorded in the census of 1930: mestizos ("mixed blood"), 9,040,-590; "pure-blooded" Indians, 4,620,880; "pure" whites, 2,444,-466; foreigners, 160,000; unknown origin, 140,094.

By any standards the average Mexican is essentially Indian. The great majority of Mexico's population may fall into the mestizo,

[20] *Cf.* Basauri, "La población negroide mexicana," *Estadistica*, Mexico City, December, 1943, pp. 96-97. Barranco, *Mexico: Its Educational Problems*, p. 11, offers an amusing summary of the "rapid transition" of Indian into white, as conceived by those primarily interested in the social gradient: "Spaniard + Spaniard = criollo (white) ; Spaniard + Indian = mestizo; Spaniard + mestizo = castizo; Spaniard + castizo = criollo (also considered white)."

or mixed, group, but the mestizo is more characteristically Indian than white—in blood, in attitude, in way of life. More than one-quarter of Mexico's people are pure-blooded Indians; of these the Aztecs, numbering some two million, form the largest segment. But the pattern is intricate and reveals thirteen separate and distinct general linguistic groups, with about fifty ethnic groups and numerous subdivisions.[21] Some tribes are almost extinct. The Seris and the Lacandones, for example, each have only a few hundred survivors.

Spanish is the official language, but a million Mexicans do not speak it. In many rural communities, even close to the Capital, one hears native tongues almost exclusively. "Indian Mexico," consisting of one-third of the country's more rugged and mountainous terrain, harbors nine-tenths of the monolingual, Indian-speaking people, who are located chiefly in the southern states of Guerrero, Chiapas, and Oaxaca, the Yucatán peninsula, and the plateau country south to the Pacific and west to Michoacán. Here primitive customs persist, and life is most strongly localized, traditional, and colorful. "In Southern Mexico," writes Robert Redfield, who has spent much of his life with the Mexican Indians, "there are local markets where Indians meet who speak languages as different from one another as are English, Chinese, and Hebrew."

Mexico inherits two educational tasks of far greater scope and difficulty than exist in most countries, namely, to improve national health and raise the standard of literacy.

The health program is fraught with obstacles unsuspected by the ordinary observer. In the past the isolation of sick people was secured by geographical barriers. Today new roads and more efficient means of transportation have speeded up communications, only thereby to increase the spread of infectious diseases. Miguel Bustamente, Mexico's public health authority, observes that as a result the spread of communicable diseases among the rural population, who are not yet instructed in the prevention of them, over-balances the reduction of deaths secured by measures of control.

The School of Health and Hygiene of the Ministry of Public

[21] Véjar Vázquez, *Hacia una escuela de unidad nacional.* On the ethnic and anthropological side Manuel Gamio is best: *Hacia un México Nuevo,* pp. 142 ff.

Health leads the way in training the personnel and furnishing the means for combating disease. In 1947 the Ministry of Education initiated a program of monthly "Calendarios del Maestro," containing advice on hygienic and agricultural matters. Only one among scores of similar projects, including health displays and programs on the prevention of disease, the calendar represents a vital and productive co-operative effort of the ministries of education and public health, evidence of which is clearly visible in every Mexican community.

The literacy crusade in Mexico is the more complicated, because it involves the gradual elimination of many folkways which are opposed to educational progress and national unity. It is not always easy to convince the Indian that learning to read and write in Spanish is worth the effort he must put forth. Estimates of average illiteracy are conflicting, since the figures for districts differ greatly and depend on varying concepts of just what constitutes illiteracy. In the urban-settled Federal District there is an estimated illiteracy (1940) of about 20 percent, while in the far reaches of the Republic it is not impossible to find rural communities with totals of well above 90 percent. Official data of the Ministry of Education indicate that for the country as a whole 40 percent of people over ten years of age and 65 percent of those over six years of age must be judged illiterate.[22]

The first serious nation-wide attack on illiteracy occurred in 1938, with the initiation of a three-year program. A national office was established in the Ministry of Education, where a dozen teachers were in charge. The country was divided into zones, and literacy committees headed local campaigns. Other agencies taking part included a Children's Educational Army and a Youth Army, the latter enrolling normal school students and apprentice teachers. The organization was elaborate enough, and the movement had many sincere supporters, but like so many well-meaning Mexican experiments it failed for lack of co-ordination and follow-through. Guillermo Bonilla y Segura, chief of the Cultural Missions Department of the Ministry, is somewhat bitter in his official report:

[22] *La obra educativa en el sexenio, 1940-1946*, pp. 45-46.

"The limited collaboration of the states was always requested [of] and received from the governors as a favor. The same may be said concerning the participation of business." Bonilla laments that the only way in which Mexican commercial interests apparently can be induced to provide proper educational facilities for their workers is by legislation similar to that existing in such fields as medical services, accident compensation, and schools for workers' children.[23] There were other reasons, of course, for the program's limited degree of achievement, among them those two perennial Mexican obstacles: lack of funds and indifference on the part of so many in a position to help. What remained of these first efforts were turned over by the federal government to the Literacy Office of the Cultural Missions Department, while state governors haphazardly fathered the program in state educational institutions.

Finally, in 1944, by edict of President Avila Camacho a huge public campaign was launched amid typically colorful Mexican fanfare. Illiteracy was given only five years more to live. The Chief Executive commanded every literate Mexican out of loyalty to his country to teach at least one illiterate fellow-citizen how to read and write or to pay for his professional instruction. Officially called the "Emergency Law" ("Ley de Emergencia"), August 21, 1945, the wording of one of its provisions is sententious: "In a land where only half the citizens can read it becomes a privilege for those who cherish their duty to the state . . . to save the other half of their compatriots from the perils resulting from lack of elementary knowledge, and hence participation in social activity."

Though warmly supported, the latest campaign has been handicapped by the wide prevalence of monolinguality. The task, known of old to colonial teachers, still remains twofold: to teach the Indian to read and write in his own tongue, and then to use the acquired alphabet in learning Spanish. Yet progress to date has

[23] Bonilla y Segura, *Report on the Cultural Missions of Mexico*, pp. 38-40. Bonilla presents a worthwhile list of suggestions which educational authorities might well work out: a compulsory hour-a-day class in all employment centers, reading rooms, increased professional rating as a reward for teachers who teach thirty people to read and write, special primers and magazines to be published by the Ministry, and material contributions from business interests.

been encouraging. Out of an estimated eight million illiterates, one and one-half millions had been taught their letters by the end of the first two years of the program.[24]

The campaign against illiteracy is also meant to serve as a trial ground for extensive and ambitious extra-school programs, to be launched when the great majority of the people have become literate. These programs are expected to effect a greater cohesion among Mexicans and to put an end to the present deplorable schism between those who can and those who cannot read. In the telling words of Torres Bodet, the success of an illiteracy campaign is reciprocal: "If the lettered free the unlettered, how effectively will the unlettered in return free the lettered from their prejudices, superficiality of enjoyment, and material interest?"

Illiteracy, then, persists as an obstinate challenge to Mexican educators; and a solution to the problem, as Rafael Ramírez warns, lies not in specialized campaigns, or in armies, but in schools—in providing an elementary school education, at least, for all children.[25]

So much for extrinsic influences on education. What about the Mexican's intrinsic characteristics?

The extreme heterogeneity of cultural and ethnic development in Mexico makes a psychological portrait of the average Mexican, that is, the mestizo, as much of an abstraction as one of the average American; but it is important to obtain some overall picture. That Mexico is a land of mixed breeds is, of course, a reality which the country's education inevitably must face.

Mexicans are very much given to self-analysis and are ever ready to expound on their national character. Among the hundreds

[24] Specifically, the literacy program included thirty-two district committees working through 2,416 municipalities and 37,722 specially founded community centers. In the single year 1945-46 this heterogeneous organization distributed 7,614,109 readers and 8,000,000 copybooks. Human effort, measured in numbers of instructors and pupils, is equally impressive, although still somewhat short of actual need. The most recent treatments on illiteracy are to be found in *La educación fundamental, op. cit.*, pp. 88 ff.; and Larroyo, *Historia comparada de la educación en México*, pp. 400 ff.

[25] *Cf.* Rafael Ramírez, "Mexico," in *International Yearbook of Education*, p. 218. Military service is compulsory in Mexico, and the Ministry of National Defense must be given adequate credit for its conversion of thousands of illiterate draftees and recruits.

of available expositions, that of Véjar Vázquez is, perhaps, among the most useful for present purposes:

There is in the Mexican an exaggerated distrust of things, which provokes hypersensitivity and easy susceptibility, rendering him restless and concupiscent, bringing him to desire the more immediate ends of life, thus making him improvident. . . . We also discover in him a weak will which, not always able fully to control his movements, converts him into a passionate, aggressive, warlike individual. . . . He is too susceptible to the criticism of others and possesses an immoderate passion for slander and obloquy.[26]

Vasconcelos adds that the mestizo has

a great vivacity of mind, quickness of understanding, and at the same time an unsteady temperament; not too much persistence in purpose; a somewhat defective will.

But this fluidity has educational advantages:

From a purely intellectual point of view I doubt whether there is a race with less prejudice, more ready to take up almost any mental adventure, more subtle, or more varied than the mestizo, or half-breed.[27]

The gifted commentator Pablo Martínez del Río makes this observation:

Not unto us, indeed, the middle of the road, the golden mean, the Aristotelian sophrosyne. For good or for ill . . . we Mexicans have always been children of wrath, extremists.[28]

Observations such as these do not imply any intrinsic Mexican biologic deficiency, since hybridism may produce better as well as poorer types. A study of historic development, cultural tradition, and physical environment is therefore a necessary preliminary to genuine comprehension. Examining Mexican history, the anthropologist Manuel Gamio points out the inherited social bias against

[26] Véjar Vázquez, *Hacia una escuela de unidad nacional,* p. 91.

[27] Vasconcelos, "The Latin-American Basis of Mexican Civilization," in *Aspects of Mexican Civilization,* p. 92.

[28] Martínez del Río, "Mexican-American Relations," in *Mexico's Role in International Intellectual Cooperation,* p. 18. Further estimate is obtainable in Manuel Barranco, *Mexico: Its Educational Problems,* pp. 70-71. A professional psychologist, José Gómez Robleda, analyzes the interests of the contemporary Mexican in *Tiempo,* August 22, 1947, and grimly concludes that "the Mexican needs to be reformed. . . . He is too interested in the sexual and the neurotic."

mixing the breed: "In the nineteenth century, interbreeding was still considered (as it is today) an abnormal, unsocial thing. Its defective genesis supposedly resulted in a convergence of the bad in two races, not the good." That this false doctrine persists is explainable in many ways. In the first place, the mestizo got off to a bad start. The mating of his parents usually had few ethical, cultural, or social aspects; it was purely physical. The white father ultimately abandoned the mother, leaving her to bring up her half-breed child alone. Thrown back on the indigenous side of his origin, the child was forced to share in body and spirit the fate of the masses. The inevitable consequence was a struggle for personal, hence national, maturity set against a backdrop of racial discrimination in favor of the white race. The pure-blooded Indian was allowed this consolation: he could point with some pride to the inviolate purity of his ancestral strain, a comfort which was denied the half-breed progeny.

A third, more trenchant, explanation has already been suggested. Poverty, poor food, and lack of security produce a physiologically badly proportioned, psychologically deficient people. Véjar Vázquez may complain that the "inherent" lack of physical beauty in the Mexican is one of the factors which aggravates a national inferiority complex; but it is the *causes* of this lack of physical beauty that need to be remedied. When he laments that the Mexican "lacks a proportionate sense of values representative of a healthy and harmonious development of the human figure," he does not and cannot mean that the Mexican is incapable of such achievement. There are other explanations of Mexican psychological aberrations, of course, the lack of urbanization being among them; the sophistication of Mexico's larger cities has done much to increase extraversion among Mexicans. And when one adds to all these circumstances the fact that intellectual activity has been almost exclusively carried on within a background of unsympathetic European determinants—that the country has been ruled by people whose eyes were turned back across the seas—it is surprising that the Mexican is not more unstable and undefined than he is. Characterized as evasive, irresponsible, lazy, suspicious, improvident, unrealistic, hypersensitive, the average Mexican's psychology is that of the oppressed and rejected. A slave morality necessarily produces such character defects. From long dependence upon his exploiters, the delinquent develops a childish inability to see beyond *mañana*. That perennial adolescent the Mexican automobile driver—temporarily crazed by power of possession and freedom of movement—is thus easily understood, as he wildly honks his horn and scatters hapless pedestrians from his private path. So long without such a wonderful material possession, he glories in advertising it to the whole world. Given, for once, even so little long-denied power, he cherishes any outlet of personal importance and private achievement. His egomania and irresponsible behavior are symptomatic of his dependent status. The scientific world has largely renounced its inherited concepts of racial superiority, but in the case of Mexico the damage remains in the lives, superstitions, and behavior of her people.

The task of education, then, is to dispel from the mind of the Mexican all shadows of an illusory inferiority and bring him to grips with the genuinely pressing difficulties of his economic and social environment. If his physical wants are satisfied, his psychological aberrations will tend to disappear. On this point nothing is more pertinent than Gamio's bald recommendation: "These pariahs need, and need badly, not alphabets and theoretical postulates, but something which will show them the way to get enough to eat."[29]

[29] Gamio, *Aspects of Mexican Civilization*, p. 132. *Cf.* Pedro de Alba, *Del Nuevo Humanismo y otros Ensayos*, pp. 203 ff.

II. The Struggle for Education

COLONIAL IDEALISM AND DECLINE

I stood in reverence face to face with the august panorama that is our history. From the pre-Cortesian epoch and through the struggles of the Conquest, our predecessors were characterized by the tremendous courage with which they lived and died in defense of their rights. Their memory is a lesson in heroism, and in it we find permanent stimulus to combat servitude. —Manuel Avila Camacho.

Our educational history has lacked coherence (enlace), *method, and continuity, and our best laid attempts at reform are the result of the unforeseen and the accidental; in the march of our government everything has been contingent, capricious, never solidified by constitutional law.*—Pedro de Alba, essayist, 1937.

Spain was impelled to militant action at that momentous period of her history; the one militarist the other spiritual, both combative and eager to conquer . . . in the latter, the prime aim was to win adherence to Christianity. There was an interweaving between the two, a mutual aid that engendered phenomena of social symbiosis of great juridical and political importance. A realization of that permanent interrelation between two organisms, each of which depended for its existence on absorbing a part of the vital juice of the other, is quite fundamental for the understanding of Spanish colonization.—Fernando de los Ríos, professor of law, The University of Madrid.

THE PREVIOUS CHAPTER has presented the elements, natural and unnatural, of Mexico's inheritance and environment, setting forth the issues as frankly expressed by leading authorities. The present chapter will deal with Mexico's national and educational progress to the present time. Mexican history is a grim story of power politics, bloodshed, and waste of human life that is a blot on the record of those who colonized to spread civilization and enlightenment.

The foreign invaders merit no commendation that is not balanced by an equal measure of censure and dispraise. This is true of the church, the lay liberators, the "benevolent" imperialists, the economic exploiters, of a dozen types of overlords, and even of the full-blooded Indian presidents themselves, once they came to power.[1] In general Mexican historians are left to disclose the sordid reality which most foreign observers tend to romanticize or otherwise distort.

Following Cortés' invasion, in 1519, Mexican history falls into three main periods: (1) from the Spanish occupation to the winning of Independence in 1810; (2) from Independence through the rule of President Díaz, 1911; and (3) the "revolutionary era" from 1911 to the present. Education has undergone countless transformations and adaptations in conformity with the prevailing objectives of these periods. Mention has already been made of education prior to the Spanish invasion. This chapter will concentrate on the significant events from 1520 to the present.

At the time of the discovery, the Spanish Crown and the Catholic church were inseparably united in every enterprise. As a world power, Spain could draw on the best intellectual resources of Europe. Humanism, at its peak in southern Europe at the time of the Conquest, aimed at an appreciation of the good, the true, and the beautiful, not only in relation to art and literature, but also in connection with an increasing, though still limited, respect for the rights of the individual.

The liberalizing tendencies of the time were to a large measure reflected in the early colonial schools of New Spain. Historian John Tate Lanning, of Duke University, in a number of places shows that contrary to the general impression there was no great cultural lag in New Spain's educational institutions, but only a "hiatus of one generation" between advances in Europe and their repercussion in Mexico. In discussing the transfer of fundamental humanism to the colonies, Lewis Hanke compares Spain's Charles V with

[1] Ebaugh, *The National System of Education in Mexico*, p. 3: "The most prominent motive of almost every man who came to power in Mexico . . . was personal ambition— save, perhaps Benito Juárez." MacFarland, *Chaos in Mexico*, p. 13: "There is considerable doubt as to whether many of Mexico's leaders since Juárez have been characterized by scrupulousness and integrity."

the modern sociologist who tries to discover truth through experiment, since this monarch did his best to understand the Indian before trying to "humanize" him.[2]

On the other hand, the Spanish occupation brought a number of changes which were deleterious to education. The first of these was the *encomienda* system, under which whole communities were "commended," or granted, by the King to individuals and to the church. Limited to only two generations of a family, these grants could be revoked for a number of reasons, among them, for nonuse of the land. The *encomenderos*, desiring quick and profitable returns, compensated for these royal restrictions by holding the Indians in virtual slavery. Worse in practice than feudalism in Europe, the encomienda system, originally conceived on the idea of mutual consent and service, soon belied its altruistic genesis. Though they were held responsible for the education and well-being of the natives who had been entrusted to them, the encomenderos too often demonstrated little interest in anything beyond the ability of their charges to work and produce. Francisco Larroyo, Mexico's outstanding educational historian, cites the native rebellions of the colonial period as proof of "this unjust and grievous situation."[3]

A second calamity occurred with the introduction of European diseases—smallpox, tuberculosis, syphilis, yellow fever, and

---

[2] Lanning, *Academic Culture in the Spanish Colonies*, p. 85. Hanke, *The First Social Experiment in America*, Preface. According to Hanke, the question in the King's mind, and that of his servants was always (p. 8): Should the natives be incorporated in the Catholic faith as equals? Hanke brings his own sociological ingenuity to bear in the deduction that all intrusive or invading nations tend to condemn the conquered as weak and stupid, and consequently seek to substitute their own customs as superior and more advanced.

[3] *Encomienda* is defined by Haring, *The Spanish Empire in America*, p. 44, as "the patronage conferred by royal favor over a portion of the natives . . . with the obligation to instruct them in the Christian religion and the elements of civilized life, and to defend them in their person and property; coupled with the right to demand tribute or labor in return." Land was only occasionally involved, p. 62: "The *encomienda* was not a landed estate . . . Indians were declared to be proprietors of their houses, lands, and animals, and neither the *encomendero* nor anyone else might dispose of them." However, in practice (p. 45) "the obligations of the *encomendero* became a mere gesture"; and (on pp. 62-63) "the Indians were in practice held to all sorts of exactions." *Cf.* Larroyo, *Historia comparada*, p. 72: "The *encomienda* . . . under which the Indian was in the service of his master for life . . . and the *repartimiento* were the methods of exploitation."

others. Subjected already to arduous toil in mine and field and exposed to the ravages of these new maladies, the Indian suffered violent and permanent injury to his health and well-being. Lesley Byrd Simpson reports, for example, that "the first century of the Spanish occupation was marked by the disappearance of millions of Indians, who had little protection against the diseases of Europe and Asia. Some of these epidemics depopulated whole provinces."[4]

A third difficulty arose from the imposition of the worst elements of the white man's moral code. Though in their more wholesome aspects the morals of the invader counteracted many harmful native excesses, nevertheless they were far too frequently destructive. As Ebaugh so correctly states: "Marriage [despite Catholic strictures] was not a strong institution even in Spain, and it will not be supposed that the Spanish soldier acquired a more discriminating, or less immoral code of conduct while on his avowed conquests." Half-breed foundlings did not testify favorably to the general morality of the conquistador.

To offset these evils, the early clerics and friars embarked with evangelical zeal on countermeasures. The native first had to be converted to Christianity. For this purpose it was essential that such European culture as was approved by ecclesiastical authorities be grafted onto the indigenous cultures. This required the introduction of a written alphabet to transcribe Indian sounds—an accomplishment of which Francis Borgia Steck writes in commendation: "Not even the Aztecs with all their supposed culture had a written language. Before they could teach the art of reading and writing, the friars had first to transcribe the spoken language of the natives phonetically into written form."[5] Considerable progress resulted from these early efforts of the church. Schools were founded, all of them as by-products of convents. The countless churches and convents which today are characteristic of Mexico's

---

[4] Lesley Byrd Simpson, *Many Mexicos*, p. 177. Haring, *The Spanish Empire in America*, pp. 215-16. Kelley, *Blood-drenched Altars*, p. 68, is of opposite mind: "This wholesale guardianship of Indians had its abuses. . . . It had one outstanding result: it did actually preserve the race . . . the Indians did not begin to die out." Similar conditions prevailed, of course, in other parts of the western hemisphere.

[5] Steck, *Education in Spanish North America during the Sixteenth Century*, p. 9. The Indians did, however, have hieroglyphic language.

architectural landscape sprang from the devoted labor of the Indians, for whose services the Fathers paid in education and the ineffable gift of Christianity.[6]

The first elementary school in the New World, the San Francisco school, was founded in Texcoco, in 1523. Two years later it was moved to Mexico City by Fray Pedro de Gante (Peter of Ghent). At San Francisco there were almost a thousand students, many of them of Indian nobility. Gante gave them religious instruction, elementary instruction in civil affairs, and apprenticeship training in the trades. A decade or so later Archbishop Juan de Zumárraga was instrumental in launching the first printed publications to appear in America, with the result that by 1600 the booktrade was actually flourishing. This same Bishop Zumárraga devoted his life to providing educational facilities for natives as well as for Spaniards. In the eight or nine towns of his diocese he maintained centers for teaching the Christian doctrine to the sons and daughters of the native chieftains and leading men. The historian and Hispanophile Charles Lummis rightly praises this "policy of humaneness which no other nation colonizing the New World had ever copied."[7]

Ostensibly to combat the evils of the encomienda system, the idealistic and resourceful priests approximated what some educators term "activity programs . . . conceived long before Pestalozzi or Dewey came onto the scene." George Sánchez, North American dean of Mexico's educational commentators, refers to Juan Vives' educational realism in relating how Father Pedro de Gante "created a true 'school of action.' At Texcoco and later in Mexico City, two hundred years before Pestalozzi, three hundred years before Froebel, and almost four hundred years before John Dewey, he had an activity school based on current life."[8] A little more cau-

[6] Magner, *Men of Mexico*, p. 135. Lesley Byrd Simpson, *Many Mexicos*, p. 107. However, Sanford, *The Story of Architecture in Mexico*, denies that the church Fathers had to teach the Indian how to build. He declares that hundreds of thousands of natives were artisans already trained in the great tradition of building.

[7] The outstanding work on Zumárraga is that by Icazbalceta, *Don Fray Juan de Zumárraga*. Green and Leonard, "On the Mexican Booktrade in 1600," *Hispanic Review*, IX (January, 1941), 1, favorably review Mexican accomplishment in book publishing during the first century of colonization. Lummis, *The Spanish Pioneers*, pp. 17 ff.

[8] George I. Sánchez, *Mexico; a revolution by education*, p. 38.

tious in his interpretation, James Magner commends the "activity" work of the utopian Fray Vasco de Quiroga, quoting him directly: "After school hours, twice a week, their teacher should take them out to the country or to some field near the school set aside for this purpose, and for two hours in the manner of fun, play, and pastime, teach them the culture of the soil, even though the school hours are diminished, for this also is doctrine and good morals." But González Peña warily observes: "These schools can be considered the cradle of Mexican culture, primarily because of the efforts and activities of the teachers, rather than the diligence of the students."

The Church Fathers were supported by the unselfish and devoted work of liberal lay leaders, among them the remarkable Cortés himself, who not only solicited the aid of the clergy in teaching the natives but also commanded the training of Indian leaders for posts in the civil government. Thus, concludes Sánchez, "that crusty and resourceful warrior, tempered his sternness and ambition with a measure of liberal vision and a feeling for social values."[9] The first two viceroys, Antonio de Mendoza and Luis de Velasco, also receive commendation, since, as the historian Teja Zabre and others observe, they "stood for the desire of the Spanish crown to save Indian races from absolute extinction, or unmitigated slavery." These men, confirms Sánchez, "exemplify Spanish leadership at its best, cast upon these shores as the flower of Spanish humanism was beginning to fade and wither."[10]

The success of early educational efforts is praiseworthy and irrefutable, but only in consideration of their limited sphere and avowed purpose. That these isolated accomplishments were unrepresentative of general educational achievement throughout Mexico is a matter on which Manuel Barranco comments severely:

[9] However, Gessler, *Patterns of Mexico*, p. 13, sees little humanitarianism in Mexico's conqueror: "Hernán Cortés had come to the Indies athirst for adventure and fortune. Legend gossips, 'I came not for work but for gold. . . .' There was not much gold, and so they extracted wealth from labor of Indians."

[10] Sánchez, *Mexico*. A depressing note in this rhapsody on Spanish humanism is sounded by Lesley Byrd Simpson, *Many Mexicos*, p. 144: "Society and public service became so corrupt (1550-1600) during the silver age, that thoughtful men saw nothing ahead but final dissolution, and the great Quevedo dipped his pen in bile and wrote 'Poderoso caballero es don Dinero!' (Sir Money is a doughty knight!)."

"The scanty popular education in the Colonial period assumed a pronounced religious character. . . . There was no well defined plan of organization and instruction—each priest working isolated in the way that he thought best." Indian schools, small, few, and far between, were located chiefly in Mexico City and vicinity, and there were only sporadic efforts in the provinces.

The so-called "activity," or "progressive," schools of the early period deserve the title only in connection with manual labor. If we understand, as Dewey does, that the term "activity" refers also to mental and spiritual freedom, the high praise bestowed by these commentators is not wholly justified. For what thoughts would have been tolerated that questioned eternal truth divinely revealed? The chief educational aim was to inculcate proper moral doctrine, which perforce meant the kind acceptable to the church. One is forced to conclude that the Catholic doctrine determined the course of general education, though it must be recognized that valuable service was done the Indian by teaching him to read and write.

For the rest, the educational accomplishment of the white invader is exaggerated by many authorities, who tend to extoll too highly the restricted efforts of early educators. Actually, as church education became established, scholasticism became the basis of curriculum and method rather than "progressivism." This is not to be taken as a censure of the work of the early Spanish fathers, who did what they thought just and proper in accordance with their faith. In their lifetime intellectual freedom in the modern sense did not exist; its supporters were usually burned at the stake. Nor must it be supposed that contemporary schools in other parts of the world had much to contribute that was more liberal or constructive. Indeed, the educational theocracy which prevailed in the English colonies in America was far more stereotyped, intolerant, and rigid than that in Mexico during the same period.

During the seventeenth century, the church's interest in education was subservient to the economic demands of landlordism; it neglected the training of the native peoples to concentrate on the education of an aristocracy which would exercise continued control. Abroad, the Protestant Reformation influenced the mother country to buttress the Catholic faith with teachings of a more rigid scholastic nature. Political unrest led to further state absolutism, which in turn fostered a more doctrinaire type of instruction. The Spanish Inquisition tended to isolate New Spain from cultural and spiritual contact with the rest of the world; all concern for the indigenous populations that had stemmed from Spanish humanism vanished; and Spain's colonial possessions were used as treasure houses to bolster the nation's declining position as a world power. Schools thus became a negligible factor in the life of the country. No longer permitted were the older, more liberal ideals of the friars who had accompanied the conquerors and for whose devoted services many commentators are so grateful. The result was a traditional, ready-made, catechistic curriculum affording little opportunity for native genius or challenge to the educationally enterprising.[11] González Peña laments that the period through 1750 was one of "decadence, whose monotony is relieved by a few figures of literary importance": Juan Ruiz de Alarcón, "whose comedies have greatly enhanced the luster of the Spanish literature of the Golden Age"; Juana Inés de la Cruz, Mexico's *Decima Musa*, "notable for her defense of the rights and dignity of women"; and Carlos de Sigüenza y Góngora (1645-1700), "distinguished in mathematical sciences, Indian languages and culture, enemy of the peripatetic, and adherent of the Cartesian philosophy." Sánchez observes that this change was "astonishing. . . . Fervid initiative, a liberal social outlook" that characterized the educational scene of the sixteenth century disintegrated into "narrow institutionalism . . . and indifference to the goal of the schools as a social institution." However, one is forced to observe that such astonishment would, perhaps, not have been experienced had the dross originally been detected in the "golden age." Codification of thought usually leads to stagnation and decay—a fact which is axiomatic rather than astonishing.

Brightening the picture somewhat was the work of the Jesuit order, which after 1572 contributed a slightly modified traditional and scholastic curriculum. Jesuit schools multiplied during almost two centuries of predominance, establishing their characteristic

[11] Larroyo, *Historia comparada*, p. 73; and James, "Spanish American Literature and Art," *op. cit.*, p. 201, who terms it "slender production . . . in three centuries."

preference for classical studies, theatrical representations, philosophy, literature, and public arts. In full support of their work, Alfonso Toro reports that they "succeeded in modernizing teaching, introducing modern philosophy, and with it the study of physics and national history."[12] Much the same point of view is expressed by Jerome Jacobsen, who, limiting his observations to the sixteenth century, cites the "unheard of" problems arising out of the complexities of race, customs, interests, and situations. Jacobsen commends the Jesuits for bringing Indians and Creoles into contact with the European thought of the period. Theirs was "a feat overshadowed only by their attempts to give all classes the wisdom of the ancients."[13] Magner joins these authors in expressing regret that the dissolution of the Jesuit order in 1767 deprived New Spain of twenty-five or thirty schools of "free education," with their corresponding libraries and churches. On the other hand, Gabino Barreda characterizes Jesuit education as "static," "incomplete," "partial"—"it neglected the scientific attitude."[14]

The Jesuit order did much to win over the Indian and give him schools for his children. Simpson claims, indeed, that Jesuit schools were "at all odds the best in the country." However, Jesuit education offered little that emancipated either mind or body in bondage to New World feudalism. The encomienda system was abolished in 1720, but the Indian still remained a slave to debt, his whole being and that of his family mortgaged for generations to the crown-appointed *corregidores*—community overseers whose professed task it was to advise and protect the native.

[12] Alfonso Toro, *Compendio de la historia de México*, p. 461. Lesley Byrd Simpson, *Many Mexicos*, p. 173: "Before their expulsion in 1767 the Jesuits were supreme in the preparatory field, operating some twenty-three institutions, of which the College of St. Peter and St. Paul in Mexico City competed with the university in influence, and was almost superior to it in accomplishment. The granting of higher degrees was a jealously guarded monopoly of the Royal and Pontifical University of Mexico."

[13] Jacobsen, *Educational Foundations of the Jesuits in Sixteenth Century New Spain*, pp. 237-38.

[14] Barreda, *Estudios*, p. 14. Barreda, born in 1818, was one of the early organizers of the National Preparatory School. González Peña, *History of Mexican Literature*, pp. 5-7, reveals the educational exclusiveness that bears out the above conclusions: ". . . creoles were not allowed to attend the schools for Indians and mestizos. Spanish instructors . . . taught the fundamentals." Augustinian monks specialized in schools for Spanish and Creole children. Larroyo, *Historia comparada,* pp. 107, 109. On p. 112 Larroyo cites Augustinian Friar Alonso de la Veracruz for founding the Colegio de San Pablo, 1575, with its "magnificent library, the first in America."

By the end of the first two centuries of occupation the plight of the Indian, educational, economic, or otherwise, had changed but little. "It is a grim thing to have to report," writes Larroyo, "that after two and a half centuries of conquest . . . little progress was made in 'castellanizing' the Indian . . . Elementary education was prostrate to the end of the 17th century. Actually, the bulk of the native population was considered unfit for the rights and opportunities of citizenship and by nature incapable of learning. As a peon, the native was actually worse off than he had been as a slave. "Peonage," comments the historian and labor leader Roberto Haberman, was "worse than slavery. Slaves cost their masters money, and some provision is made for them when work is slack."[15] Not so the peons, who, left to forage, vegetate, or perish, continued to drown their sorrows in *pulque*.[16]

CHURCH TO STATE CONTROL

In the second half of the 19th century our national history is characterized by a tendency to define and universalize the Mexican. Local chronicles no longer predominate over those of the provinces; we hear less about local history. Joint efforts, founded on national enlightenment, succeed in over-coming rigid tenets of the Church.—Octavio Véjar Vázquez.

[15] Baron de Humboldt, assessing the situation in the early 1800's veers from his usual optimism to report: "Mexico is a country of inequality. Nowhere does there exist such a fearful difference in the distribution of fortune, civilization, cultivation of the soil, and population." And later: ". . . the caste of the Whites is the only one in which we find anything like cultivation." John Taylor, ed., *Selections from the Works of Baron de Humboldt*, pp. 35-36. Humboldt's praise goes mostly to technical achievement in "higher" education, especially in mining.

[16] About pulque, Ebaugh, *The National System of Excavation in Mexico*, dutifully reports, p. 143; "Millions of acres are given over to the production of the plant [maguey] from which this liquor is obtained practically 'ready to drink,' since only twenty-four hours are required for fermentation. The fact that it must be drunk within twenty-four hours thereafter or else grow stale and useless is ample reason to the average peon for imbibing unbelievable quantities." Further evils of pulque are laid bare by Booth, *Mexico's School-made Society*, pp. 35-37: "Pulque takes a tremendous toll on the Mexican nation from the standpoint of health, culture and economics. The method of obtaining pulque is unhygienic to the highest degree. The 'national curse' is in evidence in every stratum of society. Mothers frequently wean their children on pulque because it can be obtained for twelve centavos a liter, while milk is thirty. . . . Church festivals are often little more than drunken orgies that frequently last two or three days. . . . President Calles had to admit defeat when it came to abolition of the pulque industry."

Americans set out on their historical career from a basis of dissent, social, religious, eventually political, and began getting together when they became independent; we Mexicans started from a foundation of unquestioning conformity and began to fall out the moment we shook off our European vassalage.—Pablo Martínez del Río.

Education and Mexican culture in general entered on a new path. Independence spelled the end of the Inquisition, the Index of Prohibited Reading *and other medieval institutions. Mexicans could now employ free thought and modern science, although economic poverty and old intellectual habits retarded for some time a long awaited evolution.*—Francisco Larroyo, director of the National Normal School, 1947.

Victory is ours because God, and not man, is the caudillo *of our civilization.* —Benito Juárez, 1858.

Mexico's bells ring out every year on Independence Day, September 15; for on that date in the year 1810 Father Hidalgo severed relations with Spain. The second period of Mexico's history dates from 1822, when Spain officially recognized Mexican Independence, and the brief reign of the caudillo Emperor Iturbide began.

The impetus toward independence had been rooted in popular revolt; Indians had sacrificed their lives that the land might at last be theirs again. However, as with contemporary revolutions elsewhere, the essential relation of the castes remained unchanged; Mexico's masters, not her people, turned out to be the sole beneficiaries. Manuel Gamio asserts that when Mexican independence had been declared, the great mass of natives and halfbreeds had been rifled of their national resources, and the most brilliant phases of their culture had been erased: "Mexico achieved her independence from Spain in 1821, but it was a movement which favored only the white minorities, for the indigenous masses remained in the same miserable situation, or perhaps worse, as during the colonial period."

Thus is explained the continued struggle for emancipation, fitfully brought to a head in 1910 by the "true Revolution." For fifty long years previous to the presidential inauguration of General Porfirio Díaz, in 1876, the nation staggered under the bloodiest of political and social upheavals, which augured miserably for

Mexico's position in the family of nations. Everywhere dubbed a land of perpetual revolution and banditry, Mexico has not as yet been able completely to live down her reputation.[17] Under such circumstances, endeavors to promote mass education failed dismally. Francisco Larroyo observes: "The education of native peoples throughout this entire period (1810-1857) was neglected. . . . Governments possessed neither the inclination nor the money to attack the problem, and the efforts made during the Colonial period in the manner of incorporating the Indian into national culture were unfortunately forgotten."

Independent Mexico's first constitution, conservative in nature, was written in 1824 along the lines of the constitutions of the United States and Spain. This document envisaged a unified federal state, but through the years it suffered violent revisions involving the rights of man, religion, property, individual welfare, popular suffrage, and education, all with regard to their relation to the federal government. Tracing the fate of this constitution, Manuel Gamio concludes that it reacted to the extremes of federalism and centralism and to the ebb and flow of the struggle between the forces of progress and reaction, culminating in a return to federalism under the Constitution of 1857, which reflected the ideology of Mexican liberalism. Federalism was abandoned in 1835, and a highly centralized form of government was established in 1836 under the so-called *Siete Leyes* (Seven Laws). Following the *Siete Leyes* there came, in 1843, the *Bases Orgánicas*, which were even more centralistic than the Laws. During the turmoils of the Mexican War federalism and the Constitution of 1824 were restored. Finally, after a brief relapse into centralism in 1853,

[17] The details of Mexico as a country of revolutions and insurrections are confessed in Antonio Caso (former rector of the National University), *Discursos a la Nación Mexicana*, Mexico City, 1922, pp. 93-94: ". . . 225 acts of insurrection . . . 2.5 revolutions per year." He quotes Schopenhauer to the effect that Mexico is a place where "every one thinks of himself foremost . . . without bothering about his nation, which is marching straight to ruin." González Peña, *History of Mexican Literature*, p. 153, interprets the effects on literature: ". . . they stamped on literature a new character: a political one, which dominated all writing during the period. Proclamations, edicts, manifestos, speeches, appeared both for and against the insurgent movement. Prose writers were . . . political writers; poetry assumed qualities in harmony with the warlike atmosphere."

when Santa Anna rounded out his final term of office, a return to
federalism was effected under the Constitution of 1857.[18]

Political revolutions led to educational aspirations. The various
governments needed schools in which to disseminate the prevailing
political ideals and to provide as solid a front as possible for
Mexico's newly won sovereignty. The church was the first to feel
the blow. In 1829 a law was passed completely secularizing education, at least on paper. Actually, since no schools were provided
in which to pursue this secular education, the law was abortive.
Only the church possessed schools; but in official Mexican attitude,
"Better no education at all than Catholic education."[19] A Department of Public Education *(Dirección General de Instrucción
Pública)*, created in 1833 by vice-president Gómez Farías to
implement the ideal of freedom of instruction, was ineffective.
Commenting on the education of the period, historian Ezequiel
Chávez regrets that "the schools were converted into noisy barracks
and the money allotted for their support diverted to purposes of
war; periodicals and manifestos of independent chiefs were substituted for schools and became the real education."

The political education begun by Gómez Farías was continued
by Manuel Baranda, who in 1843 organized methods of instruction under what came to be known as "The General Plan of
Studies"; but it was not until Benito Juárez assumed control that
the people became interested in education. Maximilian and the
invading French had been driven out in 1862 only by means of
unified national effort; the need for a national education to preserve and foster this national unity immediately became apparent.

[18] Gamio links liberalism with federalism, and centralism with conservatism, as does
González Peña, *History of Mexican Literature*, pp. 187-88: "Those who, for the most
part, possessed special privileges, that is to say, the conservatives, chose centralism. The
puros—those who were opposed to the riches and privileges of the Church and the
old Spanish party, and who had been infected by a desire to imitate the United States
—declared themselves federalists." Larroyo, *Historia comparada*, p. 155, depicts the
part played by the Masonic lodges, which "intervened actively in Mexican politics.
The Scottish Lodge was centralist; the Yorkshire Lodge federalist."

[19] Bishop Kelley, *Blood-drenched Altars*, p. 110, seizes upon this charge to warn
that "the blame for illiteracy in present-day Mexico cannot be placed on the Church
but justly must be charged to those who confiscated the endowments and, after seizing
and closing schools and colleges, did nothing to replace the work these endowments
supported."

The Reform Laws of 1867 granted universal suffrage; education was taken over as a function of the state, and under the *Ley Orgánica de Instrucción* (Organic Law of Education), elementary education became statutorily free and compulsory. Concerning this law, Larroyo brings out the delicate fact that though it did not expressly state that education should be lay, it nevertheless forbade religious instruction: "Thus," Larroyo rightly concludes, "elementary education in Mexico acquired three modern characteristics: it became obligatory, free, and lay." The nationalization of education, characteristic of contemporary Mexican administration, may therefore be said to have begun at this time.

Like the great statesman's enlightened Constitution of 1857, Juárez' Reform Laws turned out to be a legislative mirage. Antonio Caso, former rector of the National University, states that the Constitution was an ideal enough document, but "not for a half-hour has it been what it should have been—the fundamental law of our government, and the supreme norm of our national behavior." The central government, as before, was not in a position, financial or otherwise, to cope with the administration or supervision of instruction; hence only nominal progress was made in education. Barranco relates that the *ideals* of the new school had changed a great deal: "Before, the task of the popular school was to make good Catholics; now its aspiration was to produce fine Mexicans, better men. The methods changed little, since there was the same lack of trained teachers, and no normal schools to educate such teachers . . . public education dragged along painfully."

Thus, schooling was left to the family, the community, the state, the religious organization, or any other agency that had sufficient enterprise to take it on. Regardless of constitutional reforms, neither the Indian nor his political ally the mestizo was prepared to reap the benefits of independence. The root of the trouble lay in the lack of conviction, both on their part or on the part of the privileged classes, as to the necessity for schools. On this point Juárez himself gives full expression to the prevailing attitude:

The man who cannot supply his family with food views the education of his sons not only as something remote, but as a positive impediment to his struggle for existence. Instead of sending them to school, he hires out their frail labor-power to alleviate, even if only to a slight extent, the misery which engulfs them. If that man had a few conveniences, if he could squeeze the least profit from his toil, he would from that day on be eager to educate his children and provide them with a solid instruction. The desire to learn and to become illustrious is innate in the heart of man. Strike off the fetters of misery and despotism that oppress him and he will naturally achieve greatness.

There is ample documentation to prove that Juárez' ideals attained a meager success. W. H. Callcott, following the authority of Justo Sierra, brings out that in 1843, fourteen years after the legal secularization of education and ten years after the establishment of the Department of Public Education, only 1,310 schools had been registered with the national government; but that by 1874 this number had been increased sixfold to 8,103. A good part of the increase was due to well-intentioned, though too often negligent, local town councils. Although these institutions served less than one-fifth of the school population and were unsatisfactory in many ways, Mexico's record in founding popular schools through local initiative, though fifty years behind that of her northern neighbor, compares favorably with that of other countries where public schools were opened without centralized finance and organization. Callcott statistically concludes:

. . . about 2,000 were private schools, but only 117 were sustained by the Church, and 5,200 were unofficial. Less than 550 were for both boys and girls, and of the remainder the ratio was about four to one in favor of boys' schools. Assuming that the total population was 9,000,000, the school population must have been about 1,800,000; but unfortunately the reports showed only 349,000 in schools in spite of improvements recently made.

On private-school progress Barranco lauds Mexico by citing that in 1851, out of 122 elementary schools in Mexico City with 7,636 pupils, only four schools with 488 pupils were owned by the government. Two belonged to convents, and 116 schools with 6,955 children operated under private initiative. "It is a fact worth noting," concludes Barranco, "that Mexico is the only Latin-American nation in which the beginning of popular education was due mainly to private initiative."

The latter half of the nineteenth century was characterized by frequent attempts, most of them unsuccessful, to eliminate all agencies that interfered with the nationalization of education. Church properties were expropriated, stripped of their works of art, desecrated, and converted into barracks. Their clerical protectors were derobed and sent into exile. The thoroughness and resolution with which this destruction was perpetrated, still evident to visitors today, leads one to wonder to what extent the church, after three centuries of conversion, had actually won over the natives. Or was this devastation a certain compensation for a long period of subjugation? On this José Fuentes Mares contributes another sample of Mexican straightforwardness: "Our country from the very beginning of its independence seems to consider itself condemned to drowning in blood and destruction every creation, venerated or not, which has contributed to its historical life, even at the price of moral and material ruin." The destruction was, indeed, rudely complete, and the best that could be expected was that out of the ruins would rise educational structures better adapted to the country's needs and more in tune with educational progress elsewhere in the civilized world.

During the long regime of Porfirio Díaz (1876-1911) the country settled down to law and order, but only under armed compulsion from a strong central government, abetted by the passivity, indifference, and acquiescence of a dejected people. Anarchic ambitions passed away, discouraged by a controlled press or liquidated by the assassination techniques of modern firearms. Díaz' "benevolent dictatorship" may be credited with a few measures for the economic betterment of Mexico, but the general worth of its social and political legislation is still a matter of grave controversy.

Díaz believed himself a champion of sound material development. His regime presented a superficial façade of growth: material progress was concentrated in the larger cities, but in the provinces rifts widened in the national structure. So haphazard was the development of railroads and highways that even Díaz' finance minister, José Limantour, was moved to complain that some areas were being served excessively, while others were totally

neglected. Since intercommunication and transportation were vital
to national unity and intercultural contact, it was manifest that
the cornerstone of national enlightenment was being chipped and
split at the very time it was laid.

Agricultural development remained in control of the favored
hacendados, the landed gentry whose indifference accounted for
much of the continued backwardness of rural education and culture. Rural schools at the end of the Díaz regime were practically
nonexistent. In 1900, 85 percent of the population were still illiterate. The much-heralded educational achievement of the Federal
District, that glittering showcase of heterogeneous culture, remained only a distant ideal for the back country; it was equaled
nowhere else in the Republic.

On the constructive side, Don Porfirio believed that Mexico
lacked a solid middle class. He explained his policy as patriarchal
—guiding and sustaining popular tendencies in the conviction that
under an enforced peace, education, industry, and commerce would
develop elements of stability and union in a people naturally intelligent, submissive, and benevolent. To achieve his ends, Díaz decided that there was little benefit to be gained from antagonizing
the church; it was more useful as an ally. Leading the way as
always in Mexico's counter-revolutions, the clergy regained the
properties that had been expropriated under the Reform Laws of
1867. Church taxes were resumed, and in return the "state within
a state" at times denied religious sacraments to political offenders.
With the turn of the century, convents and seminaries reopened
and they were soon flourishing again in defiance of laws secularizing education. Don Porfirio's school inspectors deemed it wise to
pass by on the other side of parochial schools operating without
benefit of law.

Díaz must be given credit for minor concessions to education,
for he was well aware that schools were ideal agencies to propagate
political ideas. With wise foresight, Don Porfirio generously entrusted the schooling of his people to educational leaders who were
clever enough not only to obey their master but also to carry out
plans of their own. Though not blessed at all times by the dictator,
the educational experimentation of such pedagogues as Rébsamen,

Laubscher, Carrillo, and Torres Quintero was allowed fairly free rein, with fruitful results in the later revolutionary period.[20] Educational leadership was chiefly in the hands of ministers Joaquín Baranda and Justo Sierra, both of whom favored education for national unity through an emphasis on statism. "The state," said Baranda, "must become a vital element in all that is taught." As minister of education, Baranda implemented his views by establishing a system of general primary instruction as a "sure defense and protection of Mexico's artistic inheritance." In 1885 he laid the foundation for a program of nationally supported normal schools "for the worthy creation, exaltation and appreciation of a teaching corps professionally trained and adequately remunerated"—an ideal not realized, of course.

The consolidation of primary schools, officially initiated in 1891, eliminated the economical Lancastrian, or monitorial, system then in vogue and brought an increase in schools and enrollments by secularizing them and centralizing their controls.[21] Schools were made free and compulsory, this time under direct federal administration and supervision. As a result of the driving leadership of Justo Sierra, Subsecretary of Education under Ba-

[20] Larroyo, *Historia comparada*, pp. 226, 231 ff. Rébsamen, a Herbartian, was a forerunner of an education for intellectual and moral national unity, which meant the substitution of a national ethic for that of the church. Carlos A. Carrillo paved the way for a nationwide system of elementary education based on analytic, objective, and inductive instruction. Laubscher is noted for his model school at Orizaba, and Torres Quintero for his intuitive instruction and the onomatopeic (sound) method of teaching reading and writing.

[21] Barranco, *Mexico; Its Educational Problems*, p. 47, explains the Lancastrian system: "The first conscious effort toward the organization of the elementary school in Mexico was made by an Englishman . . . Lancaster. He came to Mexico in 1822 and . . . opened a school in the building in whose halls the Inquisition had lived . . . a a little later, January 1923, they formed a Society—La Compañía Lancasteriana—that had for its aim the diffusion of education among the people. In Article 2 of its statutes it is stated that 'the object of the company is to give free primary education to the children and poor classes by means of schools established at its expense.' . . . The Lancastrian School never had any pedagogical pretentions. Its end was to educate the greatest number with the least expenditure of money and time. Its monitorial system was recommended for economical rather than for pedagogical reasons. The influence of the Lancaster school in Mexico was profound, and even today there are many country schools in which the old monitorial system is practiced in a true Lancastrian fashion, and for many a little community an ideal school building is a house with one lonely but spacious hall, which was characteristic of the Lancastrian schools." *Cf.* Larroyo, *Historia comparada*, pp. 161-67.

randa, government programs took official form in the First Organic Law for Compulsory Free Education (1893) and the creation of the Department of Elementary Schools (1896).

Not one to truckle to the whims of a dictator, the "illustrious" Sierra loudly proclaimed that education was a "social process" which had to be disseminated to all the people. Yet despite super-human efforts, Sierra was able to effect major improvements only in the Federal District, with a net profit of one primary school for every thousand inhabitants, and a general enrollment of 112,078 students and 3,614 teachers, public and private. However, rural education continued in a state of what Larroyo calls "deplorable abandonment."

As head of the Ministry of Education in 1910, Sierra realized his cherished ambition by re-establishing the National University to serve as a centralized agency for unifying the nation's teaching personnel. The new university was launched on a career meant to furnish inspiration and leadership in Mexico's national and cultural life. In the words of Sierra, "We do not wish that in the temple erected today an Athenian be worshipped without eyes for humanity and without heart for the people; our desire is that Mexicans come here to pay homage to Atenea Promakos, the science that defends our country."

Statistics for the nation as a whole reveal that though enrollments in public and private elementary schools doubled from 1874 to 1907, and expenditures more than doubled, the expansion of school facilities only kept pace with the growth of population. At the turn of the century barely one-fourth of Mexico's elementary school children were enrolled in the schools. For political reasons public education remained confined to the cities, and for economic reasons to the lower middle classes. Progress in any case could be reckoned only quantitatively. Private schools remained the "better" institutions, and nobody who was anybody thought of sending his children to public schools.

As for its specific achievement in advancing public morals and enlightenment, the Díaz period, with the exception of limited individual education enterprise, may well be summed up in Sierra's trenchant pronouncement, "The people are hungry and thirsty for justice"; and in the sanguinary verses of the literary modernist Gutiérrez Nájera:

> In this tremendous struggle, crime has its code:
> It matters not that truth with error strives.
> If an arm is raised—cut it off!
> If a brain thinks—kill it![22]

EDUCATION FOR NATIONHOOD

It was now time that out of Mexico we should form a nation and that we make this nation the absolute sovereign of its own destiny.—Andrés Molina Enríquez, historian.

In the revolution that now is taking place in Mexico, the people are not fighting just for the love of war. At the bottom of it all is the hunger of our peasants for a piece of land of their own and a free government.—Manuel Barranco, 1915.

National tranquility and security depend for their existence on the clear intelligence of a citizenry; in consequence, this government will undertake to spread public education throughout the land . . . permitting the establishment of private schools only when conforming with our laws.—President Venustiano Carranza, 1915.

Mexico's Revolution, begun in 1810, revived in 1857, subdued under Díaz, reasserted itself in 1910. Peasant bands roved the country under the leaders Orozco, Villa, Zapata, Obregón, each of whom posted manifestos demanding political rights, a new deal for the common man, and the restoration of lands monopolized or held idle under the hacendados. In five months insurrectionists had swept aside Díaz' sublime superstructure and exposed the fundamental degradation into which the country had sunk. Slogans of the Revolutionary period voiced the creed of a new social religion, which included regional self-determination; popular sover-

[22] From González Blanco, *De Díaz a Carranza*, pp. 31-32, quoted in Callcott, *The History of Liberalism in Mexico*, p. 104. See also Kelley, *Blood-drenched Altars*, p. 223, deprecating Díaz as a nation-builder. Others, of course, still maintain that the era was a blessed one of "peace, order and progress." González Peña, for example, *History of Mexican Literature*, p. 349, maintains that the tranquility of thirty years had been beneficial to culture and letters *per se*.

eignty; "effective suffrage, no re-election"; "emancipation of the masses"; "land and learning." Mexico was no longer to remain the stepmother of Mexicans.

Three major obstacles lay in the path of revolutionary aims: (1) the church, which, though forcibly reduced to a secondary position in the broad struggle for social change, was still a primary factor in the spiritual life of the nation; it maintained active interest in landed property and in the field of education; (2) an ever-growing foreign commercial influence, which lent its weight to conservative elements; and (3) the mass of Mexican people themselves, who were no more advanced politically in 1910 than they had been in 1810. Political power, as elsewhere, gravitated to those who were in position to seize and use it.

The Madero government, 1912-13, fell before the Huerta counterrevolution, but popular control was given another chance under Carranza, whose main contribution was the memorable Constitution of 1917. A federalist document, perhaps the most advanced that the world had thus far seen, it codified rather than fulfilled the sweeping promises of the Revolution and limited the central government to encouraging reforms already initiated by the states. The most controversial of its provisions, Article 27, nationalized land and vested authority over its distribution in the federal government. Articles 3 and 130 declared education to be a function of the central government and made religious elementary schools illegal. Educational control and finance, however, remained in the hands of state and local governments. Article 123 recognized the educational rights and needs of the children of workers in communities without schools by creating a special type of Mexican institution called "Article 123 schools." For all the difficulty involved in its implementation, the 1917 Constitution afforded the people a brighter vision of things to come. Termed the "star agitator," it crystallized native demands that were centuries old and set down in black and white the essential terms on which the new nation was to function.

Educational historians find little to commend in the period from 1910 to 1921 outside of sporadic attacks on illiteracy and some progress in technical and rural education. Shifting political conditions engulfed one educational program after another. Plans for the establishment by the federal government of 5,000 elementary schools were shelved when the Constitution of 1917 abolished the federal Department of Public Education and lodged the responsibility in local administrations. The forced closing of more than 2,500 private primary and secondary schools maintained or conducted by religious organizations left nothing of consequence in their place, so that education under government auspices reached a low point indeed.

On the credit side, the governing classes and monied interests began to recognize the potential power of what little education they had granted and came gradually to appreciate that their own wellbeing varied in direct proportion to that of the underprivileged. Tangible evidence of this appeared in a recommendation issued by repatriates of the Huerta group:

> ... the number of Mexicans who can read and write is but slightly in excess of 3 million, while the remaining 12 million of the population are sunk in illiteracy. The first group is fit to engage in democratic government. ... Is it reasonable to say that the second group . . . can realize what is meant by a ballot, a federation, the independence of the branches of government? No one can longer ignore that if these human groups co-exist it is because one group, by force or acquiescence, is subordinate to the other. *Justice and liberty are only to be attained when the great backward group is redeemed by the small civilized group. . . . The light of education must be diffused throughout the masses so as to open to them horizons now hidden.*[23]

Subsequent efforts to "redeem the great backward group" and implement this recommendation were tangible but feeble. The direct relation between educational benefits and increased consumer demand was recognized by certain commercial interests desirous of creating markets, but others could not make up their minds as to which was the more profitable, an educated consuming proletariat or a continued supply of cheap labor. For them, this dilemma, even today, remains unsolved.

Educational inadequacy was most evident in the rural schools. Ebaugh points out that all states maintained a few rural schools,

[23] Jorge Vera Estañol, "Education," in *Essay on the Reconstruction of Mexico* (New York, 1920), pp. 39-42. Italics supplied. In this same article the author deplores the Carranza regime's reliance upon the states alone for educational efforts.

whose course covered three years of five or six months' instruction each, but that these schools were highly inefficient and for the most part inaccessible to pupils. Even the existing schools failed signally to adapt themselves to the special needs of Mexico's agrarian economy. Instead, traditional systems prevailed, with emphasis on memorization and recitation, and drill on academic matters far removed from the peon's daily needs. This type of education continued to be practically useless to rural pupils, who needed a training which would prepare them for the demands of an essentially agricultural life.

It remained for the Obregón administration of 1921 to apply remedial measures. Not one to be content with paper plans and revolutionary proclamations, Obregón entrusted the educational redemption of the masses ("educar es redimir") to a man thoroughly equipped for the job—José Vasconcelos, revolutionary student leader and rector of the National University. Often regarded as a visionary and an irresponsible enthusiast, the new minister nevertheless contributed a type of leadership, personal drive, and follow-through that had been rare among Mexican idealists. It was his conviction that Mexico could be raised from its depths by the lever of education. Already, states Bertram Wolfe, Vasconcelos "was at working planning publications, fomenting the popular arts, warring on illiteracy, teaching the trades, building schools, opening libraries, *forjando patria*, as he put it, forging a fatherland." To his job the new minister brought practical experience gained in his work with the "honorary teachers," a group of volunteers organized by him to wage war on illiteracy at a time when the federal government was financially impotent.

Among the more formidable tasks facing Vasconcelos were: (1) to redeem schools from the chaos of conflicting systems by initiating a regulatory federal program; (2) to provide adequate teacher training institutions; and (3) to revise programs in rural education. Attacks were made simultaneously on all fronts. Under the minister's leadership the constitution was revised in 1921 to permit greatly increased federal participation in education. The centralization advocated by the new constitution, together with increased appropriations, enabled Vasconcelos to rescue countless recalcitrant, bankrupt local systems. From one percent of the national budget during the Carranza administration, federal appropriations for education climbed to 12 percent in 1922 and 15 percent in 1923.

Concentration on rural education gave rise to Mexico's original and much-publicized "cultural missions." Devised on the principle of the itinerant schools, these missions aided rural teachers in the realization of educational aims and in the application of agricultural, hygienic, and industrial techniques. In 1923 the first formal mission, under the direction of Rafael Ramírez, undertook a three-week program at Zacualitipán, consisting of rudimentary instruction in sanitation, pest control, crop rotation, the significance of the Revolution, and sports and games. Included in the mission were an instructor in soap-making, a tanner, two agriculturalists, a carpenter, and a homemaking teacher.

Cultural missions have since become a permanent feature of Mexican life with their own special organization, personnel, and techniques. Under Elena Torres, Chief of the Bureau of Cultural Missions, six missions served more than two thousand rural teachers in 1926. In the following decade the number grew to eighteen missions serving more than four thousand teachers. From 1938-42 the program was temporarily discontinued, but since that time traveling missions have covered every corner of Mexico, bringing to outlying communities their first tangible understanding of the benefits to be gained from association with national life. An imported cell of specialized organization, the cultural mission creates its own village system and lends focus and direction to amorphous communities wherever it goes. With the assistance of cultural missions more than one thousand permanent rural schools by the end of 1924 were breathing life and enlightenment into the remotest hamlets. In practical application, each school became a community cultural center, a "house of the people" *(casa del pueblo),* for in order to bring about the desired reforms not only the children but also the entire population had to be reached.

"Forging the fatherland," as Vasconcelos had designated his

task, was to be effected not by schools alone but by other cultural agencies as well. The diversity of native languages, the dead-weight of illiteracy, and the inertia of public indifference pointed to the need for a simple, appealing medium, recognized by Vascon-celos in his promotion of a national art program. The Revolution had given birth to a rich variety of themes of suffering; and if public education was to provide the solution to Mexico's social problem, art was to become one of education's chief mediums. The middle twenties saw every important painter in Mexico on the pay-roll of the Ministry of Education, with assignments as drawing instructors, art-school inspectors, and so on, but actually working for the government on canvas or wall. World-famous artists such as Rivera, Orozco, Siqueiros, and others of the Revolutionary Syndicate of Painters donned overalls and, in Anita Brenner's terms, covered the walls of public buildings with interpretations of the Revolution thrice human size. Working directly under the Ministry of Education, they became the first spokesmen of the new Mexican national spirit through the realism of their massive frescos and murals. The aim was educational and revolutionary; the spirit, one of national brotherhood and the glorification of work and the worker. "Art for art's sake" was considered an aesthetic fallacy. "Art for the people" was termed hypocrital and sentimental. In-stead, art was a thing *of* the people, not an abstract concept or a vehicle for simply exploiting whims. At Chapingo, for example, the Agricultural College bears the motto, pictorialized by Rivera: "Ex-ploit the earth, but not your fellow man." In the Ministry of Educa-tion frescos portray the history of Mexico in a cycle of pictures from exploitation to salvation—from hacendado to teacher—uni-fying the nation behind the accepted method for working out its own redemption.

The educational accomplishment of the Obregón administration is striking enough in statistical terms but merits special commen-dation for having improved the attitude of the nation toward public education. The 1,089 rural schools of 1924 were still inadequate, but they were a welcome contrast to the half-hearted, unsupported paper program of 1911. More important still was the fuller recog-nition of the necessity for including isolated, neglected rural peoples.[24] Whereas cultural efforts previous to 1910 had centered upon engrafting alien modes, postrevolutionary education came to grips with existing problems, defining educational objectives in terms of local needs and national aspirations. Art, with federal encouragement and under the aegis of the mystic Best-Maugard, turned from exotic themes of limited interest to become the evangelist of work, nationalism, and healthy living. New standards of beauty took the place of the old. Vasconcelos, who had been held up to mild derision as a quixotic figure, "tilting at the windmills of economic desolation with lances of votes, letters, painting," responded by constructing a national system of education which to a very tangible extent amalgamated the divided castes and races, reduced illiteracy, created skills, and gave the people an awareness of common purpose.

During the next decade and a half the school system became a storm center. The Calles administration planned for a thousand new schools a year, but achieved only half that number in five years, raising the total to 3,594 by 1929-30. However, included in Calles' program were twenty-four model elementary schools, which assisted so greatly in the improvement of teaching methods that Hubert Herring speaks of Calles' educational adjutant, Moisés Sáenz, as the "ablest educator in Mexican history." Sáenz, subsecretary to education minister Puig Casauranc (1924-28) and a follower of Dewey's vitalist theory, resolved that federal efforts to establish schools should not signify a "mere change of supporters." What Sáenz referred to, of course, was the renewed campaign on the part of the government for landownership reform and for the elimination of the church in politics and education. In conflict with the church on two points, landownership and the control of education, Calles declared the Catholic church to be "a perpetual menace to the Mexican state and a permanent obstacle to social progress."

[24] Ebaugh, *The National System of Education in Mexico*, p. 20: "During the last years of the Díaz regime, May, 1911, a bill was approved by which the federal government accepted, for the first time in Mexican history, the responsibility for rural instruction throughout the Republic. Ability to read, write, and speak the Spanish language and to perform fundamental operations of arithmetic were to be the aims of the schools . . . expenditures of 160,000 pesos was authorized for the first year, but the figure was afterwards reduced to 80,000 pesos—a ridiculous sum for the extent of the proposed undertaking."

His indictment led to as wanton an anticlerical campaign, in the name of improving the lot of the masses, as the country had experienced. Calles stated his guiding creed in terms of the Revolution:

The ideal of my government is to save the great masses of the population from misery and ignorance, to raise their social standard, to teach them to eat better, to give them schools and culture, to raise them to a higher level of civilization, so as to construct a homogeneous nation, closing the existing gulf between a handful of Mexicans who enjoy comfort, refinement and well-being, and the great mass of Mexicans exploited by every tyranny, abandoned by every administration, buried in misery, darkness, and suffering. I prefer to carry on this humanitarian task—even if by so doing my government is marked with the name of Bolshevist, which propaganda is giving it. I leave to time to pass the difficult final judgment.

Calles was determined. On June 14, 1926, he issued a decree making practically every act of Catholic worship or expression of opinion on public affairs a criminal offense. In an all-out drive to gain final control of education, he closed Catholic institutions and prohibited religious instruction in the public schools, evicting, arresting, and in some instances inflicting the death penalty on teachers and pupils. Residences, seminaries, schools, convents, and other properties belonging to the church or to religious associations were forcibly and often brutally transferred to state ownership. Students were expected to adopt anti-Catholic views; priests were required to register with the government.

The Archbishop of Mexico retaliated by denouncing and rejecting Calles' constitutional restrictions against Catholicism. In this attitude he had the unswerving support of large segments of the people, native and conservative, who were indignant that Calles should attach godlessness to his program along with his other alien importations. On July 31, 1926, the church officially boycotted public education, and according to Father Parsons "a whole system of clandestine schools sprang up." These "home schools" were groups of nine or ten children assembled in private houses, there to be trained in the three R's by former public-school teachers or by laicized Sisters. Catholic bishops informed the people that it was their "grave obligation of conscience" to stay away from the public schools. Parents who kept their children in socialistic schools were "committing a grave mortal sin which cannot be absolved in Confession until the children are removed from these establishments." Laymen, too, demanded a revision in the law. Organized defenders of the Faith, called *cristeros*, though restrained by the church, nevertheless retaliated for government atrocities by raiding government schools, killing and maiming "socialist" teachers and leaving their bodies labeled with placards proclaiming "Christ is King."

Not until 1929 did a compromise quiet the violence of church opposition. This agreement provided: (1) that the government would not register clergymen except with the approval of their respective creeds, (2) that religious instruction might be given, but only inside church buildings, and (3) that the members of any church might petition the proper authorities for the amendment, repeal or passage of any law. Within half a decade, however, the conflagration broke out again, kindled by education minister Narciso Bassols' insistence not only on observing to the letter Article 3, but on actually combating religion in the schools. Mexico was by no means ready for church-state conciliation.

GROUNDWORK OF A SYSTEM

A school is planned which will respond to all the aspects of the life of man and society, so as to create a new type of man with ideals of an equalitarian society.—Extract from the first *Six-Year Plan*, 1934-40.

The socialist school creates a concept of personal, family, and civic ethics which supplants superstitious dogma, to the direct benefit of our people.— Lázaro Cárdenas, 1938.

Mexican teachers worthy of being called Christian will cooperate with parents . . . by educating in the Christian faith; they will deviate in no manner from the norms prescribed by the Church.—Don Pascual Díaz, Archbishop of Mexico, 1932.

To President Lázaro Cárdenas (1935-40), fell the task of coordinating the conflicting desires of his troubled land. Declaring that the state was to become "an active agent in the management and direction of the vital phenomena of the country, and not a mere custodian," the socialist-minded chief executive advanced a Six-Year Plan, three main objectives of which were: (1) to speed agrarian reform; (2) to effect the full organization and increased co-operation of labor; and (3) to provide adequate educational facilities for all Mexicans, young and old.[25] Under Cárdenas the Mexican state became not merely a guardian and a policeman but also a high priest and a teacher, professedly superseding the church in controlling even the spiritual lives of the people. In this connection Wilfred Parsons, half-tragically, half-humorously, presents a creed which he says was taught the children:

I believe in Almighty Socialism. . . . I believe in the Ejido . . . which descended to the miserable huts of the peasants, and sitteth at the right hand of General Cárdenas, the proletarian throne, and from thence shall come the division of the lands, which up to this have been in the hands of the Spaniards and creoles to the amount of 60%. I believe in the extinction of all religions inspired by the cowardice of mystical spirits. . . . Instead of Amen, there is *Tierra y Libertad,* the old device of Zapata, "Land and Liberty."

At best, the Six-Year Plan assured focus and continuity in educational activity. It called for 2,000 new schools a year, plus an increase in educational appropriations to 20 percent of the national budget. The federal government was bound to fix educational appropriations at a minimum of 15 percent, while state and local agencies were urged to maintain their 1933 expenditures at a minimum. Actually, not one of these aims was fully achieved, though the spirit that actuated them lived on as a challenge to succeeding administrations.

The Six-Year Plan put teeth into Article 27 on land distribution, leading to the establishment in 1935 of agricultural credit banks. Commenting on this sweeping measure, Clarence Senior writes: "Cárdenas learned that, in addition to the smallness of individual plots, two other factors had worked against the success of the land

[25] El Comité Ejecutivo Nacional, *Plan sexenal del partido nacional revolucionario,* p. 17. See also *El plan sexenal,* 1935, extracted in *La educación pública,* I, 19-25. Harold Benjamin, "Education in Mexico's Six-Year Plan," *School and Society,* XL (November 17, 1934), 666-68.

distribution program—the lack of financial aid and technical assistance." The purpose of the banks was to advance money for wages, improvements, and machinery; they organized markets, fostered technical achievement, and conducted agricultural schools. In addition, more than one million peasants in ten thousand villages received parcels of land totaling fifty million acres. This radical alteration in the distribution of Mexico's wealth naturally resulted in a considerable extension of educational opportunity among rural areas.

For industry and industrial workers, an institute of vocational guidance was established, together with a system of fellowships for technical students. A campaign was launched to force ranches and factories to provide schools for their workers, thus creating at least 1,500 more new schools. Other activities called for were a greatly enlarged public health program, public works projects, and specific measures for popular enlightenment designed to supplement the school system.

Thus, the political philosophy dominant in the 1930's was essentially materialist, and this accentuated the trend toward practical activities in the schools. Officially termed the "socialist school," the goal of this institution was epitomized in an important though abstruse statement issued by the Ministry of Education in 1935. Elementary schools, designated the country's first concern, consequently turned from book-learning to concentration on environment and community needs. Also, rural education facilities were expanded, as is evidenced by the large number of schools now bearing plaques to President Cárdenas, their builder. Finally, a Technical Council of Agricultural Education was created to supervise the program of the new agricultural schools.

The socialist school is the logical result of all the forces which have brought the school into harmony with the various aspects of recent reform in educational theory and the social movement in favor of the masses. Almost simultaneously with the beginning of the Revolution in 1910, a socialized school was envisioned which would not dwell on the fringes of society but would overcome its deficiencies, and work in defense of dispossessed classes.[26]

[26] *La educación pública en México*, I, 527-30. The author confesses to a streamlined translation of the original heavy-footed Spanish.

As might be suspected, dual standards for rural and urban education were incompatible with Cárdenas' socialized education, since a sense of community and all-round training for national citizenship of necessity superseded regionalism and provincial effort. Helpful in removing extreme differences was the success, however slight, of the campaign against illiteracy and rural backwardness. By 1939 the union of rural education with urban education was complete, at least in its federal-administrative and ideational aspects. A split occurred again in the early forties, but at present rural education is fused with the general elementary educational program, specialization being reserved for higher levels of training.

As the general success of the Six-Year Plan became assured, socialist doctrine gradually gave way to the more fundamental democratic interest which had inspired most of the Plan's features. James Magner, strong critic of the socialistic and antireligious aspects of Mexican revolutionary education, notes this change: "Cárdenas himself became impatient of the extravagant language of the proletarian pedagogues, and in 1938 began to order a stressing of 'democratic,' in place of the sectarian, 'socialism.' "

Under Cárdenas and his education ministers Ignacio García Téllez and Gonzalo Vázquez Vela the achievement in education was significant, at least in its physical phases. The number of rural schools, teachers, and pupils was doubled in less than a decade, and the per capita cost rose from 15 to 18 pesos per year to 28 to 30, a fact which induced Goodwin Watson to comment: "In proportion to per capita income, Mexico is now spending a larger share for education than is the United States." Libraries, following the successful pattern of the cultural mission, took to the road. Eight motor-truck libraries sent out from the Ministry of Education in 1937 circulated 57,000 books, gave 300 cinema performances, and 150 concerts. Adult education, originated in 1833 by Gómez Farías, awoke from a century of slumber to become in 1927 a permanent functioning branch of government schooling on all levels.

Commentators were, however, not by any means all in approval. James Magner, sympathetic to the suppressed Catholic schools, observed that from the standpoint of quality, the schools, both primary and secondary, declined pedagogically from those under Díaz. However, as others suggest, educational opportunity must remain a myth if economic need prevents it. The fact that 90 percent of Mexico's children, even as late as 1940, had never reached the sixth grade would indicate that increased educational opportunity was more needed than pedagogical refinements. The poverty which Juárez had blamed for poor school attendance ninety years before could scarcely be said to have disappeared with Cárdenas. And until children could be adequately fed and clothed, their schooling would have to remain a secondary matter, pedagogical or any other principles notwithstanding.

Conciliation of Mexico's many and bitter antagonistic camps was the professed purpose of Manuel Avila Camacho's administration, 1941-46. In the matter of religion, legal restrictions upon church activity were relaxed. Thus the way was paved for the greater religious freedom prevalent today, though the clergy are still expected to eschew political matters. Legal restrictions persist against church ownership of land; the number of priests has been limited to one for every 45,000 inhabitants; and well-defined regulations govern the conduct of church authorities. Officially, religious education is still prohibited, though at the present writing schools under church auspices function openly. In the capital alone there are at present some eighty Catholic schools in operation, all filled to capacity.

It was chiefly to the tangible, practical needs of Mexico that the Chief Executive turned his attention. In a desire to lessen the materialism of the socialist school and in answer to strong Catholic appeals, he appointed the conservative Octavio Véjar Vázquez as minister of education (1941-43). Government policy, expressed in Véjar Vázquez' speeches and writings, involved an education for national unity and for social equity, with new emphases on spiritual phases: "There can be no education," pronounced Véjar, "without the sign of the Cross behind it." At best the Véjar Vázquez interval was a healthy antidote to the ultramodern alien educational attitudes pervading the schools under Véjar's socialist-minded predecessor, Luis Sánchez Pontón. Véjar's main contributions were the Organic Law of 1942, the National Academy *(Colegio Nacional)*, the Commission for Scientific Investigation, and the Normal School for Special Education, further discussion of which is reserved for later chapters.

In response to the technological demands of the time, industrial and technical aims were superimposed on Cárdenas' agrarian reforms. The reason was clearly expressed by Avila Camacho in his announcement of the Second Six-Year Plan, 1941-46:

We live today on the margin of applied science, which in the production of wealth renders benefits which raise the public welfare and give foundation to human dignity even in the most humble home. . . . We need to construct, produce, industrialize ourselves, to take advantage of our national resources, the great expanse of our wild unexploited territory and wealth of water power.[27]

The spirit of conciliation, of seeking fuller participation by all groups, with greater emphasis on national educational planning, was manifested by Jaime Torres Bodet, who assumed office as minister of education in 1944. Education, according to Torres Bodet, was not to be confined to an office of education or to educational specialists: "It is a task in which all agencies concerned must participate: newspapermen, writers, professional men, artists, theater and radio managers," all of whom should be prompt to understand that their efforts, their contributions, are necessary for the proper integration and functioning of the schools.

A shift from controversial socialism to something more essentially Mexican was discernible in the minister's statement concerning textbooks: "They should develop ideas of unquestionable democratic worth for our nation as a whole; and their content should feature national tradition, national reality, and local color." The individuality of local regions was not to be destroyed in the process of national amalgamation. Notable during Torres Bodet's administration was the provision in Article 3, approved December, 1945, for the establishment of numerous institutions destined to improve the quality of teachers and teaching and for a renewed, large-scale campaign to eliminate illiteracy.

[27] Secretaría de Gobernación, *Segundo plan sexenal*, 1941, pp. 10-11. Larroyo, *Historia comparada de la educación en México*, p. 399.

Miguel Alemán, the present presidential incumbent, elected in December, 1946, carries on his predecessor's emphasis on industrialization and land improvement. In Alemán's six-year program, irrigation, communications, roads, and manufacturing loom large; his greatest interest and energy are to be absorbed in the production of material goods for increased home consumption. In the field of education, this means greater efficiency, increased productivity, and a closer integration with the economic strength of the nation. A consolidated national education program will be geared to a growing economy. The talented Torres Bodet, former subsecretary of foreign affairs and an intellectual in the tradition of revolutionary ministers, gives way to a man who in Alemán's opinion is more adapted to the new task, Manuel Gual Vidal, appointed in January, 1947. The present minister, selected with an eye to uniting business interests in support of educational efforts, is a professor of law and finance and chairman of the very important committee for the National Charity Agency *(Monte de Piedad)*, an organization which handles and distributes to charity large funds derived from the sale of pawned goods.

Gual Vidal's pronouncements to date have concerned what he terms the "unified school" *(escuela unificada)* and programs for the modernization of agricultural, technical, and normal schools. Agricultural education, which still lags behind the growth of population, must be stepped up. "Our agricultural education," he states, "without question does not conform to the needs of the country; there are too few rural schools, and they have not been properly equipped. . . . These schools will have to be converted into working farm schools of a productive type." To set these schools on their feet again, the new minister relies on the missionary agricultural credit banks: "The existing schools are being provided with agricultural machinery and cultivating implements, school supplies, and other necessities for sound functioning. Procedures have been initiated for the agricultural credit banks to finance these schools in order to convert them into productive plants." Physical evidence of progress in technical and normal education is visible in the recent additions to the vocational schools and in the inauguration of the imposing and modernistic National Normal School, 1947.

It is yet too early to measure Gual Vidal's accomplishments, but he may at least provide a workable solution to the fundamental problem which has always frustrated Mexican educational leaders —the lack of adequate wherewithal. It is certain that Mexico's educational salvation will come, not from fond hopes, pedagogical niceties, or spiritual blandishments, but from an adequate provision of the necessary material means for its very existence.

III. Contemporary Thought and Organization

PREVAILING IDEOLOGIES

All education has a double purpose, human and national; because every man is bound by tradition to his people at the same time that he is part of humanity. It is false to educate solely for the nation. . . . But to educate solely with a view toward humanity, excluding sacred patriotic traditions, constitutes on the face of it a grave and serious error.—Antonio Caso.

Mexican ideology resolves the philosophic debate as to who owns the child, the family or society, by answering that neither owns him. He is a free member of society from the moment he is born, and he is under a reciprocal agreement with both family and society.—Plan de Acción de la Escuela Primaria Socialista.

It is the final goal of education to produce the spirit of co-operative brotherhood among our people; and to prepare them for liberty and justice, so that they can rule themselves.—Manuel Gual Vidal, 1947.

THIS SECTION concerns itself with the thought, the ideology, and the principles which, chiefly in the last generation, have brought the public school system to its present status. This thought has come mostly from those in government offices who have been responsible for the direction of public education. Philosophic concepts of a more strictly academic order have been confined almost exclusively to higher education; they have penetrated the lower schools only through the medium of higher school preference.[1] In this respect, the type of learning that was foisted on Mexican public-school

---

[1] "French literature and philosophy overflowed the intellectual world in Mexico. Its influence upon the privileged classes was strong. . . . But this intellectual activity did not go down to the popular school." Barranco, *Mexico; its Educational Problems,* p. 47.

students has nearly always proved overacademic, inapplicable, and unattainable; hence it has constantly been under attack.

Recurrent throughout Mexican educational thought has been the theme of national and social integration. Among the first to sound the keynote was Benito Juárez, who, though by no means anti-religious, concluded that after centuries of hunger and deprivation the Indian needed to be fed on more than spiritual food. Instead of continuing to entrust the education of Mexican youth to the clergy, he applied himself to the training of lay teachers secured from the ranks of his people. Thus was born the principle of *laicismo* in Mexican education in place of *clericismo,* an emphasis on lay training by lay teachers rather than on education with a clerical bias.

The philosophy of Juárez was not so important as his personality. For the first time in Mexico's history a full-blooded Indian, early orphaned and poor, and possessing all the virtues, feelings, attitudes, and yearnings of Mexico's native peoples, came to the helm of an orphaned country and, by warring against foreign aggression—imperialistic, political, cultural, and ecclesiastic—attempted to make Mexico an independent, self-determining nation. Here at last was a man who in his native soul felt the heartbeat of Mexico's native populations, a Zapotec Indian who expounded a political and educational philosophy that was rooted in the country's very blood and soil.

Juárez' educational program was dedicated to the double purpose of emancipating the Indian and setting Mexico on the high road to nationhood. But Benito never succeeded in vanquishing provincialism and ecclesiasticism. Mexico's states, jealous of their rights and suspicious of supergovernment, may have been aware that union makes for strength, but they chose to keep the house divided. And Catholicism, its hold already shaken by the failure of France and Spain to maintain political control in Mexico, could hardly have been expected to support a state system which was pledged to undermine the church's very foundations.

Following Juárez, the supporters of national and social integration resolved to throw off all foreign dictation, active or latent. They agitated for a popular education which would recognize regional preferences and take into account local thought as the groundwork on which to build a broader native culture. Only on a sound basis of regionalism and local preference could there arise a Mexico strong in all its parts. Supporters of this idea were accustomed to point to the United States as a shining example, overlooking one essential difference, the fact that Mexico's states were less artificially created.

The Díaz administration theorized about national integration, but practiced reaction. This regime clearly demonstrated the extent to which philosophers and philosophies may be used as apologists for those holding the power. Díaz' positivistic *científicos* ("Let us be scientific; let us be realistic") were an ideal front for a system that was at heart retrogressive. In contrast to the apologists for Díaz' authoritarianism, the revered humanitarian Justo Sierra stood out in lonely dignity. A democratic follower of the democrat Juárez, Sierra was an alien spirit in Don Porfirio's oligarchy. Sierra combatted an educational automatism which stressed repetition, recitation, and *memoriter* learning, and advanced social integration by introducing German developmental methods and encouraging the work of native humanist thinkers.

Sierra's antipositivism was continued by José Vasconcelos, who considered the work of the científicos to be mainly an excuse for educational secularization: "The Comtian system imposed itself upon us almost literally, because it contradicted the orthodox Catholicism always latent in our culture, and because . . . it represented a 'new era,' a 'definite creed,' that of SCIENCE in capital letters, the new fetish."[2] Positivistic teaching, Vasconcelos decided, was unfertile for Mexico. Instead, he substituted a modern philosophy of practical values. A philosopher in his own right, he recognized the qualitative necessities of education; but in the early period of organization he saw clearly that quantitative demands had to be satisfied first of all. The guiding thought of Vasconcelos' administration was therefore one of practical adjustment and empirical accomplishment: "We have all the ideas we need," he asserted, "more than we can use. What we need is money, resources, people, details, persistence." Under Vasconcelos, education ceased

[2] Vasconcelos, *Historia del pensamiento filosófico*, p. 357.

to be a foreign institution artificially grafted onto the body politic and instead became an integral, active agent for nationhood. Educational aims had always been a part of national policy. The speeches of politicians had long referred to the need for unity and economic prosperity; now effort was concentrated on school improvement as the chief means of attaining that end. The present Ministry of Education, its power, its structure, its purpose—all may be traced directly to Vasconcelos' driving energy.

Native and national integration implies the unification and coordination of all school systems, but ideas as to how this could and should be done have undergone considerable variation with changes in political administrations. Since 1921 the ministry of education has occupied the key place in determining the thought which shall guide Mexico's educational life. The minister of education is first of all a cabinet member and must of necessity be a politician close to the administrative center of political gravity. It is axiomatic that a change in presidents is speedily followed by a change in educational ministers. It does not follow, however, that the official educational philosophy is based entirely upon political expediency. The education minister's judgment may strongly influence his colleagues, inducing adjustments throughout the government to the demands of the educational program. Education is thus elevated to full participation in the total national progress, a status it has not yet attained in the United States.

By and large, the ministry's fundamental aims have remained fairly constant in the last twenty-five years. Aside from the principle of national and social integration of the indigenous peoples, they include: (1) the extension of elementary schools throughout the Republic; (2) the spread of elementary education to the adult population; (3) the elimination of illiteracy; (4) the formation and training of teaching staffs "on the basis of a Mexican culture and a recognized pedagogy"; (5) the co-operation of the family; and (6) the co-ordination of federal education with that of the states and municipalities.[3]

[3] Adapted from Secretaría de Educación Pública, "La educación en México," MS, Mexico City, 1943; and based on the *Ley Orgánica*, pp. 60-62. For comment on these MSS and others which follow see Bibliography. *Cf.* José Vasconcelos in Véjar Vázquez,

Fulfillment of these purposes has left little room for purely pedagogical experimentation or educational adventure, though in the late twenties certain foreign educational ideologies (Dewey's activity program, for example) were drawn on with no conspicuous success to "redeem the nation through education" *(educar es redimir)*. By the middle thirties the ministry's program had become more social-minded, more class-conscious. The question of this period, "What kind of education redeems?" received its answer in a revised doctrine of socialism and a Mexican interpretation of the objective, scientific approach. The purpose of education, according to Article III of the Organic Law, was to create in youth a "rational, exact concept of the universe." History, as well as physics, chemistry, anatomy, and cosmography, was to be taught rationally and as a means of demonstrating the mechanism of human society. It was to be made evident, for example, that if misery exists, it is not because "God so wills," but because the condition is the logical and inevitable result of society's defective economic organization.

There then descended on the country a veritable barrage of pamphlets, invading every intellectual corner of the land with the essence, much diluted, of dialectic materialism, social justice, educational egalitarianism, "co-operativism" and a whole array of those salvation-centered "isms" which always seem to enshroud countries in the depths of economic and psychological despair. Widely prevalent was the feeling that the country needed a complete social transformation, attainable only by educating a new generation away from the "old, evil ways" and concentrating on broader social welfare.

In 1935 Luis Sánchez Pontón, later minister of education, systematized current thought by urging educators to "create *(crear)* the personality of students."[4] According to him, national education had two major objectives, the first of which was "to adapt the in-

---

Hacia una escuela de unidad nacional, p. 183: "The home constitutes a school of supreme socio-biologic type. Without the preparation given by the home, the greater part of the educative drive of the state is wasted."

[4] Sánchez Pontón, *Hacia la escuela socialista* (La reforma educativa en México), pp. 272 ff.

dividual to the conditions of life in his own community, identify him with its aspirations, and enable him to influence social progress through the action of his own free personality." Sánchez Pontón's second general objective was to "form the socio-economic man, who is the sum-total of the ideals of socialization, equalization, and unification in the modern world." Toward this end he urged: (1) the use of scientific, rather than metaphysical, explanations of the universe; (2) constructive social criticism in teaching; (3) the creation of concepts of social justice based on equitable material distribution; (4) the elimination of unfounded prejudices and superstitions, especially with regard to race, class, and sex differences; and (5) the awakening in pupils of their responsibilities as members of a community through productive intellectual and physical effort.

Thus, in the mind of the socialistic minister the new Mexican personality was to be co-operative, tolerant, and vocationally and culturally skilled. Above all, he was to be a useful citizen of Mexico. This view had already been reflected in the reasoning of more moderate socialistic educators, such as the anthropologist Manuel Gamio. Eschewing "social-ism," yet mindful of the need to reinforce efforts toward national integration, Gamio concentrated on what he termed "integral education." According to Gamio, the school must include all those community activities which would integrate the individual into the life of the group "socially, economically, politically, linguistically, and artistically."

Sánchez Pontón and Gamio were agreed on the need for learning to live more productively and more co-operatively, and both stressed a more than merely mechanical co-operation. The existence of man as an individual or as a member of a group was measured, they thought, in terms of his activity, of his personal production and its effect on society. But Sánchez Pontón revealed a greater preference for philosophic existentialism, exemplified in his educational goal: "To follow the objectives of general education in the development of all the powers latent within every individual, and to educate with a clear vision of what constitutes human plenitude."

Recognizing that co-operation, economic efficiency, and most of all the achievement of "human plenitude" depended upon experience and activity, Sánchez Pontón admittedly followed Dewey in declaring that "the school must be a workshop and a community in miniature." He therefore offered a new approach, in contrast to the "academic" type of training favored by the church and other private agencies, an approach that recognized the responsibility of the school to create in students those personal characteristics which would correspond to national, rather than to group, norms.

Sánchez Pontón's well-meaning objectives proved impractical. To create a "socio-economic man," modern in all respects, was difficult enough even for Mexico's brighter citizens, but to adapt this formidable creature to a system essentially capitalistic and to the vicissitudes of life in the country's more deficient areas was well-nigh impossible. Educational theory, in this instance, was too far removed from the existing circumstances. Socialist educators such as Sánchez Pontón propounded reforms that were much too novel, much too alien for an unprepared populace to grasp.

The reaction to socialism was violent. Such modern ideas, most of them only half understood, outraged traditional minds and threatened Mexico's whole social structure. Catholics cried out against the rival religion which threatened to banish their creed from the minds of innocent children and devoutly religious parents. The idea of sex education and coeducation shocked Indian and Catholic alike.[5] In order to create a concept of social justice founded on the equitable distribution of material and social goods of the community, the teachers were obligated to advocate the precepts of Marx, Bakunin, and related social philosophers whose teachings they improperly understood. Over the interpretation of the term "socialistic," as employed in Article 3 of the Constitution, gallons of ink and tears were shed, though much opposition arose because the expression was really an error in terminology. To be precise about it, the Mexican Constitution did not, and does not, deny the right to private property; instead, it reserves the right to determine in what instances private ownership has ceased to serve the general welfare. In any case, the socialistic educators of the Cárdenas ad-

---

[5] MacFarland, *Chaos in Mexico*, p. 88, states that it was not the teaching of sex in itself that was so offensive, but "the crude way in which it was sensationally announced by a former secretary of public education."

ministration found that changing the face of a nation was not the work of a single generation. And it scarcely helped to have their concepts stigmatized at home and abroad as communistic to the core.

Socialistic education left an indelible mark on Mexican schools. Certain theses were retained which actually acquired the character of law, among them:

(1) Efficient participation in the work of the community in order to understand, transform, and control the forces of nature; (2) Permanent participation in the rhythm of the historic evolution of the country, contributing toward the fulfillment of the postulates of the Mexican Revolution essentially with regard to the liquidation of latifundismo and to the creation of a native economy benefiting the masses of the people; (3) Fervent struggle for a more human and more just social understanding on which economic organization can be constructed, in a way favoring the general welfare and forsaking the system of exploitation of man by man; (4) Consolidation and perfection of democratic institutions and raising the material and cultural level of the people.[6]

With the passing of time socialistic utterances were considerably toned down, but the revered Rafael Ramírez could still say in 1942 that "today education has a meaning definitely proletarian; the disinherited masses come to the schools because they feel and understand that education is one of the principal instruments for their redemption." In other words, a course of moderation had taught the country that though Mexico had rejected pure socialism, a modified socialism could offer the schools benefits that perhaps had been too long delayed.

We have already indicated how, commencing in 1940, this moderation was transformed into a sincere desire to conciliate opposed groups. Avila Camacho placed the responsibility on every individual: "If we desire to become free, we must begin by making ourselves individually worthy of the liberty to which we aspire." A "healthy individual understanding" was the indispensable proviso for national progress. Prosperity and social order, he considered, might best be achieved through solid technical attainments rather than by the study of erudite doctrines. The President's prime concern was thus to develop educational skill and precision: "We

[6] *La educación pública en México,* 1934-40, "La nueva escuela en México," Dirección General de Estudios Tecnicopedagógicos, I, 24.

have not yet succeeded in acquiring a public education which in quality and kind satisfies the peculiar necessities of our people." But certain that true progress could not be made until all programs and institutions were adapted to the Mexican environment, he insisted on an education "grounded in the social sense of the people."

Exercising his talents as a conciliator in the educational branches, the Catholic conservative Octavio Véjar Vázquez sought to restore to the schools and schoolteachers a lost appreciation of religion. With buoyant heart and zealous spirit, this minister, formerly a military lawyer and a government strong man, embarked on a policy of resurrecting what he considered were forgotten virtues. His writings reflect a preference for traditionalism and a strong feeling for the "natural hierarchy of man."

Avila Camacho had declared himself a "believer," without clarifying the extent to which his belief adhered to traditional church doctrines. But the destructive effect of socialism on traditional schooling lay heavily on Véjar's heart, and he felt himself chosen by the President to redeem the loss. His indictment that attacks on traditional schools had turned the child's mind against his home and family, was a passionate protest against the legal secularization of schools and a plea for the church.

Véjar Vázquez was convinced that the schools could not remain indifferent to moral principles, to ethics, aesthetics, and the other values directly concerned with human conduct. Education had to have a positive moral content as the only sound and abiding foundation for a full and meritorious life. The socialist ethic, Véjar decided, had failed, and in its place "a hard materialism has lowered our national morals . . . turned us toward fleeting pleasures that weaken the soul and dilute the character. The need for the moral reconstruction of our country is imperative." In Véjar Vázquez' philosophy positivism was a strong component. His definition of moral order was based essentially on ecclesiastic tenets. However, Véjar's fervent self-dedication to the old ideals could not prevent him from criticizing traditional method:

In the past, learning was developed from foregone conclusions, from truths, from erudite encyclopedic information—and not from the proper exercise of those functions which create culture. The present situation reveals an absence of men technically prepared for economic endeavor; this gives us our opportunity to plan an education in accordance with vital reality, benefiting from the hard experiences of other peoples.

The restoration of moral order also called for a conciliation of the privileged classes, who were warned to become more aware of their obligations. Vested interests were to "countenance the social advancement of all types of worthy people," so as to prevent social degeneration. Indeed, Véjar Vázquez rejected educational aims which catered to a single social group: "The schools must not be used to impose upon new generations the type of life and culture peculiar to any one group."

What solution did Véjar offer for settling the angry conflict between classes? Love, he was confident, would conquer all. The schools would teach Mexicans to love one another despite differences in creed, party, or class. Just how Véjar intended to foster this love and at the same time call for an end to coeducation puzzled many a skeptical Mexican student, who twitted him in typical undergraduate style. For, paradoxically enough, Véjar's catholicity with respect to national instruction did not extend to both sexes. The "natural requirements" of men and women were found to be so vastly different that he preferred to reduce educational opportunity rather than continue what he termed the "socialist" policy of educating males and females together. In this attitude he had the support of the President and of the Catholic church.

In the matter of the individual's relationship to society, Véjar's thought was liberal. It was his conviction that the object of education was the individual as an end in himself. On the other hand, since "man is what he is only through society," the Mexican school was obligated to inculcate in youth a love of country and an active interest in one's fellow citizens, regardless of religious or other preferences. The place of the individual in the educative process received varied definition. Demanding a "functionally complete" education, the President had declared that he was opposed to an education restricted to eliminating illiteracy and "snatching children from the obscurity of their cradles—only to submerge them in primary school automatism." To educate, Véjar interpreted, "is to make every man a personality endowed with resources for worthy use in exercising his hierarchic position in creation."

Such was Véjar's protest against an education which to his mind was not only void of spiritual uplift, but was actually failing to achieve its much-touted vocational goals. "Hierarchic position in creation," an expression far removed from socialism or social humanism, implies, of course, the existence of a well-defined and proper place for every human being. Véjar's own definition testifies to this. Mexican society, he taught, was divided into four main groups: the army, the privileged classes, the workers, and the Catholic church. Furthermore, "Education does not mean the imposition of a new being at the root of every individual existence, but the unfolding of what was original, influenced by environment and history, and aiming to reach a higher grade of natural perfection."

Thus Véjar Vázquez confessed his devotion to revealed truth, which "history and environment render ever more resplendent." The individual, he charged, would do well to acknowledge this fact, for his growth and development take place naturally only when free rein is given to what was original. This meant, presumably, that what was original was natural; and this originality began, of course, with Cortés. For, strangely enough, only the events subsequent to Cortés' act of salvation could contribute to the Mexican's "natural perfection"—at least in Véjar's reasoning.

Véjar Vázquez failed to remain in office chiefly because he underestimated the strength of socialism's educational residue and because the conciliation of all parties among Mexico's antagonistic camps demanded a greater compromise between conflicting educational doctrines. Véjar's monistic leanings did not permit him to tolerate opposing points of view or to modify his own. In his sympathetic Introduction to Véjar Vázquez's *Hacia una Escuela de Unidad Nacional,* José Vasconcelos, himself recently a convert to monistic preferences, could not refrain from sympathizing with Véjar's definition of the true foundation of civilized human existence: "Whenever a profound social crisis moves the very foundation of human existence [and brings us] face to face with danger, then our eyes turn back to those institutions which centuries have proved to be creative and beneficial in their effects." Thus, in Mexico, as elsewhere, one experiences the desire on the part of many to rely essentially on traditional values rather than on the unknown and the uncertain. The Véjar Vázquez era was to them a return to morality, on which all culture must finally rest.[7]

Véjar Vázquez had served his time, but did not move along with it. New worlds were in the making; Mexican leaders stirred to the pipes of pan-Americanism and the hope of discovering international brotherhood, peace, and social justice in a world at war to achieve it. Avila Camacho accordingly summoned the suave career diplomat Jaime Torres Bodet to assist in the national reorientation toward hemispheric solidarity and the "good neighbor" policy. To his appointed task Torres Bodet remained faithful; yet, however devoted to internationalism, he did not harness the schools to alien ideologies. Mexico, he argued, must not be a slave to imported academic disciplines. Internal unity should not, moreover, be sought by catering to vocal pressure groups and ardent minorities. The new minister condemned the specious uniformity which sacrificed harmony among all groups to the rigid control of a single faction.[8]

Torres Bodet conceived the special task of the school to be that of serving as a "mental transformer" of historical forces, adapting these forces to the necessities of the present and employing them with foresight toward the solution of the problems of the future. He held the school responsible not only for maintaining the continuity of tradition but also for selecting those traditions which gave promise of greater national prosperity. Neither traditionalism nor progressivism, however, was to predominate. Traditionalism he considered incompatible with the natural forces of human society, the latter being distinguished from its animal counterpart by its aptitude for change. On the other hand, to ignore tradition would

---

[7] José Gómez Robleda, *Tiempo*, August 22, 1947, writing from a psychiatrist's point of view, elects two education ministers to the hall of fame: Narciso Bassols, and Véjar Vázquez, the former for his "sex education," the latter for his "school of love." "Both of them shattered the average Mexican's irritable neuroses."

[8] Torres Bodet, *La escuela mexicana*, pp. 14, 49. *Excelsior*, March 19, 1944, distinguishes, "three critical phases" within the preceding decade: (1) "The communist, anti-Christian" ministries of Vázquez Vela and Sánchez Pontón; (2) the communist purge under Véjar Vázquez—needed "to make teaching more national, inspired by the necessities and desires of Mexico"; and (3) internationalism under Torres Bodet, especially pan-Americanism and "buena voluntad."

be to "minimize the extent of our task and incur the danger of destroying our national life."

To Torres Bodet, a school system which hoped to serve as a passage to the future had to remain close to present reality. This was not to be a bland and doctrinaire "realism" which ignored the locale and background of the students. Declaring that no culture could be "cicatrized" by universal customs, he pointed to the peculiar circumstance of the isolated native peoples. "What support and loyalty can be expected of the Indian boy," asked Torres Bodet, "when we try to teach him reading from a book that contains examples of things he has never seen, and fails to incorporate the objects, people, and customs with which he is familiar?"

Torres Bodet recognized that common learnings were the basis of a sound nationalism. Effective articulation (*vertebración effectiva*) throughout the nation's school curricula was imperative; and this articulation should follow the mellowing course of the Revolution. "Education must teach us to appreciate our own national soul."[9]

Achieving "integral development of the total personality" proved to be a vexatious task for the unsettled philosophies of Mexico,[10] so much so that Torres Bodet found it necessary to systematize his ideals in a functional six-fold program: (1) The development of physical strength through individual and team sports; (2) the training for sensory alertness through manual activities; (3) the elevation of attitudes and sensitivity through aesthetic expression in poetry, music, and painting; (4) the refinement of intelligence through a scientific apprenticeship in which knowledge is not simply memorized, but is verified by experience; (5) the strengthening of character through personal initiative; (6) the cultivation of a sincere altruism through common action, interdependence of interests, and solidarity of ideals.[11]

Torres Bodet was more than an education minister; his influence

[9] Torres Bodet, *La escuela mexicana*, p. 15; also *Educación mexicana*, p. 239.

[10] In 1943 a critic complained of residual "positivism" in the public school system, because "positivism establishes norms for the control of thinking, but not of sentiments or the will; that is to say, it does not establish norms of conduct."—González Garza, *El problema fundamental de México*, p. 79.

[11] Secretaría de Educación Pública, *La obra educative en el sexenio 1940-1946*, pp. 10-12.

in national affairs approached that of the President, to the benefit, naturally, of the schools. His mental horizons were wide, his counsel was valued in all matters pertaining to national welfare. Eschewing excesses and disdaining personal prerogatives, Torres Bodet became a popular minister, admired for his scholarliness and for the dignity and sense of balance he lent the ministry. In 1947 he was returned as minister of foreign affairs under President Miguel Alemán, and in November, 1948, was named Director-General of UNESCO to succeed Julian Huxley.

To transcend, rather than merely to co-ordinate, Mexico's irreducible differences is the present ambition of President Miguel Alemán's energetic administration. A new official note of national individualism, sounded lightly by Avila Camacho, has become the dominant theme; but it is an expression born of war and inflation. Industrialization and economic development are now the determining factors in educational policy. The early speeches of Alemán's minister of education, Manuel Gual Vidal, financier and lawyer, suggest that the educational planning of the next six years will accentuate practical values and those functions of the schools which contribute to the success of Mexican big business.

In defense of democratic education and the "unified school," Gual Vidal expresses himself in favor of a system founded on the social and cultural betterment of all Mexicans. This means an end to self-determinative provincialism, which Gual Vidal castigates as "the limpid poison of Mexican originality, physiognomy, and progressive cultural continuity." Regional cultural attainment must be preserved, but only as it contributes to the commonweal.[12] Yet nothing will ensue from the new program if the people are unwilling to work to achieve its goals. The minister addresses a special appeal to young people:

You cannot close your eyes and ignore the pressing needs of Mexico, its problems so easy to formulate and so difficult to resolve because of their gravity and depth. We must turn promises into realities; but to that effort each and every one of us must contribute work—with an enthusiasm and courage inspired by faith in our national destiny.

[12] Gual Vidal's views are expressed in his *Diez discursos sobre educación. Cf.* also Larroyo, *Historia comparada*, pp. 406 ff.

In Mexico, as elsewhere, official eyes turn hopefully toward the younger generation for national salvation.

Mexico, Gual Vidal asserts, is maturing. Her institutions are sound. What is needed for the future is an interval of peace and order during which the ideals of the Revolution may be brought to fruition. The implication here is that certain national standards have already been achieved and that the chief need is now for law codification. Says Gual Vidal: "Without legal order, there is no social life possible, either national or international."

These are, of course, the words of a practical business man, speaking to be understood by others like himself. Of the harmonious development of character, the transformation of indigenous cultures, the social adaptation of isolated individuals through group expressive arts, the regeneration of maladjusted persons from families oppressed and ill-functioning for generations, and the further rehabilitation of the church, he has spoken only suggestively.

It has been shown that the type of educational thought and planning which has yielded the most profitable returns in Mexico has been that which dealt with methods of adjusting the public school system to the very tangible and urgent needs of Mexico's masses. A quick survey reveals the directional lines of this thought to be somewhat as follows: (1) from absolute control by the church to absolute state control; (2) from ecclesiastical education, dogmatic and exclusive, to social education, "rational and scientific"; (3) from abstract and verbal methods to activity and life-oriented teachings; (4) from education as the privilege of the dominant classes to public education for all.[13] Inherent in this development

[13] Tirado Benedí, "Panorama educativo de México," *Nueva Era,* 1944, p. 288. MacFarland, *Chaos in Mexico,* p. 81, quoting Ignacio García Téllez, minister of education, 1935, reveals the typical Mexican official interpretation: ". . . the historic periods of our education. These were: theocratic in the period before the conquest; overpowered by religious dogma during the colonial period, and until the time of the separation of the Church and the State by the Reform Laws; predominantly positivist in the official establishment and theological in the private schools during the Porfirio Díaz regime. With the publication of the Constitution of 1917, the state instituted lay teaching, and limited the ascendency of the clergy, who, under the protection of liberty, mutilated the intelligence of childhood, imposing traditional dogmas which were contrary to scientific progress and to the principles of the political, economic and moral emancipation of the masses."

has been the drive to integrate into the Mexican nation every member of every remote tribe within its wide borders.

Educational thought has not been purely academic or contemplative in nature. The delicate web of philosophy has been far removed from the politically controlled progress of Mexico's public-school education, where "practicalism" has been the only "ism" to succeed. Foreign ideologies have bloomed in educational experimentation only to wither and die in the harvest-time of practical application. Over thirty years ago Manuel Barranco, outlining what he considered essential to the educational progress of the Mexican, wrote as follows:

First, he must be physically fit to work and to form a family. Second, he must have ability enough to be a sound producer and consumer. Third, he must possess, intelligently, a sum total of knowledge sufficient to give him an idea of the civilization in the midst of which he is living, with a conception, a simple one, of the struggles of humanity to get where it is now. Fourth, he must keep in his heart *con amore* the moral and esthetic ideals of the group or society in which he lives, to help him to form his character. Recapitulating in three words, he must be able to do, to think, and to love.

A simple and prophetic ideal this is, indeed, and founded on the down-to-earth needs of the people and of the land. Debate still rages, however, on the exact meaning and connotation of such expressions as "love" and "think." Though little question is raised nowadays as to the functional purposes of Mexican schooling, commentators loyal to tradition and to religion do not sanction Barranco's ideas or those of his followers, especially as regards moral training. Parsons, Kelley, Steck, MacFarland, and other representatives of the church, Catholics and Protestants alike, protest against the type of spiritual teaching advocated by the Mexican state. Nor does any Catholic agree that the general education taught in church schools excludes a "rational, scientific approach" or believe that Catholic schools are, or have been, barriers to Mexico's social progress. Deploring the trend toward atheism and the worship of "material gods," MacFarland clinches the issue when he concludes: "The government has taken possession of education." Instead of being a church monopoly, education has now become a state monopoly, a "capture of intellects," in Parsons' terms, a "totalitarian form of schooling." Any educational dictatorship, these critics pertinently observe, is objectionable, since no government which imposes it can properly be called democratic. It becomes all the more objectionable to the religious mind when governmental legislation compels schooling to become antireligious.

Whatever point of view is taken, there should be no hesitance about giving full credit to the various religious groups and private agencies for the struggle they have waged to preserve their hold on Mexico's educational life. Despite confiscations, persecutions, and endless political interference, they have valiantly and persistently maintained their right to exist. That Mexico's government interferes with them less often is eloquent testimony that this restrictive legislation was, and is, contrary to the popular will. As may be seen in the final chapter, it is perhaps time for both church and state to acknowledge that neither can monopolize the education of young people and that in a democratic society parents will tend to choose that type of training which to their mind promises assurance of the fullest all-round development of their children. The deadly conflict of the past may, of course, resolve itself into a healthy competition among the schools. Certainly both church and state can point to better schools and schooling than existed before the struggle began —not solely as a result of normal progress, but to a large extent because of the sincere desire of both public and private interests to prove the intrinsic merits of their chosen type of schooling.

THE FRAMEWORK OF EDUCATION

It will be useless to perfect our educational methods if this perfection is not accompanied by the cleansing of our political system and our cultural institutions.—Manuel Avila Camacho.

The workshops in which the soul of a people is forged are the homes and the schools. And when one of these workshops is tossed about at the mercy of political tempests, the equilibrium is destroyed and partisanship is satisfied only at the cost of national progress.—Jaime Torres Bodet.

Mexico calls herself a constitutional republic like the United States, but from what has been said thus far it should be obvious that historically, at least, this claim has been more of an ideal than a reality. Since the achievement of independence in 1810, Mexican constitutional history has been littered with the wreckage of despotisms. Presidents, good and bad, have been as expendable as ammunition, and lesser men have in all eras fallen from power when their politics veered from the line of the dominant group, or when they lost their toga as commander-in-chief of the armed forces. Mexican elections, have historically been orgies of vote manipulation, shot through with strong-arm tactics and every kind of skulduggery at the polls. The election of Miguel Alemán, in 1946, probably the cleanest and fairest to date, nevertheless met sharp criticism from the opposite camps for the methods used by the victors.

The force and violence which have characterized Mexico's political history are totally incompatible with the usual republican ideals of behavior. Throttling the opposition can scarcely be considered conducive to the attainment of the "government by consent of the governed" by which the general welfare is best served. But for many reasons democracy is not yet a firm concept in Mexico. For one thing, the idea of full voting representation has never completely been established. Citizenship and the right to vote are vested in all male nationals who are 18 years of age and married; or 21 years if unmarried and having an "honorable means of livelihood." Full woman suffrage has not yet been granted. Of the chosen electors, too many are politically ignorant—literate enough, perhaps, to read the names and pictures on campaign broadsides, clever enough to use a gun or a knife, but too poor to resist a peso or a pot of pulque in return for their vote. Mexico's essay in democracy is very young, indeed, and beset by many of democracy's characteristic frailties.

The Mexican government is in theory representative. As in the United States, the national congress is bicameral. The chamber of deputies is popularly elected for three years on a basis of one representative for every 100,000 inhabitants. The fifty-eight senators, two from each state including the Federal District, are elected every six years. The president, members of congress, governors, mayors, and all state legislators are ineligible for re-election to the term immediately following. The president, elected directly by popular vote, holds office for six years.

Thus, democratic forms are present. But Mexico's political structure is tightly controlled by the Institutional Revolutionary Party (PRI), which, as Herring astutely observed of the former PRM (Party of the Mexican Revolution), "plays a role comparable to that of the Democratic party of Georgia or the Republican party in Vermont." Then too, Mexico has a democracy of her own design, in which governments have yielded to the voting masses, only to exercise a firm and direct control once their power has been assured. The opposition party, when defeated, becomes a less potent force than is usual in most democratic governments.

The explanation for this lies mostly in the way in which Mexico came to function as a nation. Identification of the Revolution with the national government has automatically given that body the broad responsibilities of common welfare and national survival. Thus, although the Mexican constitution reserves to the states all controls not expressly granted to the federal government, the powers of the Mexican national congress have become constitutionally greater than those of the Congress of the United States in such fields as public health, religion, labor, land, and education. The centralism which prevails in Mexican politics and education may, in a larger sense, be regarded as a triumph of practical circumstance over political philosophy—of national necessity over imported custom. For more than half a century, despite lip service to federalism and decentralized power, every vital problem of nationhood had gravitated toward the federal government for solution. With regard to issues of the common welfare, the various states have proved themselves administratively too weak, too indifferent, too unreliable, or too isolated. In education local governments have so far failed to provide adequate institutions.

Whether or not centralism is in itself an evil is a matter of less concern to Mexicans today in view of the need for creating an instrument capable of fusing the myriad small centralisms. Francisco Céspedes of the Pan-American Union denies that centralization in itself is an evil: "The evil lies in the subordination of education to partisan, personalistic politics. It is doubtful whether decentralization would protect education from the pernicious influence of tropical politics." Likewise, as Larrea points out, "Centralization finds its justification in the growing emphasis on the responsibility of government." It is precisely from this circumstance that a paradox arises, not, indeed, peculiar to Mexico, that education must work for human betterment, but must trim its sails with every shift in the political wind.

Unlike the Constitution of the United States, the Mexican Constitution, as the reader has already noted, embodies very definite and comprehensive stipulations concerning education that are binding not only upon state and national schools but also upon privately supported systems. The legal bases of Mexico's educational program are to be found in Articles 3, 27, and 123 of the Constitution of 1917, with revisions and amendents in 1933, 1940, 1942, and 1945.[14] Article 3 of the Constitution specifies the authority for planning and administering a program of national education. The Article was originally prefaced as follows: "The education imparted by the state shall be socialistic. It shall exclude all religious doctrine, and shall combat fanaticism and prejudice by organizing its instruction and activities in such a way as to create in youth an exact and rational concept of the universe and society." As a result of a final agreement among its many opponents, the Article was revised in 1945 to read: "The education imparted by the state shall aim to develop harmoniously all the faculties of the human spirit, and at the same time inculcate a love of country and a feeling for international solidarity, of independence and of justice." It further states that education shall remain completely aloof from religious doctrine and that it shall be democratic, national, and contributory to human brotherhood. Article 27 declares that religious associations and churches may not own or administer property and that all property formerly held by the church belongs to the state. Article 123 compels employers under certain conditions to provide schools, hygienic living quarters, and medical attention.

With the exception of the universities, certain state institutions, and professional schools relegated to other ministries, all education

---

[14] *Ley orgánica de la educación pública,* pp. 49-50.

today comes under the supervision of the Ministry of Education *(Secretaría de Educación)*. This ministry prescribes administrative procedures, constructs curricula, and regulates requirements for admission, promotion, and graduation from all schools. However, the states and municipalities still maintain much autonomous control within bounds prescribed by the ministry. In the majority of instances they share the expenses and administration of their education with the federal government. The Mexican school system of today is accordingly administered in four broad divisions: (1) federal; (2) federal in co-operation with the states (or municipalities); (3) state; and (4) local community. It is the obligation of the Ministry of Education to co-ordinate and provide help for all these groups. Just how this is done is our next concern.

THE SYSTEM IN FUNCTION

The true purposes of the Ministry of Public Education are to direct the unification of the national educational system; to improve the teaching profession by incorporating the most effective of new methods; to promote the collaboration of private initiative in the educational and social functions of the state; to develop a staff of teachers at all levels of instruction, competent, well-trained, and alert, who can perform in proportion to the confidence which the nation places in their work.—Domingo Tirado Benedí, 1944.

Only with the Organic Law (Ley Orgánica) and the national system of public education can we achieve continuity in the progress of Mexican eduction, and, consequently, in the planning and solution of the multiple problems that this progress implies.—Manuel Gual Vidal, 1947.

The Ministry of Education, located in the capital, was reconstituted in 1921 and charged with the fulfillment of national educational responsibilities promulgated with the Obregón reforms. Unlike the United States Office of Education, the Mexican Ministry of Education has direct cabinet representation; it is an administrative department with supervisory powers and a full contributory relation to all phases of national government and policy. The ministry proper has many subdivisions, which undergo frequent changes of personnel and organization. In 1946 the official listing included

ORGANIZATION OF THE MINISTRY OF EDUCATION

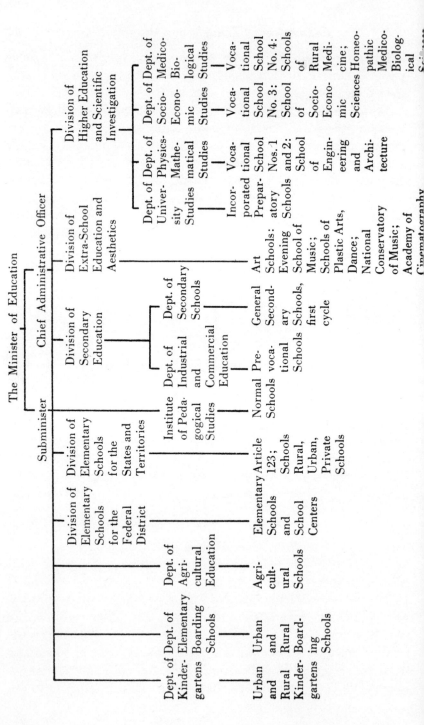

twenty-three major divisions and departments administering every phase of education from preschool through higher education, with the exception of autonomous universities.

School organization in 1946 featured five major divisions, outlined in the accompanying diagram. Three departments—kindergartens, elementary boarding schools, and agricultural schools—

TABLE 1

NATIONAL EDUCATIONAL BUDGETS[a]

Year	Federal Educational Budget in pesos[b]	Percentage of the National Budget
1921	12,296,265.00	4.9
1923	52,326,913.50[c]	15.0
1925	21,668,575.41	7.1
1937	57,364,000.00	27.3
1940	75,300,000.00[d]	11.9
1944	119,360,000.00[e]	10.8
1946	207,900,000.00	17.3
1947	220,900,000.00	13.2
1948	246,000,000.00 (allotted)	10.7

[a] Compiled from the annual *Memorias*, Secretaría de Educación Pública. See also "Datos estadístícos," MS, p. 4; *La obra educativa*, p. 333; and *La educación fundamental*, Ministry of Education, pp. 78-79.

[b] Up to 1949 the Mexican peso was worth approximately 20.5 United States cents— roughly five pesos to the dollar. Actually, financial benefits have not increased so bountifully as the figures show. Inflation up to 300 percent was reached between the years 1940 and 1948.

[c] Program of President Obregón.

[d] In 1940 the states expended 39,362,000 pesos in addition to this sum. *Cf.* Sapia M., Raúl, *México*, p. iv.

[e] Additional allotments from the states were estimated at 60 million pesos in 1944.

were separate and autonomous; other departments constituted, in reality, subdivisions. The duties and responsibilities of each of these branches are treated later in connection with the various types and levels of education over which they individually have jurisdiction. For present purposes the diagram demonstrates clearly the deliberate comprehensiveness of the ministry's activities. No educational agency is left wholly to itself, though the ministry is quick to point out that wide latitude is allowed for creativity so long as official directives are not disregarded.

Fair words make fine speeches, but money turns the wheels.

Allotments for education reached the Cárdenas ideal of 20 percent of national expenditures in only two years, 1936 and 1937. Recent budgets, though mounting in pesos, show a decline in ratio to the total budget. Table 1 reflects in limited measure the progress of education in the financial esteem of the national government.

The comparatively favorable position of education is seen in the federal budget for 1948, reported in the press December 24, 1947.

TABLE 2

FEDERAL BUDGET FOR 1948

Communications	415,500,000.00
Public debt	361,186,000.00
PUBLIC EDUCATION	246,000,000.00
National defense	240,000,000.00
Hydraulic resources	235,000,000.00
Related expenditures	226,010,000.00
Public health	115,000,000.00
Treasury	100,000,000.00
Investment	95,000,000.00
Navy	70,000,000.00
National economy	45,940,000.00
Agriculture	41,000,000.00
Foreign relations	25,845,000.00
Military industries	17,250,000.00
Legislature	15,000,000.00
Interior	13,000,000.00
Agrarian	12,900,000.00
Judicial	7,434,000.00
National properties	6,410,000.00
Labor	5,500,000.00
Attorney general	3,800,000.00
Presidency	1,725,000.00

2,300,000,000.00 pesos
(less 500,000 pesos)

Funds are derived, of course, from taxes. But in Mexico commercial enterprises occasionally donate money outright. For instance, of fifty million pesos paid out for a recent three-year program of school construction (1943-46), two million pesos were collected from private contributions. The purpose of these donations is both altruistic and practical—to stave off impending higher tax levies for schools. Financial assistance in school construction comes also from states and municipalities, some six million pesos having been pledged from this source over the same three-year period. While these statistics show the willingness of other agencies to co-operate, they also demonstrate the extent of the financial responsibility to be shouldered by the national government. Again, since much educational work is assumed by agencies other than the Ministry of Education (the ministries of Health, Agriculture, Defense, etc.) and in constantly increasing measure, the proportionate decline of the education budget may be readily understood.

Little information on per-pupil costs is available, though they may be approximated from available data. In 1946, for instance, the over-all per-pupil cost (total budget divided by total pupils enrolled) was about one hundred pesos, with the secondary school ratio at about 125 pesos. These figures (at that time approximately $21 to $26 United States currency) are, of course, low, but not inordinately so when equated with Mexico's divergent economic factors, such as the lower cost of school construction, operation, and maintenance, and general lower living standards. Mexico's climate permits the construction of cheaper buildings; labor is less expensive and is often volunteered, especially in small communities. Finally, the lion's share of Mexico's capital outlay for buildings is allotted to elementary schools rather than to the more costly fields of secondary and higher education.

The organization of instruction in Mexico, as in most countries, is based on the ladder system, with more than the usual amount of patchwork, despite the standardizing quality of central controls. This organization may be represented graphically as follows:

Evidence of educational patchwork is visible at once in elementary school organization. The outcome of the many educational experiments which Mexico, in her confusion and desperation, has adopted, the organization reveals a multiplicity of types that the ministry constantly seeks to equalize and co-ordinate. Somehow or other, the main features of elementary education should be the same for pupils in the hinterland and in the cities. It is paradoxical that co-ordination of school programs is the aim, but the varied nature of the cultural pattern militates against it.

ORGANIZATION OF INSTRUCTION IN MEXICO

Student's Age		Year of Schooling

UNIVERSITIES — ages 23, 22, 21, 20, 19, 18

POLYTECHNIC INSTITUTE AND OTHER HIGHER SCHOOLS FOR VOCATIONAL, TECHNICAL AND ARTS EDUCATION — ages 21, 20, 19, 18 / Years of schooling 17, 16, 15, 14, 13, 12

TRADE SCHOOLS — Schools of agriculture, arts and crafts, mining, nursing, social service, etc. / Years of schooling 11, 10, 9, 8, 7

HIGHER NORMAL SCHOOL

NORMAL SCHOOL FOR PHYSICAL EDUCATION

NORMAL SCHOOLS FOR PRIMARY AND KINDERGARTEN TEACHERS

FIVE-YEAR NATIONAL PREPARATORY SCHOOL

SECONDARY SCHOOL—SECOND CYCLE — Preparatory and vocational schools — ages 17, 16

SECONDARY SCHOOL—FIRST CYCLE — General, university initiation, prevocational — ages 15, 14, 13

ELEMENTARY SCHOOLS
Urban, semi-urban, frontier, boarding, rural, agriculture, Article 123, cultural missions — ages 12, 11, 10, 9, 8, 7 / Years of schooling 6, 5, 4, 3, 2, 1

KINDERGARTENS (Voluntary) — ages 6, 5, 4

NURSERY SCHOOLS — ages 3, 2

Interpreting Mexico's school organization, it is obvious that a child may attend a nursery school till his fourth birthday. From his fourth birthday to his seventh he may go to a kindergarten. His elementary school training lasts six years, after which he has four major choices on the secondary school level: (1) general; (2) "university initiation" *(iniciación universitaria)*, followed by university preparation; (3) prevocational, followed by vocational; (4) normal school.

Until very recently secondary education has been divided into a "first cycle" and a "second cycle." The first cycle lasted three years; the second, two. The first cycle also included university initiation, or pre-preparatory training, for entrance to the university. (For a time previous to 1942, the *iniciación universitaria* in the Capital was an independent unit within the National University, with the same status as the Preparatory or any other University school. At the end of 1942, the *iniciación* was integrated with the Preparatory School under a common director. See the section on secondary education below.) This cycle was followed by the two-year preparatory school, which prepared directly for the university. The present tendency is to do away with the cycle system and reserve the title "secondary education" for the first cycle only.

Prevocational education is the term given to the first cycle of vocational education on the secondary level, and is also for a period of three years. It is succeeded by vocational education, usually for two years, after which the student is ready for the higher professional schools, such as those of the National Polytechnic Institute.

Immediately upon leaving elementary school the pupil may enter the six-year normal school. Other choices include schools of technical, commercial, agricultural, fine arts, nursing, social service, and home economics type, further description of which will be found in later chapters.

Education is compulsory from the sixth to the fifteenth birthday; but the enforcement of this regulation is possible only where enough schools and teachers exist, that is, in about one-half the country. Government schools are officially free, though in practice, especially in secondary schools, a nominal fee of a few pesos a year is charged if the family can afford it. In most instances text-books and personal supplies must be purchased by the pupils.

School attendance differs greatly in different communities and in various sections of a city; percentages as low as 55 and as high as 99 are often recorded within the same community.[15] After the fourth grade there is a marked decrease in class enrollments; at least 50 percent of those entering elementary school never complete the sixth grade. More serious than this, hardly one-fourth of the students entering the first grade continue their studies beyond the elementary school. (In one primary school visited, Escuela "José María Morelos," Milpa Alta, D. F., there were four first grade groups and only one sixth grade group. Seven hundred fifty boys and girls were enrolled, divided into seventeen groups, or about 44 per group. The primary school at Xochimilco had four first grade groups and two sixth grade, but the sixth grade groups were smaller than those of the first grade.)

Economic circumstances are chiefly responsible for the high rate of school-leaving. Parents send their children to work in order to help support their generally large families. And though school-leaving has been a matter of perennial concern to the ministry, not much can be done about it until such time as adequate wages are paid to the chief breadwinners or until some other material provisions are found to keep children in school. Public boarding schools have helped in this regard.

Departments of truancy do not exist. Persistent cases are referred to the police, who may hold parents responsible and levy fines or, in some instances, actually imprison repeated offenders. Ordinarily, however, children and parents consider themselves privileged to attend school, and there are always many children waiting for vacancies.

Mexico's school year is determined by climate and locality. The majority of schools operate under the principal school calendar, or calendar "A," which customarily sets aside the month of January for administrative duties and examinations preliminary to the

---

[15] *Compendio estadístico*, Secretaría de la Economía Nacional, pp. 121-23, shows an over-all average attendance in elementary schools of 83.94 percent. The state of Colima was lowest, with 75.08 percent; highest was Tabasco, 92.75 percent.

opening of schools. Classes begin the first week in February and end the last week in November. Vacations occur during the last two weeks in May, the last two weeks in September, and the months of December and January. Calendar "B" puts the two-month holiday for regions with hot summers in July and August, the school year beginning in September. There are also many shorter holidays *(días de fiesta)*, commemorating famous historical and national events and totaling at least fifteen days throughout the year. Children attend school, therefore, about two hundred days a year, in contrast to the United States average of slightly more than 150. Classes usually meet six days a week. Saturday mornings are often used for school excursions or recreational instruction. Saturday afternoon is free for all pupils.

The school day varies greatly in length. Where possible, two sessions are provided, usually from 8 to 12 and from 3 to 5, making for a six-hour day. The early grades have shorter sessions, lasting about four and one-half hours. Some schools have only one session, five hours in length, to make room for afternoon or evening sessions of other groups—a procedure similar to the double session system in the United States. In 1948 the official school day for secondary, commercial, and industrial schools was from 9 to 2 and from 4:30 to 6:30. Night schools, beginning at 7 and ending at 9, 10, or even 11, also had one morning class at 7. Class periods in schools of all types usually last 50 minutes, with a ten-minute interval between periods and a rest and recreation period of 20 minutes in the middle of the longer session.

As with European schools, examinations are vital to Mexican school life, and are often the chief determinant of pupil success or failure. For elementary and secondary schools, examinations are held either just before the May, September, and December vacations or in the middle and at the end of the school year. Final examinations, held in November, are prescribed and compiled under federal supervision for all levels of education and are uniform throughout the country. Periodic examinations are usually set by the classroom teacher or the department head.

The grading system is constructed on the unit basis of zero to 10, or zero to 100. A grade of 10 (or 100) represents the highest possible attainment; 6 (60) is the passing mark *(aprobado)*. Grading is rigid, in the manner of European traditional schools, daily work being recorded and averaged equally with final examinations. Report cards are fairly stereotyped, and ordinarily restrict information to the student's grade, attendance, effort, and position in class. Space is also provided for teacher comment.

This uniformity is carried over into the courses of study. All classes handling the same subject matter are supposed to cover the same material, to remain reasonably abreast of each other at all times, and to accomplish similar results.

Education is supervised by the Department of Federal Supervision and Inspection, and is divided into three sections—personnel, administration, and technical. Some thirty federal directors and five hundred regional inspectors are entrusted with the task of orienting, guiding, directing, and stimulating the efforts of teachers and seeing to it that practice conforms as closely as possible with the recommendations of the administration. Federal and state governments share in this supervision, and they appoint inspectors for each department of instruction. In actual practice, the duties of these inspectors are largely administrative, confined to such matters as school attendance, personnel, and equipment. The inspectors give teachers some assistance in methods of instruction and make sporadic efforts to advise them professionally, particularly in elementary education; but school principals and heads of departments are actually closer to the teacher in this respect.

Private schools, at least on the elementary level, occupy a more prominent place in Mexican school life than in the United States, despite the legal regulations which govern them. Before 1910, and with some modification up to 1921, private education, principally under the leadership and direction of religious orders, had been accepted as the only respectable type of schooling. Today, only those private institutions may legally exist whose aims are "completely educational" and in accord with government regulations. Private schools of many varieties flourish throughout Mexico and are increasing in number, many of them having been opened as a result of popular opposition to socialistic schools. In 1934, for example, there were 150 private elementary schools; in 1941 the figure had increased to 441. Though statistics on private schools are scant and untrustworthy, it is evident to any observer that there are proportionately as many private schools in Mexico City as in any capital in the world. Indeed, there is hardly a main thoroughfare in any sizable Mexican community without its quota of private schools, gaily advertised and on the whole well patronized.

Like the public schools, private educational institutions are subject to administrative and technical inspection by the various departments of supervision in the ministry. The law stipulates that inspectors shall receive full co-operation and that information on all schools shall be readily available. Religious groups, corporate societies, and affiliates are forbidden—legally, at least—to maintain schools or to participate in school instruction. Private interests must obtain official authorization for any type of popular education, and the course of study must conform to the prescribed bases of Mexican education (Article 16). Teachers are required to satisfy the state as to their professional preparation and moral attitudes. Courses and teaching methods must conform to those prescribed for public institutions. School buildings must be ample, hygienic, and suitable for the type of instruction offered, and must provide enough space for games, sports, and physical exercise. Funds must be derived from approved sources. Other stipulations include the provision of adequate libraries, laboratories, and workshops. However, these restrictions and requirements must not be taken at their face value, for it is not to be expected that private schools will feel rigidly bound by obligations which great numbers of Mexicans oppose, and which the public schools themselves are often unable to meet.

From the foregoing, it is apparent that educational types are as numerous and as elusive in Mexico as elsewhere. Yet no account of Mexican education is adequate without some sort of over-all picture of the actual school. To begin with, there is great diversity in the quality of school buildings and equipment provided. The best schools are by no means concentrated in the capital. Indeed, many schools in Mexico City are old, shabby, and inadequate in contrast to imposing modern structures such as that at Milpa Alta, D. F. Nor does the external architecture of the buildings necessarily reveal the quality of the classrooms within. As in the United States, a schoolroom, even in a modern building, may be cold and barren; while an ugly, ramshackle structure may house warm, inviting rooms. In Mexico, more than in the United States, classroom decorations are likely to reflect the initiative, the industry, and the artistic ability of the teacher. Only a few stock furnishings and decorations can be supplied by the ministry.

A representative Mexican school may be visualized as a two- or three-story building with a patio in the center. It is often a former convent, private residence, or other converted structure. Staircases located within the patio lead to classrooms facing on the inner court. This arrangement is most convenient for shutting out noises from the street and for presenting a cloistered area of privacy. The patio lends itself to a number of purposes. Hard-surfaced, it furnishes space for outdoor games and recreation. Cultivated, it is used for instruction in gardening, planting, harvesting. As a thing of beauty, accessible from every room in the building, it may harbor a flower garden, a lawn, a fountain, or a statue. In some schools, the patio is neglected altogether—mute testimony of administrative indifference.

Though visitors are free to enter any Mexican school, they are expected to submit to the guidance of the principal or some other administrative official. When the visitor enters a classroom, work usually stops, and the children rise as if ready to entertain. After the teacher is persuaded that what is wanted is business as usual, a warm and assuring *"sentaditos, chicos"* returns the pupils to their seats.

The children's faces reveal many types of skin coloration. No race discrimination is evident, though social cleavage is discernible in the absence, generally, of a more privileged type of child, who usually attends private schools. Mexican youngsters win their way into the stoniest heart. They are well-behaved, ingratiating, demure. Hands and faces are shiningly clean. Their clothing is simplicity itself—often a uniform, particularly in girls' schools—and neatly laundered. One wonders, however, just what kind of breakfast the average child has eaten—unless he eats government-subsidized school meals—and at what sacrifices his parents are sending him to school.

Normal classroom procedure reveals the extent to which the teacher's ingenuity is drafted to make up for the lack of working tools. With few books, teaching aids, or formal demonstration materials, the Mexican teacher's inventiveness assumes paramount importance. In this connection the North American teacher finds much to learn from his Mexican colleague.

The teacher's personality is always arresting. Mexican teachers are usually endowed with a seriousness of purpose, an ingrained respect for the missionary quality of their calling, and a driving energy—qualities that often display themselves in outbursts of impatience with pupils who are slow to learn. The experienced observer cannot but reflect how much better oriented this abundant enthusiasm would be if the latest findings in educational psychology were more frequently applied—an accomplishment which Mexico's professors of education are making every effort to bring about.

The departing visitor must not forget the formal courtesies which mean a great deal to the Mexicans. As one leaves, *"con permiso, señorita,"* and with a handshake, one must also remember the children with a cordial *"adios, niños."* These polite gestures, especially from *Norteamericanos,* make lasting impressions on the minds of Mexicans; the omission of them is put down to crude behavior.

Mexico has some of the best schools in the world, and some of the best teachers. It is a rare visitor, however, who does not feel a burning desire to help. The patent signs of poverty are indeed pitiable. Yet in the wise words of a modest kindergarten teacher, pronounced to the author with utmost sincerity: "It would not be right for Mexico to take money from other countries to build our schools, because they would then no longer be Mexican. Our institutions must arise and grow from Mexican soil and Mexican labor. They must be the natural outgrowth of Mexican progress—however slow, however difficult."

IV. The Early Years

THE KINDERGARTEN

The kindergarten establishes a bond with the home and reaches out to take its proper place in Mexican society; it creates an environment calculated to encourage the growth of the child's experience in his early years.—Rosaura Zapata, Chief of Kindergartens.

In this full phase of Revolution, the kindergarten, previously limited to the rich and privileged in the large cities, extends its benefits to the children of city workers and farmers—Indian, and mestizo.—Ley Orgánica de Educación Pública.

THE PLANT that would grow tall sinks deep roots. Although pre-primary school education *(educación preescolar)* is still considered a luxury, the Ministry of Education tends more and more to think of it as a desirable downward extension of the educational ladder. In view of the need for early emotional and hygienic training where home backgrounds vary greatly, it is the intention of the Mexican government to spread preprimary education to all sections of the Republic, not as a substitute for, but as a supplement to, parental training. This type of training is not, however, at present a requirement for entrance into the primary school (Article 54).[1]

Nursery schools *(guarderías infantiles)* are under the direction of the Child Welfare Bureau *(Asistencia Social Infantil)* of the Ministry of Public Health *(Secretaría de Salubridad Pública)*, which also administered the kindergartens from 1937 to 1942. These institutions care for youngsters between two and six years of age. Working mothers leave their children at eight in the morn-

---

[1] Secretaría de Educación Pública, *La obra educativa en el sexenio 1940-1946*, pp. 63-64. See also *Compendio estadístico 1947*, Secretaría de la Economía Nacional, p. 102.

ing and call for them as late as six in the evening, assured that during the day they have received the best in medical, health, and educational services. Today, practically every sizable government office and industry in Mexico's larger communities possesses a nursery school. This phase of child development is not, however, considered to be a function of the educational authorities.

The first kindergarten, "Federico Froebel," was established in Mexico City in 1903 by Estefanía Castañeda; the second, "Pestalozzi," was opened the following year by Rosaura Zapata. Though not the only attempt at education on the preprimary level, kindergartens were the first to achieve articulation and continuity and to gain governmental recognition. Their beginning was auspicious, and they have since become well established in the educational system.

As with other phases of national education the ministry establishes kindergarten objectives and provides for supervision throughout the entire country. Objectives are centered on physical, mental, moral, and aesthetic development in relation to social mores (Article 49). Games, singing, dancing, light rhythmic physical exercises, and manual and artistic activities introduce the child to the materials and attitudes of later academic instruction. Group activity in a simple, creative, and natural atmosphere leads to easy adaptation to social living. An understanding of the child's world is fostered by conversation, tales, simple historical narratives, short excursions, and practical chores suited to his age (Articles 50 and 51). Parental assistance and co-operation are sought and utilized (Article 53). Kindergartens are not considered schools in the usual sense, but establishments concerned principally with creating a better understanding of the life that a youngster has to live from four to six years of age. They are expected to contribute to the integration of child capacities for better achievement in later life.

Kindergarten organization is determined by local requirements. There is no schedule, as such, for instruction. The distribution of time is subordinate to the interests and needs of the children. There is likewise no "method" as such. Froebelian, Montessorian, and other methods formerly in vogue are still utilized, but they have been adapted rather than adopted. Systems of instruction derive from Mexican originality of thought and from the nature of the environment; about this the Department of Kindergartens is most emphatic.

Enrollments are officially limited to thirty or forty pupils per teacher, but actually a single instructor may have as many as fifty children in his or her charge. Requirements for admission are confined to good health and the permission of parent or guardian. An entering kindergartener must not be under four years of age, nor can he remain after his seventh birthday. Unlike public kindergartens in the United States, which commonly form part of a primary school and occupy a schoolroom indoors, Mexican kindergartens are picturesque units in themselves and are generally held out-of-doors. Enrollments as high as four hundred in one school are not uncommon.

The essential purpose of the kindergarten is to ease the passage from the home into society. In a miniature community the children plant gardens; harvest vegetable crops; wash clothes; build model houses, boats, and toys. Their program, in fact, comprises any activity which contributes to child growth through play. In the cultivation of plants, for example, "the child becomes patient and steady, and learns that after great hopes and constant care the harvest may yield a great measure of personal satisfaction."

Health objectives are achieved through open-air play, medical attention, hygienic school surroundings, and instruction leading to the formation of healthful personal habits. Stress is laid upon sound physical growth through play: "The child builds with water and sand; runs, jumps, extends his movements, and exercises his whole body—prudently—so as to render him free and happy."

Recreational experience includes reading and dramatizing stories. Excursions and parties *(fiestas)* are frequent, but of a developmental nature and adapted to the tastes of the child. Puppet shows are designed for the same end, that of "placing the child in contact with reality and nature *(la naturaleza)*."

Civic education begins in the kindergarten with flag salutes and hero stories to "impress enduring affections in the heart of the child." Contact with Mexican cultural achievement contributes to this understanding; the National Children's Museum *(Museo del Niño)*, in Mexico City, affords the child an opportunity to capture the world around him.

Music, too, serves a patriotic purpose. An example from the songbook is the "Flag Song."[2]

Ban - de - ra   de tres co - lor - es   yo te   doy mi cor - a - zón, etc
(Flag   of three colors   I give you my   heart, etc.)

Of great value in the emotional life of the child, music includes singing, musical games, appreciative listening, and participation in juvenile rhythm bands—all under specialized leadership. Music is linked with physical education through a well-developed dancing program and with civic training through the use of popular historical ballads and educational nursery rhymes. Various kinds of productive labor are also recorded in song.[3]

Es-ta ri - ca   cre-ma   que voy a ba - tir   es   sa - bro-sa man-te - qui - lla, etc
(This   rich   cream   that I am going to beat is   tasty   butter, etc.)

The kindergarten's three grades are also planned to provide academic foundation for entrance into the primary school. Features of the language program will serve to illustrate this objective:

Program for the First Grade of the Kindergarten—Language: The child's oral expression is corrected within the limits of his years. He gives his full name, those of his parents, and the first name of his teacher; tells where his home is; transmits simple messages, repeats little rhymes with suitable gestures; dramatizes episodes of child life and incidents from picture books.

Program for the Second Grade of the Kindergarten—Language: The child practices the correct use of words; performs simple errands; says the full name of his teacher; interprets and repeats the stories which his teacher tells him; tells of visits which he has made with his family or teacher; repeats simple quatrains with appropriate gestures; describes and

---

[2] Secretaría de Educación Pública, *Cantos para los jardines de niños*, p. 1.

[3] *Ibid.*, p. 11, "Haciendo Mantequilla," ("Making Butter"):

draws pictures; dramatizes stories; takes the place of puppets in per-
formance.

Program for the Third Grade of the Kindergarten—Language: The
amplification and correction of the child's language through conversation,
stories, rhymes, riddles, etc. The child recounts stories; recites in dramatic form; describes scenes of child life, animals, the home, etc.

Parents or guardians usually accompany their children to and
from school, a custom which provides opportunity for close parent-
teacher contact and for co-ordination of effort. Recognizing that
"the home is necessarily the place where the work of the kindergarten must begin," the ministry has encouraged a greater measure
of co-operation between families and teachers. The latter are expected to aid and advise mothers concerning the hygiene, diet,
recreation, and education of children in the home. At the end of
the school year, in November, an ambitious exhibition of the year's
work permits the townspeople to observe for themselves the concrete results of kindergarten training; conversely, it focuses the
children's attention upon the adult standards against which their
work will eventually be judged. Perhaps no other method is so
successful in acquiring a sense of one's potential usefulness as a
future citizen.

Financial and legal restrictions upon the acquisition of buildings
for school purposes have limited the development of these praiseworthy institutions. Impatient with routine progress in view of the
"transcendent importance of play in the life of preschool children," the ministry has responded by opening kindergarten facilities to all children of the community. Musical programs, radio
shows, and movies are featured at "children's Thursdays" *(jueves
infantiles)* which offer to all children, whether in school or not,
moments of joy and satisfaction in the medium most suited to their
age. "Brigades of Joy" *(Brigadas de Alegría)*, which stage puppet
shows, songfests, and games in public parks and gardens, provide
the means for profitable recreation and other early educational
values in the poorest precincts. Professional preparation for the
popular Children's Theater *(Teatro Infantil)* is offered at the
Women's University of Mexico, and, commencing in 1948, in the
new Normal School for Kindergarten Teachers.

Kindergarten growth is favorably revealed by statistics. In 1920 there were only 19 kindergartens in all Mexico; the number increased in 1936 to 257. By 1944, 86 public kindergartens dotted the Federal District alone, and there were another 220 in the states. In 1946, 620 kindergartens, attended by a staff of 1,492 directors, teachers, and assistants, enrolled 46,783 children. While this enrollment is almost double that of 1943, it nevertheless reveals the distressing fact that only one-fiftieth of the nation's school population of kindergarten age (four to five years old only) is at present in attendance. Kindergarten organization and instruction are at an advanced stage in Mexico, but there is a crying need for more plants and more teachers and for a much wider distribution throughout the Republic.

In sum, the Ministry of Education, eager to elevate the educational standards of the nation, reaches out toward the toddle-age group for the foundation of its effort. The extension of the three-year kindergarten program to the more backward communities aims to eliminate age-old superstitions and hygienic deficiencies injurious to the child and to modernize child-training methods on a nationwide scale. Yet, however much the ministry may desire its extension, the kindergarten is still far from its goal; at present, lamentably few children are receiving the enriched experience and early educational advancement which this medium offers.

ELEMENTARY EDUCATION

Elementary education aims at the fullest development of pupils in such a way as to provide all inhabitants of the Republic with a minimum cultural attainment.—Octavio Véjar Vázquez.

In planning the curriculum let us leave alone the "mental faculties" of the poor little Indians, and not try to develop them with infinitesimal doses of something abstract, bitter, insipid.—Manuel Barranco.

The organization of the school of activity and manual work which our democratic system demands leads logically to the integrated elementary school, which is the cornerstone of our ideal of national unity.—Manuel Gual Vidal.

The elementary school *(escuela primaria)* is the chief educational institution of Mexico. Since the vast majority of citizens attend no other school, the attitudes, skills, and information upon which the nation depends must be propagated within its six short years. Previous chapters have recorded the multiple problems involved in this process. Fundamental national objectives—unity, prosperity, institutional adaptation—require a common education, a common language, and a common purpose throughout all the diverse and isolated elements of Mexico's heterogeneous makeup.

Before the Revolution, local communities insisted on preserving full responsibility and control of their schools. The result was that outside the Federal District the country was an educational desert. Sheltered in isolationism, local tradition proved itself narrow, bigoted, and opposed to change. This condition, it is recalled, furnished the primary argument for the establishment of the National Ministry, which immediately proceeded to adapt localism to the newly found national spirit. In this endeavor the elementary school has played the leading role.

It has not been easy to discover the means or the extent to which the subordination of local custom is desirable and practical. Torres Bodet, always with keen insight, observed that "elementary education can lead us continually toward greater homogeneity; but it is important to incorporate regionalism without destroying it." It is vital, in other words, to determine the extent to which the national education system must yield to local custom in order to insure co-operation and bring about the successful adaptation of children to their environment.

There has also been the question of just how much imported ideology could profitably be used. The doctrinaire socialistic regimentation of the middle thirties had led to conservative and provincial reaction in the early forties. The ministry consequently chose a policy of adapting alien political and educational modes to a program of modified regionalism. Work activities and vocational education presented themselves as the most suitable avenues toward this goal. Since the welfare of the nation depended upon basic vocational rather than purely academic skills, the ministry considered it wisest to concentrate on the trades, even in general education. The government thus won the support of a people whose educational needs were expressed in hard economic terms.

Mexican schools have been criticized for their stress on manual arts and crafts. But such simple skills as basket-weaving and pottery-making are basic to the country's needs; they are an indispensable medium for developing productive attitudes and techniques. The ministry points out that the co-ordination, sensory training, and confidence gained in manual arts are vital to the entire educational program.[4] There is, however, another, more pertinent reason. In most European nations elementary school training has been hardly more than a preparation for an established secondary education; Mexico's elementary training is mainly terminal, not essentially a preparation for the higher levels.

The Organic Law of Public Education prescribes that "all inhabitants of the Republic shall have equal right to an education and that the state shall provide equal opportunities for acquiring it" (Article 5). The state is obligated "to establish, organize, and maintain schools in accordance with local needs throughout the entire Republic" (Article 6). Deference to local conditions is a legal proviso for expanding the school system. Elementary training by law (Article 57) shall develop the total personality of the child—intellectually, physically, aesthetically, socially.[5] The child is to be prepared for a beneficial, productive life in and for society.

Administration is shared among four agencies: the Division of Elementary Education in the Federal District, the Division of Elementary Education in the States and Territories, the Department of Elementary Boarding Schools, and the Department of Cultural Missions. These offices supervise several different types of schools: urban, semi-urban, rural, federalized, Article 123 schools, and boarding schools. "Semi-urban" is a comprehensive term applied to schools falling into neither the urban nor the rural category. It includes frontier schools *(escuelas fronterizas)* which sponsor a program suited to border communities. The aim is to accentuate loyalty

---

[4] Secretaría de Educación Pública, *Programas para las escuelas primarias de la República Mexicana*, p. 103.

[5] Torres Bodet, *La escuela mexicana*, pp. 45, 46. Articles 49, 57, 61, 66, and part of 188 of the Organic Law of December 31, 1941, ordain the bases, principles and norms of elementary education.

to Mexico and love for things Mexican; these schools are supposed "to counteract or nullify foreign cultural penetration." The federalized school *(escuela federalizada)* is organized and administered under joint state and federal control.[6]

In deference to local choice and the prevailing religious faith there is provision for segregating the sexes, except as determined by school population, financial exigency, or lack of facilities or teachers (Article 62). That this is not only a matter of fundamental educational policy but is also a diplomatic gesture may be inferred from an additional directive: "Education for boys and girls shall adhere to the same plans, programs and methods, without prejudice to those activities which tend to affirm the specific qualities of either sex." The law clearly directs the ministry to "weld Mexicans into a single spiritual nucleus"; but forbids it to construct its program in such a way as to destroy productive cultural diversity.

Pursuant to the need for unity, the ministry, in 1946, reformed the entire elementary school curriculum. The latest official programs expressly advise local adaptation by "alert and ingenious" teachers. They designate the content of instruction, but make little mention of method. The ministry restrains all attempts to be of such assistance to teachers as to destroy their originality or induce stereotyped instruction. Published programs deal with (1) the "tool subjects" *(materias instrumentales)*—basic vocational and communicative skills; and (2) informational subjects—facts and knowledge involving a world of reality, nature, and culture. Tool subjects include language, arithmetic, geometry, drawing, manual training, and, for the girls, domestic science. "Of vital importance" is training in music, singing, and physical education. Informational subjects embrace natural and social sciences—history, civics, and human geography—"in which it is given us to know the creations of the human spirit and the organization and purposes of social activities."

Acknowledging the essential unity of the pupil's thought processes, the ministry exhorts the teacher to integrate all segments of the curriculum: "The programs may be co-ordinated in such a way as to establish the maximum connection between content and exer-

[6] *La educación pública en México*, pp. 49-50. See below for Article 123 schools.

cises, knowledge and activities, information and practice; the student then develops as mature an understanding as possible of the unity of knowledge and the harmony of nature's diverse elements." The teacher must also recognize the unifying value of application: "The programs have been designed, not from the point of view of an abstract child generically considered, but with a view toward applying them concretely to the children of our native environment." The teacher is obligated to modify the programs in accordance with the aptitudes, tendencies, and ability of his students. The school in turn takes its direction from the local social and economic environment, and from the aspirations, goals, and ideals of Mexican culture. A standardized plan, the ministry points out, is advantageous in that it places the student in a "constantly developing, unitary contact with cultural reality." Curricular materials are graded in accordance with their difficulty; but more important is the "cyclic co-ordination" of studies at different levels, each cycle containing a full complement of general studies, which is broadened with each successive cycle.

Thus, the national program for elementary education rests upon curriculum co-ordination and community contact and promotes an educational integrity which will not sacrifice the unique values of local custom and community need. Illustrative of this broad approach is the statement in part of the aims and methods of citizenship training.

Citizenship I—Aims: (1) to contribute to the formation of the student's personality as the foundation of future activity as a citizen; (2) to strengthen the student's concept and appreciation of his country; (3) to study the lives of men whose civic activities have served to stimulate better citizenship and a vital, vigorous concept of Mexican nationality; (4) to create habits of order, of individual and collective work, of discipline, etc., and moral attitudes of proper conduct—urbanity, and good manners, which permit co-operative and responsible behavior in society; and (5) to instruct the student concerning the political and administrative organization of the country.

Thus the ministry distills the last precious dram of curricular value for purposes of individual and national development. Thus, too, is exemplified the drive for unity in differentiation, the harmonic growth of the individual, and the infusion of integrated general knowledge—all within the profoundly real orientation of the local community and conjoined with the values of a citizenship firmly grounded in vocational utility.

In method, child interest is to be the guide. The official approach begins with a center of interest, followed by pupil projects on the center of interest, and finally its application to life. The ministry insists that the structure and arrangement of this curricular material has little value in itself. "The efficacy of the whole program lies in its application . . . and the practical use of each one of its phases within the educational process of which it is the basis. . . . The aim of teaching is not to heap up knowledge in the minds of students, but rather to prepare them to acquire it themselves." Apart from this injunction, teachers are expected to rely on their own talents and preferences rather than to adopt formalized methods not clearly understood or incompatible with the teacher's personality. Schools are not to become laboratories for experimentation in pedagogical methods; institutions annexed to normal schools are entrusted with that function. Elementary schools must become applied workshops: "The school as a social institution . . . is a true community of work."

So much for glowing desires and ingenious ends. What syllabi does the ministry provide to help the teacher attain them? Returning to the citizenship outlines, we find three sections dealing with (1) general topics; (2) suggested activities; and (3) a detailed curricular outline covering three cycles of two years each. The course of study in the first cycle (grades 1 and 2) is concerned with home-school relations and an elementary nationalism of flag salutes, hero tales, and the national anthem. Here, also, begins vocational instruction in various occupations, including the manufacture of books, of games, and of the various realia with which the children work. Ideas on home, school, family responsibility and social relations pervade all studies. In the second cycle (grades 3 and 4) activities lead directly into community life, where the child is introduced to the principles of local and federal government. Fundamental habits of contribution and participation are encouraged, with a strong emphasis on such attributes of good social behavior as discipline, neatness, punctuality, co-operation, responsibility, and urbanity. In the third cycle, the ministry hopes to achieve full community orientation and participation. Economic "co-operativism" *(cooperativismo)* is taught in theory and practice. Other subject matter concentrates on family customs, on the status of women in the arts and sciences, and on the significance of the school in Mexican society. "Affirmation of correct habits" recurs at this upper level.

In the specific art of government, students in the third cycle are taught the individual rights which are guaranteed by the constitution. In this connection Article 27 on "expropriation for reasons of public welfare" and "the particular case of petroleum" receive appropriate treatment, along with the ubiquitous Article 123 (the federal labor law). The outlines stress the advantages of a democratic government, and the pre-requisites, rights, and duties of Mexican citizenship. Instruction in the importance of ethical unity as the foundation of nationality and the key to successful citizenship completes the training of the model citizen.[7]

On the whole, these demands, though somewhat formidable, do not vary greatly from those of an elementary school in any part of the world. As elsewhere, the degree to which the school extends its activities into community affairs depends largely upon the administrative and inspirational qualities of the principal and the individual teacher. Years ago, Manuel Gamio's "integrated schools" had achieved considerable success in employing local resources as teaching matter. Woe betide the program, however, if the teacher prefers the traditional approach!

The elementary school curriculum also attempts to develop unitary objectives from compartmentalized knowledge. Science teaching, for example, trains pupils not only in techniques but also in

[7] *Ibid.*, p. 94. With regard to activities, see George C. Booth, *Mexico's School-made Society*, p. 122: "Posters and newspaper murals are made up in schools all over the nation, the newspaper mural taking the place of the school paper in the United States. The mural is a class project and usually requires a week to produce. It comes out on a regular date as does a newspaper." Among other activities are educational trips to factories and workshops in the vicinity; visits to districts which lack water, drainage, sanitation, electric lights, etc., in order to demonstrate the necessity of such public services; visits to asylums, homes, railway and telegraph offices, etc.; inter-school visits; visits to nearby co-operative farms; participation in the celebration of national holidays and civic festivals; business transactions with appropriate authorities, etc.

appreciation of the social and aesthetic uses of science. Geography induces love of country. History is expected to concern itself not only with facts but also with sentiments and affections: "It creates an attitude of solidarity, collective responsibility, and an understanding of other peoples of the world."[8]

With so much emotional training spread throughout the curriculum, it is not surprising to find that music, drawing, and manual arts are enlisted for their expressive, artistic, and co-ordinative values—values which are consciously used to support other aspects of instruction and to furnish outlets for pupil interests. Physical education is to be given greater attention, but its aims are to be more individual; among them are personal hygiene, physical growth and co-ordination, courage, self-confidence, and the proper use of leisure. Art combines with physical education to strengthen the feeling for rhythm and beauty. Finally, the defense of the nation is of crucial importance: "Military values will be served by the discipline of wills."

The question now arises as to how far all this curricular utopianism penetrates into the actual classroom. The answer is as varied as Mexico's schools and teachers. Certain outstanding schools exceed the basic aims of the ministry; others pay them only lip service. Statistics on the pupil-teacher ratio would seem to indicate a none-too-favorable relation between the established aims and their fulfillment.[9] Classes of fifty are prevalent in urban communities, so that while the approach may be genuine and liberal, the practical circumstances confronting the classroom teacher tend to preserve routine behavior and formalized methods. The teacher is obliged to keep and use a plan-book *(cuaderno diario de preparación)*, which is supposed to include the lessons for the day, together with an account of achievements and observations, the latter preferably corrective and constructive. Homework is assigned and recorded, but kept to a minimum. Few textbooks are available; consequently, the teacher must lecture and dictate for notebook copying. The notebooks, supplemented by drill and boardwork,

---

[8] *Programas para las escuelas primarias de la República Mexicana,* 1944, p. 61.

[9] *Compendio estadístico 1947,* p. 120, shows a national average ratio in 1944 of approximately 42—1, ranging from 31—1 (Lower California) to 63—1 (Oaxaca).

constitute the bulk of the information to be mastered for examination purposes. As such, they are eagerly, proudly, and unfailingly exhibited to every visitor.

The use of diagnostic and achievement tests is urged to measure accomplishments objectively and to check the methods, techniques, and procedures used in the learning process. But accomplishment and progress in this field are slow.[10] Reports are customarily sent to parents every month. Cumulative in make-up, the report is ordinarily a standardized card containing academic grades. In addition to subject matter, other items listed are conduct, cleanliness, promptness, and attendance. Studies in the national language are divided into reading (subdivided into speed, comprehension, and expression), oral expression, written expression, penmanship, and spelling. Three grades are given in arithmetic and geometry under the headings "concepts," "habits and abilities," and "problem solving."

The new curriculum is especially important for its application to Mexico's world-renowned rural education, born officially in 1921.[11] Throughout the twenties the educational methods adopted by rural teachers tended to accentuate rather than to relieve the unfortunate effects of isolation. Bonilla's dictum that "rural education was to prepare children for rural, not urban, life" turned out to be a handicap to those peasants who in later life moved to urban surroundings; "practical" education had not enabled them to adapt to new conditions.

Today, school programs subordinate rural education as an entity in itself. The ministry strives to unify all types of primary education in such a way as to facilitate a transfer from one environment to another. Recent programs allow few exceptions or special arrangements for special types of schools. Furthermore, rural education, with its modified aims, is no longer to be considered

---

[10] Further treatment of psychological tests and testing is included under the section on psychopedagogy, Chapter VI.

[11] On rural education of a decade or two ago see Smith, *Education in Mexico*, p. 40. Katherine M. Cook, *The House of the People*, p. 3. Herring, "Education in Mexico," p. 330. Probably the best treatment on issues previous to 1930 is Ebaugh, "The National System of Education in Mexico," chapter on the "Rural School." Two of the most recent books are *Educación fundamental*, pp. 37 ff., and Larroyo, *Historia comparada*, pp. 297 ff.

"inferior" to urban education. Warns Torres Bodet: "We must no longer shrink from raising the dignity of the rural school. It no longer makes peasants, but rather citizens of Mexico." There is no reason why youngsters of the country should not enjoy the same fundamental training as do their fellow citizens in the city. However, deviation from general objectives is permissible to rural educators, as the ministry advises:[12]

Arouse in the child an interest in rural occupations, preparing him for later intelligent participation in rural life. . . . Awaken a love of nature and feeling for the beauty of the country. . . . Exalt the advantages of a simple life, in an effort to keep children within their rural environment and to counteract the present exodus of laborers from the fields to the cities. . . . Combat the peasant's barren mode of life, springing from ignorance and skepticism, by substituting a profound faith in scientific method and discovery. . . . Provide the elements and equipment necessary to modify the environment, such as circulating libraries, conference halls, radios, sport centers, demonstration centers for agriculture, simple laboratories, etc. . . . See to it that manual activities are not used for the purpose of transforming the rural school into a workshop, but of serving as a basis for investigation, for scientific co-ordination, for the development of aesthetic tastes, prevocational training, and the formation of acceptable social habits.

The administration of rural schools is now co-ordinated with that of urban schools under the Department of Elementary Education for States and Territories; while the minimum plan of action for both types of school is significantly entitled "Programs for Urban and Rural Primary Schools *(Escuelas Primarias Urbanas y Rurales)*." The integration of rural with urban education thus becomes another well-laid plank in the ministry's educational platform.

Another type of elementary school is the Article 123 school, inspired by the famous "labor law" of the Mexican Constitution. Under Article 123 and the Organic Law of 1942 (Articles 67 through 71) employers are held personally responsible for the social, cultural, and educational welfare of their employees. Article 67 specifies that owners of agricultural, industrial, or mining

[12] *Memoria de la Secretaría de Educación Pública,* "Orientaciones didácticas—la base del trabajo en la escuela rural," MS 1932.

organizations, or associated industries, located more than three kilometers from the nearest town, must establish and maintain elementary schools for the community in which they operate, provided there are more than twenty children. Schools founded under this law were federated in 1934. Aims, programs, procedures, and methods are set by the Ministry of Education to accord with those of other elementary schools throughout the nation (Article 68). The law imposes definite obligations upon employers; they are required to furnish complete and hygienic school quarters, adequately equipped with minimum necessities, such as libraries, textbooks, and general school materials (Article 70). They must also pay the teachers the same salaries as those paid by the Ministry of Education (Article 71). The number of teachers to be appointed must be in the ratio of one for every fifty pupils or fraction thereof greater than twenty (Article 69). Thus, a school of 120 pupils normally would have two teachers, and a school of 121 pupils would have three.

Considerable difficulty has been encountered in keeping employer-owned schools open and adequately staffed in view of the conflict which exists between employers and government agents on educational aims. Many industries simply process raw materials for export to centers of finished manufacturing; thus, skilled labor is less in demand. The educational objectives of the national government, involving ready vocational transfer, personal excellence, and a degree of skill appropriate to technical development, go beyond the needs of agricultural and mining operators, who naturally resist any capital outlay on educational benefits that are not directly to their advantage. Nevertheless, these schools are actually increasing in number.

Government boarding schools play an important part in the ministry's program, and are designed to overcome the disadvantages suffered by pupils who live at great distances from day schools. Prior to 1942 boarding schools had sprung up haphazardly in response to temporary demands. For example, the "Sons of the Army" schools had been organized to take care of boys and girls whose fathers—incapacitated, or serving in the army away from home—were unable to support their families. But there were other reasons. The famous Francisco I. Madero school in Mexico City was founded as an experimental school to foster the ideas of the Revolution by assembling in one locality a cross-section of the country's less-privileged youth, particularly those of the working class *(obreros)*.[13] Boarding schools on the normal school level were established to attract more young people into teaching by offering virtually free board, room, and tuition.

Since 1942 it has been the policy of the ministry to favor the admission of all needy children to the boarding schools, without regard for class or political preference. Nevertheless, the schools themselves remain functionally specialized. Ten are essentially industrial, four essentially agricultural, five agricultural and industrial, and three essentially female. Thirteen institutions admit boys only, three are girls' schools, and six, including the Francisco I. Madero school, are coeducational. Regulations emphasize the desirability of promoting schools in which considerations of wealth and sex may be set aside and where representatives of Mexico's diverse population may come together to share an integrated educational experience. Opportunities, though meager, are thus provided for children who would otherwise be deprived of an education, either because their home conditions were poor or because they lived too far away from a school. Recognition of the value of the boarding schools has led to increasingly ambitious plans and larger budgetary allotments, so that today there is a definite trend toward establishing them as a fundamental and necessary part of Mexican national education.[14]

Cultural missions were reinstated in 1942 after a lapse of two

[13] Avila Garibay, *La Escuela Francisco I. Madero*, pp. 33-34. An entire, practically self-contained community of interests is found in this school.

[14] *Resumen de los informes*, "*Dirección General*," pp. 45-47. See also Manuel Gual Vidal, *Tiempo*, May 2, 1947, p. 29, where a brief reference is made to the importance of "increasing the [food] rations of the boarding school pupils who lack the money to pay for their education." The growth of boarding schools is represented in the following table:

	BOYS		GIRLS		TOTAL	
	1943	*1947*	*1943*	*1947*	*1943*	*1947*
Boarding	3,407	5,000	1,229	2,000	4,636	7,000
Non-boarding	220		106		326	400
					4,962	7,400

The pupil-teacher ratio in 1947 was about 17 to 1.

years. These institutions, sixty-one strong in 1946, are concerned with the "economic, cultural, and social improvement of isolated communities, preferably those which geographic and social conditions keep on an inferior plane of life." Of varied types, these mobile educational units transport specialized workers and equipment thousands of miles. For the most part, no group stays in one location longer than four to six weeks, since there is more need for extensive than for intensive effort. Contemporary aims of the cultural missions may be summarized as follows: (1) to regenerate the nation physically; (2) to elevate the general spiritual tone of the home; (3) to co-ordinate the home with the school; (4) to promote individual well-being and community solidarity; and (5) to develop local initiative.

The rural cultural mission usually consists of a chief (ordinarily a normal school professor with at least five years' experience), an instructor in recreational activities, a social worker, a music teacher, a registered nurse, an obstetrician, an agricultural expert, a teacher of handicrafts, a master mechanic, a motion-picture operator, and two industrial instructors. Not very different is the type of mission sent out to industrial communities and mining centers. Fully motorized missions carry an imposing array of equipment, including moving pictures and projector, a radio, a public address system, phonograph records, a small library, propaganda and educational pamphlets, a full surgical kit, medicines and drugs, seeds and plants, and vaccines and serums for domestic animals. Still another mission brings the latest agricultural techniques to rural teachers. The latter consists of a normal school professor of "brilliant" professional preparation, a graduate nursery-school teacher, a recreational supervisor, a professional musician, a social worker, a teacher of plastic arts, and an expert in mental testing and pedagogics.

Cultural missions have historically been associated with land cultivation and the improvement of the living habits of the peasant class. Of late, other purposes have been added, such as the exaltation of national welfare and patriotism. During the recent war the need was especially urgent for collaborating with those institutions in charge of pre-military education of the peasant class. Courses were organized to safeguard those democratic principles which sustain the institutional life of the nation. The cultural mission was to demonstrate methods of increasing production, strengthening the domestic economy, and improving the health of the people.

All these individualized endeavors—special schools, boarding schools, cultural missions, the literacy campaign—constitute the means by which the government has sought to overcome deficiencies in and barriers to nationwide elementary education. It is evident that these special types of school will have to be preserved for another generation at least. The goal of "equal opportunity" set by the Organic Law has not by any means been attained. Even in Mexico City, where the beacon light of education shines brightest, Gustavo Viniegra, the head of school construction, could point to the ironic plight of 85,000 children "who still await schools which our constitution says are free and compulsory."[15] The herculean task still facing the ministry is suggested by the table below. In 1945 the total number of children of elementary school age not in schools was almost three million. Of the 54 percent enrolled, the majority was attending one-room schools—a happy circumstance for many, but actually an all-to-vivid reminder of the school construction problem still facing the country. Despite praiseworthy accomplishment in the building program from 1944 to 1946, only 40,000 additional pupils had been housed.

TABLE 3

ELEMENTARY SCHOOL POPULATION AND ENROLLMENT[16]

Year	School Population (6 to 14 years)	Enrollment	Schools	Classroom Teachers	Teacher-Pupil Ratio
1940	4,688,410	....	23,434	.....	..
1943	5,022,422	2,352,502	20,170	48,817	48
1945	5,143,838	2,394,950	20,783	52,091	45

The over-all picture of Mexican elementary school education

[15] Gustavo Viniegra, *Tiempo*, March 28, 1947: "The fact remains that there are today two and one-half million children in the whole country without schools, despite repeated government efforts and commendable private initiative." See also *La obra educativa en el sexenio*, 1940-46, pp. 281, 286.

[16] *Compendio estadístico*, 1947, pp. 89, 104 ff.

is one of hopeful effort and progress. But despite progressive aims, despite an awareness of what constitutes intelligent educational advancement, it is painfully clear that the Mexican school, like so many of the world's schools, must remain quasi-traditional in approach. Heavy teaching loads, lack of equipment, inadequacy of teacher-training, all tend to preserve old patterns of behavior. The educational scene, therefore, is one in which conservatism is being modified by progressive effort. Much reliance is placed on the individual teacher, who in order to effect the individual learnings proposed by the Ministry must be more inventive, resourceful, and energetic than ever.

The body of Mexican elementary education is still plagued with growing pains and wounds that remain unhealed. Yet once the economic means have been found to bring cherished ideals to practical realization, the results should mark Mexico for distinction in urban as well as rural schools. To the Mexicans, schools have become far more than reading and writing institutes. With curricula founded on agriculture, soil conservation, sanitation, hygiene, crafts, bookkeeping, and with equipment consisting of hen coops, pigeon houses, beehives, rabbit hutches, pig sties, and vegetable patches, modern Mexican elementary schools are training a receptive nation in the vital arts of living.

V. The Education of Adolescents

The secondary school throughout history has been oriented to a theoretical and academic approach in conformity with university requirements; but it should be dissociated from this restriction so as to become an adequate preparation for technical pursuits.—Manuel Avila Camacho.

The secondary school, initially created to prepare a select few for university life, should be converted into a "school for adolescents" who are to be prepared for citizenship without distinction as to social hierarchy.—José Angel Ceniceros, 1944.

Adolescence, like all stages of human life, possesses value of its own; the boy is not a little man (homunculus) *; the youth is not still a boy, but neither is he yet a man. Boyhood and youth are stages of a continuous development . . . Education must attend with equal solicitude to each of these stages.*—Jaime Torres Bodet.

SECONDARY EDUCATION in Mexico consists of a five-year course of study following the elementary school. It is divided into two cycles: the first lasts three years; the second, two years. The first cycle is directed and controlled by the Ministry of Education; the second cycle, in its college preparatory phase, is usually administered by the universities. In some instances the universities also maintain schools of the first cycle, if they are of the college preparatory type.

The present section deals exclusively with the first three years of general secondary education, leaving vocational education and the preparatory schools for later treatment.

Secondary schools in Mexico have been much more reluctant than the elementary schools to enter into the spirit of mass education promoted by the ministry. At the root of their reluctance is a long history of exclusiveness, or aristocratic purposes, and of preparation in professional and liberal studies acceptable to university entrance authorities. They have been, on the whole, disinterested in the more unpleasant aspects of Mexico's workaday world and have felt an essential detachment from the elementary school.[1] Secondary education has been so exclusive that it was not until 1926—less than a generation ago—that its supervision was taken away from private agencies and put into the hands of the ministry. In that year secondary education became the joint concern of the Division of Secondary Education *(Dirección General de Segunda Enseñanza)* and the Department of University Studies *(Estudios Universitarios)* and was subdivided into "federal-state," "boarding," and "private" types. The result has been that this branch of education has steadily developed into a more popular, a more integral, and a more practical school experience. In the official expression of the ministry, "national unity demands a uni-

TABLE 4

ENROLLMENT IN PUBLIC SECONDARY SCHOOLS

	SCHOOLS		ENROLLMENT		TEACHERS
PUBLIC SCHOOLS	1941	1946	1941	1946	1946
The Federal District					
Day secondary schools	15	20	9,218	10,030	1,145
Night secondary schools	21	14	4,953	5,129	452
Special education	13	7	5,361	5,655	612
Fine arts	..	2	....	350	61
The States					
Secondary schools	20	38	2,659	4,411	486
Incorporated with the federal					
government	22	28	888	2,379	387
Boarding schools	7	6	721	1,064	77
Special education	17	19	7,288	5,716	440
INCORPORATED PRIVATE SCHOOLS					
The Federal District	48	53	5,400	7,955	981
Elsewhere	36	73	3,060	5,515	542
Special education	..	13	....	172	39
Totals	199	273	39,548	48,376	5,222

[1] Larroyo, *Historia comparada de la educación en México,* Mexico City, p. 127, reports that secondary education was born and nourished in confessionalism. Sánchez, *The Development of Higher Education in Mexico,* p. 83. *Cf.* Watson, *Education and Social Welfare,* p. 14: "The secondary schools have served primarily to prepare children from upper and middle class homes for entrance into colleges and professions. The attempt to bring them closer to the people has not been very successful."

fied cycle, elementary through secondary, practical and comprehensive."[2] The secondary school no longer is allowed its inherited isolation.

Table 4 lists the various types of public secondary schools, together with comparative enrollments for 1941 and 1946. There are, in addition, other secondary schools administered by various university boards.

Transfer to governmental control has brought striking progress. In 1926 only four public secondary schools were providing instruction for a total of 3,860 students—less than one percent of the secondary school age population. By 1946, 273 institutions were functioning, with 48,376 students. Financial investment has also increased: in 1946 the budget appropriation was 56 times greater than that of 1926. This budgetary increase is due, however, partly to monetary inflation, characteristic of national budgets throughout the world, partly to the acquisition of expensive permanent equipment, and partly to the payment of higher salaries for qualified teachers.

Physical growth in secondary schools has been accompanied by wide revisions in school programs. Emphasis has been on unification of effort, expansion of facilities, and the establishment of standards more suitable and more applicable to greater enrollments. There have been, and still are, the familiar difficulties of providing adequate staffs and equipment within a short space of time. There has also been the usual conflict between the values of terminal and continued education. As elsewhere, university authorities have joined with old-line secondary educators, in spite of government directives, to preserve traditional secondary education. Pressing economic necessity continues to force many apt, alert young people into the labor market before their time. Then, too, the eternal conflict has raged as to the advisability of spending sizable sums on vocational and technical education, when some maintain that this sort of training can best be done on the job by employers. In Mexico, as elsewhere, it is strongly felt in lay circles that elementary education is enough for the ordinary child and that secondary training should be reserved for those equipped with

[2] Secretaría de Educación Pública, *La obra educativa en el sexenio 1940-1946*, p. 17.

the brains and the background to cope with university preparation. Mexico's colloquia on the aims of secondary education postdate those of her northern neighbor by about fifty years, but their realization has been so greatly accelerated in recent years that the lag between theory and practice has become far briefer.

Leadership in the reassessment and the realization of secondary school aims was assumed by President Avila Camacho, who left no doubt in the minds of his people that existing procedures were not responding to contemporary demands. Conflict remained, he observed, between the practical and the cultural purposes of secondary schooling. In the President's mind a fusion of the two was desirable. In other words, he recognized no essential dichotomy between academic and vocational education; to him, secondary education meant continued training for one's life work in any field which the schools could serve. But he also declared that it was increasingly necessary for students to acquire the type of training which would prepare the way for more advanced technical pursuits.

The ministry has sought to meet this and other demands by promoting a series of experiments and adjustments designed, as were those at the elementary level, to bring the secondary school into the general pattern of the country's educational life. Frequent shifts in organization have resulted, typified by a division between general and technical education, which was effected chiefly to placate the academic-minded. In 1944 the Ministry reformed secondary school programs in accordance with the following objectives: (1) to continue the school's cultural emphases; (2) to concentrate equally on the physical, intellectual, moral, and aesthetic growth development of the student; (3) to train for the fulfillment of citizenship duties in the democratic government of the country; and (4) to prepare for the vocational, technical, and university preparatory schools.

Implementing these objectives, the ministry again revised the general secondary curriculum in 1946, as shown in the outline below. For purposes of comparison, Table 5 shows the number of hours allotted per week to each subject in the years 1940, 1944, and 1946.

The marked increase in the total number of hours in the course

TABLE 5

PRESCRIBED CURRICULA FOR GENERAL SECONDARY SCHOOLS, FIRST CYCLE

COURSE OF STUDY	TOTAL HOURS REQUIRED PER WEEK[a]		
	1940	1944	1946
Mathematics I	5	5	6
Mathematics II	4	4	4
Mathematics III	4	4	4
Spanish language and literature I	3	4	6
Spanish language and literature II	3	3	4
Spanish language and literature III	3	3	4
Foreign language I[b]	3	3	3
Foreign language II	3	3	3
Foreign language III	3	2	3
General biology	4	4	4
Zoology	4	3	3
Anatomy and physiology	3	3	3
Physical geography	3	3	3
Physics	4	4	4
Chemistry	4	4	4
World history I	2	3	4
World history II	3	—	3
World history III	3	3	—
Mexican history I	—	—	3
Mexican history II	—	3	4
Civics I	2	2	4
Civics II	2	2	4
Civics III	2	2	4
Human geography	3	3	3
Mexican geography	2	2	4
Drawing *(imitación)*	2	3	2
Drawing *(constructivo)*	2	3	2
Drawing *(modelado)*	2	1	2
Music I	1	2	2
Music II	1	1	1
Music III	—	—	1
Games and sports I[c]	2	4	2

a Hours include supervised study. All courses are allotted one hour each of supervised study, except mathematics and first-year Spanish, which have two hours.

b English has been required since 1944. German was dropped in 1946.

c Called physical and military education originally, but changed to physical and premilitary education in 1946. Two hours only are required for girls; the remaining time is usually devoted to domestic science.

TABLE 5—(CONTINUED)

PRESCRIBED CURRICULA FOR GENERAL SECONDARY SCHOOLS, FIRST CYCLE

	TOTAL HOURS REQUIRED PER WEEK		
COURSE OF STUDY	1940	1944	1946
Games and sports II	2	2	2
Games and sports III	2	2	2
Manual arts Iᵈ	6	2	4
Manual arts II	4	2	4
Manual arts III	6	—	4
Electives Iᵉ	—	—	—
Electives II	—	2	—
Electives III	2	2	2
Grand totals for three years	103	98	120

ᵈ Called "practical activities" in 1940, and "workshop and domestic science" in 1946.
ᵉ Electives in 1944: manual arts, bookkeeping, commercial arithmetic. Electives in 1946: additional manual arts, laboratory science, mathematics, art.

of study for 1946 is attributable mostly to the greater number of hours allotted to supervised study. Immediately discernible, of course, is the increase in the amount of time given to Spanish, the social studies, and manual arts. This development clearly reflects the trend toward Mexican nationalization, especially since the teaching of Mexican history as a separate subject had been suspended in the early 1940's. It also reveals the added concentration on training for Mexican practical life and a "strongly reinforced impulse" toward laboratory practice. New elective subjects have been introduced. Group studies and manual projects within classes have been especially encouraged, and flexible hours established. The ministry also requires more hours for manual arts, still retaining them as electives, but adding electives of a more academic and theoretical nature.

The first cycle of Mexican secondary education corresponds in actual years of schooling to the junior high school in the United States, but there are essential differences, notably in the number and extent of required courses and the intensity of the student's load. In terms of class hours and intellectual content the Mexican student is expected to accomplish at an earlier stage approximately one-third more than the average senior high school student in the

United States. World history, for example, is taught two years earlier than its equivalent in the usual American course of study. Mathematics and general science are similarly accelerated. The ambition of the ministry is justified in part by the more restricted student body in Mexican secondary schools (15 percent of the total age-group as compared with 70 percent in the United States). Also, Mexico's school year is longer—200 days as compared with an average of about 160 days in the United States.

The preference for a wide variety of academic subject matter is characteristic of most school systems outside the United States. The Mexican youth's secondary school experience is more strictly subject-centered than that of his neighbor to the north. Likewise, he does not as a rule enjoy the multifarious extra-curricular activities of his northern neighbor—experiences which are considered a vital part of school training. Mexican school officials have long been aware that their curricula include an excessive number of courses, and between 1940 and 1946 they inaugurated remedial measures. Their efforts soon waned, however, and finally collapsed in 1946, when the ministry settled for such reforms as a reduction in the amount of homework, the regular scheduling of supervised study, a revision of compulsory courses, the introduction of group project methods, the promotion of realistic workshop activities, and added provisions for the recognition of individual differences.

In secondary, as in elementary schools the ministry today insists upon an organic unity in the presentation of subject matter. Units of instruction must be so organized as to convert study programs from "mere lists of topics, such as the index of a textbook, into effective guides for school activity." Supervised study, moreover, is not just another activity; rather it connotes a complete change in procedures, designated to aid the student in acquiring the habits and procedures most conducive to effective study.

Serious difficulty in this regard has been encountered in the mathematics program, which consumes the lion's share of the student's time. Emphasis is supposed to be on practical application. According to official directives, mathematics, at least in the early years, must be taught in such a way as to prepare for later technical and industrial training. Actually, the intensively academic nature of the program and the preference of most teachers for dwelling on the abstract, have resulted in a high percentage of failures. Increased supervised study in the early stages is partially remedying this difficulty; but the struggle continues for better pedagogical methods and more functional teaching and learning situations. In mathematics, especially, it has been shown that emphasis on abstractions without corresponding stress on practical applications can bring little benefit to the average student, who must use the subject matter as a means, not as an end.

Education for Mexican nationalism is reflected in an increased emphasis on the Spanish language and literature. In addition to the communicative and aesthetic values of these subjects, the ministry uses them to stimulate national cultural solidarity. The first two years concentrate on grammar, reading, oral and written expression, lexicology, phonetics, and spelling. In the third year, the youngster studies the history of language and literature as exemplified by classical Spanish and modern Mexican contributions.

Expansion in the study of social sciences has occurred in response to Mexican needs as well as to educational trends in other countries. Torres Bodet, still mindful of the "rational-scientific" concepts advocated by the original Organic Law, demanded that Mexican education accord the social sciences a status equal to that of the natural sciences. Aims evolved by the Ministry for teaching world history, Mexican history, and civics stress the need for understanding, co-operation, and acceptable habits and attitudes of good citizenship in international as well as national affairs. The teaching of world history is expected to inculcate in tomorrow's citizens the democratic ideals of liberty, justice, peace, order, culture, and progress." At the same time students are to gain a clearer understanding of the world and human relations. In response to the demands of progressive historians for more interpretation and less bare fact, the ministry submits five headings under which history should be taught: (1) the *chronological,* from which the student obtains a framework for interpreting the evolution of peoples and institutions; (2) the *geographical,* which affords a knowledge of the environment and its influence upon the material, political, and cultural life of peoples; (3) the *economic,* which explores the effects of inventions and machinery, labor movements and methods, and "the organized relations of men" (slavery, peonage, free labor, paid labor, and so forth); (4) the *political*, which delineates the modes of life that have been brought about by the transformation of communities and institutions; and (5) the *cultural*, which familiarizes the student with the origin and development of religious, artistic, scientific, and juridical customs.

Beginning with prehistory, universal history embraces natural history and philosophy. It deals with the earth as a part of the solar system, with the origins of life "based on scientific theories," and with "social mores from primitive communities through neo-oriental civilizations of Greece and Rome, to the international confusions of the World War period." The teacher is urged always to teach in such a way as to train "the scientific judgment of the student, and not stuff his mind with irrelevant and memorized material."

Mexican history was prescribed by the ministry, in 1942, as an antidote to international stresses. In 1946 the requirement was doubled. This study modifies the aims of universal history to stress national environment, national leaders, and events contributory to national formation. Recommendations clearly specify that the teacher shall "endeavor to banish all particularist passions and false prejudices" injurious to Mexican unity. The central aim is to produce a generous attitude toward all the peoples of Mexico and a firm resolve to combat war and all causes of war. Emphasis is placed on a sympathetic understanding of national problems and on the creation of sound judgment and active co-operation in improving social and national conditions in Mexico today.

Methods of study include visits to original sources—museums, archives, libraries, and scenes of famous historical events. Supplementary reading is expected to clarify, amplify, and fix certain aspects of historical phenomena. Realistic teaching materials and visual aids, such as films, photographs, models, drawings, and maps, are employed "to assist in arousing student initiative." The teacher is cautioned against a simple recitation of facts unrelated to the interests of the student. The ministry everywhere stresses the pedagogical value of student participation.

The study of geography is designed to contribute a "rational explanation of phenomena in perpetual transformation." The influence of geographic factors in the life of nations is considered of prime importance. Included in the first year of study are the solar system, the earth and its structure, atmosphere, climate, rainfall, and so forth. The second year concentrates on the geographic environment of man, on the morphology and distribution of mankind, and on the production and distribution of goods, especially those of Mexico. The third phase stresses the physical, human, social, and economic geography of Mexico.

The brightest flower of the social science program is civics or "civic education." Here all the pressures of national education converge, for the major preoccupation of this subject is with the development of individual competence in a social situation. As the ministry defines it, "Civic education leads to the formation of upright, tolerant and intelligent citizens; it proceeds by stages, beginning with a rudimentary understanding of the rights and duties of the citizen. At a more advanced stage, it broadens the entire political horizon of the student. Finally, the student is brought to a true appreciation of the state and its historic mission." The most desirable values are those of democracy "as it struggles for existence against the aggression and tyranny inherent in other systems of government." The first year is concerned with institutional precepts: the individual and society, the family, the community, the school, and the nation. These units of study are succeeded by more abstract material: moral law, problems of delinquency, poverty, social assistance, labor relations, concepts of the state, government, war, peace, and so forth.

Excursions for purposes of civic understanding are made to homes and communities on various social levels. Students may visit the Ministry of Education "to investigate the state of education in the country and the number of illiterates." The Ministry of Public Welfare and other governmental agencies also "welcome the opportunity to explain their aims and procedures to secondary school students." Factories and working conditions are investigated. Pupils also form clubs with recreational, intellectual, artistic, or social purposes; they are expected to maintain an alert interest in current events as reported in the daily newspapers. Finally, personal appreciations, initiative, understanding, and socially acceptable moral habits are encouraged as aids in forming balanced, patriotic citizens. So, at least, states the official program.

Conflict between the idealists and the instrumentalists continues in the foreign language program.[3] Directives originating in 1941 have been modified many times. Formerly, reading and writing were of paramount importance; more recently, speaking and comprehension have been pushed to the fore, in response to a growing emphasis on deductive, functional methods. Traditional methods still prevail, however, and modern languages are studied in the same manner as Latin and Greek. Only really proficient language teachers are able to employ methods better adapted to modern needs, and they are all too rare, in view of the law which restricts teaching positions to Mexican citizens. Until more foreigners are legally permitted to teach their native tongues in Mexican schools, students must still endure, as they do in the United States, the tutelage of grammar-minded teachers with defective pronunciations, second-hand knowledge, and a general inadequacy in speaking and understanding the language they teach.

The biological sciences include zoology, botany, anatomy, hygiene, and physiology. The programs involve: (1) the study of living things, with an interpretation of biological laws and the evolution of organisms; (2) the study of environment and its best use from a biological point of view; (3) the promotion of hygienic living by the immediate application of biological knowledge; (4) the discovery of personal aptitudes through individual experimentation; and (5) the acquisition of realistic understanding by means of excursions and laboratory work. Today most schools have biological laboratories, a few rather well-equipped. Efforts of the ministry in this direction have been admirably supplemented by individual teacher and student effort. In the majority of instances

[3] Villagrán Prado, "The Importance of the Study of English and Spanish," in *Mexico's Role in Intellectual Cooperation.* For a discussion of the teaching of English see pp. 10 ff. The teaching of German was rare even before the ministry dropped it in 1946. Classes in Latin and Greek are practically nonexistent in public secondary schools of the first cycle.

the laboratories inspected by the author had grown directly out of local, not ministry, initiative.

First-year course content focuses on elementary subject matter: the seedling, the cell, and rudimentary botanical life. Students learn the use of the microscope and experiment with practical planting. The second year continues with vegetable and animal life. The third year concentrates on the human body: general structure, mobility, nervous system, digestive system (including the nutritive value of foods), circulatory system, respiration, secretions, and excretions.

The physical sciences are supposed to be taught with a view toward practical application; they are employed to demonstrate the fact that causes exist for all phenomena. Laboratory work is required, and opportunities for independent work are recommended. Here again the teacher is urged not to deal out facts for memorizing, but to help the student learn through his own efforts. A harder goal to fulfill, of course, than the old method of fact presentation!

Drawing, a subject particularly sympathetic to Mexican proclivities, is compulsory throughout the first cycle. The program is designed to foster observation, analysis, and manual skills; to promote habits of perseverance, precision, clarity, and neatness; and to facilitate the interpretation of schematic and spatial problems derived from other fields of study. Products of the drawing classes are exhibited everywhere throughout the school; they not only provide a most acceptable substitute for furnishings which would otherwise have to be purchased, but constitute undeniable testimony of Mexican natural ability, ingenuity, and manual dexterity. The deftness, agility, and downright affection with which the average Mexican handles tools and materials arouses the envy and admiration of all who observe him at work.

The Organic Law is, of course, the basis for all secondary education. Aside from the particularized aims and programs listed above, certain other stipulations remain in force. The law requires, for instance, that the sexes be segregated (Article 74). Teachers must be specialists in their subjects, and must possess a sound pedagogical background (Article 76). (This provision tends to

124   *The Education of Adolescents*

eliminate the amateur specialist who once predominated on a part-time basis on the staffs of most Mexican secondary schools.) By law, student organizations may exist for cultural development and in the service of economic, ethical, civic, or cultural values. But these organizations may under no circumstances interfere with school administration (Article 77). Instruction is legally free, except for special laboratory and equipment fees and a nominal tuition of some six or eight pesos, which may be set aside in case of need. This fee has two purposes: it tends to keep students in school because of the personal investment involved; and it provides the school with small items of equipment not readily procurable from the ministry.

Summary.—Efforts in the secondary field have in part been determined by national necessity, in part by student demand and maturity. Pedagogical methods advocated by the ministry in 1946, presently in force, lay special emphasis upon the genetic approach adapted to the natural course of the life of the student. Education in, for, and through the community is the official aim. Technical training within the framework of general education is receiving increased attention—a fact which is evidenced by the relatively greater number of hours now devoted to science and manual arts in contrast to the old verbal emphasis.

Serving as both continuation and terminal education, the lower secondary school is attracting more and more students and consequently a greater cross-section of intellectual ability. This has brought about a supervised study program that consumes a larger portion of school time than formerly. By and large, the whole plan is supported by excellent pedagogical principles as leading educators know them today. But here, again, the full implementation of Mexico's enlightened views depends upon more adequate staffs and better equipment. Given more teachers with professional training, more teaching aids, more schools with larger staffs and fewer students, secondary Mexican education will be in a position to respond more faithfully to national directives.[4]

[4] A useful set of conclusions, on the progress of secondary education in Mexico is to be obtained in Angel Ceniceros, *El valor democrático de la enseñanza secundaria.* Note especially p. 29: "The transformation of our secondary school is not a North American phenomenon, but also European and Latin American because it has to follow the inevitable course of progress everywhere."

THE NATIONAL PREPARATORY SCHOOL

The National Preparatory School is the very heart of University academic life. In it the adolescent receives the imprint of his future life as a man of letters or of science. Youth acquires for good or for ill the habit of work or of negligence; the spirit of personal honor or of moral indifference; the creativity of intellectual life or the sterility of talent gone to waste.— Francisco Larroyo, 1947.

Everywhere recognized as a model for the other university preparatory schools of the country, the National Preparatory School *(Escuela Nacional Preparatoria)*, in Mexico City, is here used as an example of advanced secondary school training.

Founded in 1867 by Gabino Barreda, the National Preparatory School originally gave promise of redirecting secondary education into new realistic and popular paths. Barreda was a follower of Comte, but his program envisioned a fairly broad scientific and humanistic general education which, according to Sánchez, sought to prepare the student for reasoned humanitarian social action. However, citing Alfonso Reyes, Sánchez observes:[5]

The school soon degenerated from its highly liberal purpose, giving way to the "mechanisms of method." Mathematics, natural history, science, and even the humanities themselves became dry, academic disciplines . . . Laboratory equipment was almost abandoned, and science was largely a mental discipline. So with the rest of the curriculum; and the school, the people's college, became but a mental exercise ground that served only as a stepping stone to the professional schools . . . The original broad significance of "preparatory" was soon lost sight of, and preparatory schools were thought of exclusively as the initial grade in higher education. This limited interpretation has persisted to the present day . . .

Housed since its founding in the famous old Jesuit School of San Ildefonso, erected in 1749, the institution is in reality a School of the Autonomous National University. It is therefore under the control, not of the Ministry of Education, but of the university.[6]

[5] George I. Sánchez, *The Development of Higher Education in Mexico*, pp. 94-95.
[6] The frontier preparatory schools, however, at Nuevo Laredo, Nogales, and Piedras Negras, function under the Division of University Studies of the Department of Higher Education and Scientific Investigation of the Ministry. *Anuario de la Escuela Nacional*

At present, the National Preparatory School enrolls over more than ten thousand students in day and evening courses—about five times as many boys as girls.

For a number of years the preparatory school has prepared its candidates for university entrance first in an *iniciación universitaria* program, which, as we have seen, corresponds to the first three years of secondary school. The reason for this step was obvious: as a result of governmental stress on "general" secondary training in place of university preparation, the university feared inadequate preparation for the two-year preparatory school and later for the higher university schools. More recently, the program of the first three years of secondary education *(iniciación)* was actually consolidated with that of the ensuing two years of the preparatory school. A comparison of the first three years of the latest preparatory school course of study with that of the regular general secondary school is shown in Table 6.[7]

Inspection of these curricula reveals that public school students receive, hour for hour, a training equivalent to that given in the National Preparatory School except in the field of Greek and Latin. Manual arts and supervised study account for the additional scheduled time in the public schools, though the physical science requirements of the public schools exceed those of the preparatory school. The handicaps to general secondary students desiring further education are therefore largely qualitative, since the lack of Greek and Latin should not prove insurmountable for those who aspire to matriculation in the National Preparatory School. Because of the greater selectivity of students, however, the consolidated preparatory program no doubt achieves better results for the purposes of the university. Environmentally and pedagogically, if in no other way, preparatory students are early indoctrinated in university ways and preferences, since they are as a rule taught by university instructors with university standards (adapted, of course) and in university buildings.

Preparatoria, Universidad Autónoma de México, pp. 53 ff. Many Mexican educators object to any conclusion that the "Preparatoria" is a secondary school. Some prefer to call it a junior college. But to enter the argument is, in the personal experience of the author, almost futile.

[7] Universidad Autónoma de México, *Plan de estudios,* Escuela Nacional Preparatoria, September, 1946.

The baccalaureate *(bachillerato)* is awarded on graduation from Mexican preparatory schools and the passing of qualifying examinations. This certificate, attained after eleven years of organized schooling and frequently termed the "bachelor's degree," does not, however, correspond to the B.A. degree granted by a four-year college or university in the United States after about sixteen years of organized schooling. Debate rages as to how the preparatory

TABLE 6

COMPARATIVE COURSES OF STUDY FOR GENERAL SECONDARY SCHOOLS, FIRST CYCLE, AND THE FIRST THREE YEARS OF THE NATIONAL PREPARATORY SCHOOL, 1946

	GENERAL SECONDARY SCHOOLS					NATIONAL PREPARATORY SCHOOL FIRST THREE YEARS *(Iniciación)*			
	YEAR OF STUDY			SUPER-VISED STUDY	TOTAL CLASS HOURS	YEAR OF STUDY			TOTAL CLASS HOURS
	1	2	3			1	2	3	
Mathematics	6	4	4	(4)	10	5	4	4	13
Spanish	6	4	4	(4)	10	3	3	3	9
Modern languages	3	3	3	(3)	6	3	3	3	9
Greek and Latin							3	3	6
Biological sciences	4	3	3	(3)	7	4	4	4	12
Physical science	4	3	3	(3)	7			4	4
Social science	8	13	12	(9)	24	6	6	9	21
Arts (drawing, mechanical drawing, art, and music)	4	3	3		10	7	5		12
Physical education	2	2	2		6	2	2	2	6
Manual arts	4	4	4		12				
Elective (manual or academic)			2		2				
Grand totals	41	39	40	(26)	94 (120)	30	30	32	92

graduate compares with the college student in the United States. Assuming adequate knowledge of English, a high-ranking graduate of the National Preparatory School should be able to enter the sophomore year in a standard college of the United States. Mexicans naturally demand a higher standing, while North Americans are usually not so liberal.

Once having elected a particular school or faculty of the university, the student is expected to remain with his choice throughout his preparatory and university life. Up to 1943 seven main curricula were offered in the National Preparatory School. Profes-

sional specialization dominated these curricula; only five courses
were identical in all basic programs: Spanish, logic, Mexican history, hygiene, and physical education. A realization of the costli-
ness of this differentiation, and its lack of justification, prompted
the University Council, in 1942, to authorize a simplified experimental program commencing in 1943. Under this plan only two
basic courses were differentiated throughout, namely, science and
letters. At present, the science curriculum, leading to the *Bachillerato en Ciencias* (not a B.S. degree), is a unified, composite preparation for later graduate work in biology, medicine, dentistry,
and other scientific fields. The letters curriculum, on the other
hand, provides suitable preparation for law, philosophy, letters,
the arts, and allied studies.

TABLE 7

COURSES OF STUDY AT THE NATIONAL PREPARATORY SCHOOL LEADING TO
THE BACHILLERATO IN SCIENCES AND THE BACHILLERATO IN
LETTERS (HUMANITIES), 1946

FIRST YEAR		SECOND YEAR	
COURSE OF STUDY	HOURS PER WEEK	COURSE OF STUDY	HOURS PER WEEK
Mathematics I	5	Mathematics II	4
Geography I	3	Geography II	3
Biology I	4	Biology II	4
Spanish language and literature I	3	Spanish language and literature II	3
Modern language I	3	Greek or Latin I	3
Civics I	3	Modern language II	3
Free-hand drawing I	3	Civics II	3
Modeling I	2	Music II	2
Music	2	Mechanical drawing I	3
Physical education	2	Physical education	2
	30		30

THIRD YEAR	
Mathematics III	4
Geography III	3
Physics I	4
Biology III	4
Spanish language and literature III	3
Modern language III	3
World history I	3
Greek or Latin II	3
Civics III	3
Physical education	2
	32

TABLE 7—(CONTINUED)

COURSES OF STUDY AT THE NATIONAL PREPARATORY SCHOOL LEADING TO
THE BACHILLERATO IN SCIENCES AND THE BACHILLERATO IN
LETTERS (HUMANITIES), 1946

FOURTH YEAR

BACHILLERATO IN SCIENCES		BACHILLERATO IN HUMANITIES	
Physics II	4	Spanish language and	
Chemistry I	4	literature IV	3
World history II	3	Chemistry I	3
History of Mexico I	3	World history II	3
Modern language IV or a		History of Mexico I	3
second modern language I	3	Modern language IV	3
Hygiene	2	World literature I	3
Philosophy I	2	Hygiene	2
Physical education	2	Philosophy	2
Electives[a]	7 to 10	Physical education	2
		Electives	8 to 9
	30 to 33		32 to 33

FIFTH YEAR

Physics III	4	World history III	3
Chemistry II	4	History of Mexico II	3
History of Mexico II	3	Modern language V	3
Modern language V or a		Modern literature II	3
second modern language II	3	Mexican and Spanish-	
World literature	3	American literature	3
Logic	3	Logic	3
Physical education	2	Psychology	3
Electives	10 to 11	Ethics	3
		Physical education	2
		Electives	6
	32 to 33		32

[a] The following subjects must be elected the fourth year by students aspiring to the schools or faculties of medicine, veterinary medicine, and sciences: mathematics IV (3), biological sciences IV (3), anatomical drawing (2), modeling (2); and in the fifth year: biological sciences V (4), psychology (3), ethics (3). For chemical sciences, the electives required for the fourth year are: mathematics IV (5), biological sciences IV (3), mechanical drawing II (2); and for the fifth year: mathematics V (5), biological sciences V (4). The School of Engineering and the Faculty of Sciences (except the Department of Biology) require: mathematics IV (5), mechanical drawing (2); and for the fifth year: mathematics V (5), cosmography (5). The School of Architecture requires in the fourth year: mathematics IV (5), mechanical drawing (2), modeling (2); and for the fifth year: mathematics V (5), cosmography (3), free-hand drawing (2). The Faculty of Philosophy and the School of Law require: Latin I (3), Greek or modern language (3); and for the fifth year: Latin II (2), Greek or modern language II (3). The School of Economics requires: mathematics IV (5), modern language (3); and in the fifth year: mathematics I (3), and a modern language (3).

The subject matter in classes of the National Preparatory School is prescribed in detail by university authorities. Some official syllabi even designate the precise number of lectures to be devoted to each topic. Representative aspects merit presentation in summary form.

Courses in English and French are expected to stress conversation. The student is to acquire a vocabulary sufficient for discussing the weather, time of day, calendar events, classroom paraphernalia, and so forth. He learns the words for numbers, colors, parts of the body, articles of clothing, the senses, food, furnishings, community classifications. Also emphasized is reading for visual and oral comprehension, the principal objective being to enable students to read texts which will later be used in their professional studies. English grammar is outlined under some thirty-six headings. The use of the grammar syllabus is left to the individual professor, as Villagrán states, "because of the difficult conditions in which we have to work; too many students in one class; heterogeneity of students, especially as to previous preparation, etc."

History is concerned with essential points in "the story of man in time and space"—with the exception of the history of the ancient Chinese, of the East Indians, and of what are somewhat vaguely termed the "many other peoples about whom we either know nothing or concerning whom there is little or no information." This attitude is somewhat difficult to understand, though it can, perhaps, be explained as a reluctance, unfortunately still prevalent among many Mexican historians, to embark upon experimentation or adventure in the teaching of history.

Ancient history begins with archeological discoveries in Egypt, Greece, Palestine, Assyria, and other countries in those regions, and continues with studies of the human being and his racial characteristics: Egyptians, Chaldeans, Hebrews, Phoenicians, Persians, Greeks. A study of the Roman World features economic and juridical accomplishments, and the multisecular life of the empire. Types of government and social revolutions also come in for treatment. The study of medieval history concentrates on religious revolutions, the Christian and oriental doctrines, and the influence of monotheism on economic and political development to the beginning of the sixteenth century.

Modern history is divided into "modern times" and "contemporary history," the first classification dealing with those outstanding events which bear directly on the present life of nations. Strangely enough, only Europe and America are included. Contemporary history is considered to begin with the later phases of the French Revolution and with the propagation of democratic ideas after 1848. Industrial and commercial developments and their consequent effect on the laboring classes are complementary to a major emphasis on political progress. The twentieth century is ignored (1946 syllabus), and the course ends with "The United States and intervention in Spanish America," citing territory lost by Mexico, and the Monroe Doctrine, "not recognized by Mexico."[8] However, personal observation has satisfied the writer that contemporary history is taught in actual practice.

The history of Mexico begins with Mexican antiquity—the Nahoa and Maya traditions as interpretive of Mixtec, Zapotec, and Tarasca cultures. The course of study for the first year takes the student to the War of Independence, 1810. He completes the course (at least according to the syllabi) with the Constitutional Revolution of 1917.

Programs in mathematics are arranged under three headings: arithmetic and algebra, geometry and trigonometry, and analytical geometry and calculus. The arithmetic program allots twenty lessons to the study of systems of numbers, powers, prime numbers, fractions, and decimals, with special application to the English system of measurement, and roots and elementary calculus. Sixty lessons are devoted to algebra. The course includes the binomial theorem, logarithms, functions and derivations, graphs, arithmetic and geometric progression, and so forth. In geometry and trigonometry, Wentworth and Smith's well-known texts are used. Seventy-five lessons are assigned to plane geometry; thirty-five to solid geometry, and thirty-five to trigonometry. H. B. Phillips'

---

[8] *Ibid.*, p. 140. For the bachilleratos in philosophy and letters, the biological sciences, and commerce and administration previous to 1943, a synthetic course in modern and contemporary history was offered in eight lectures, beginning with the fifteenth century and inclusive of developments among the Indians in America prior to discovery by Columbus. The French Revolution and its consequences were handled in some detail, followed by a treatment of nationalism from the fall of Rome to the present day. Contemporary social problems were next considered as a consequence of economic transformation since 1850, including the advent of machine labor and technology. The labor movement, unions, co-operatives, utopianism, Marxian socialism, anarchism, fascism, communism, and contemporary tendencies all came into consideration as part of the course.

Analytical Geometry is the text employed in analytical geometry, a course consisting of seventy-five lectures through Cartesian co-ordinates, followed by seventy-five lectures in differential and integral calculus.

Examinations follow all courses of study and are of five types: "partial," "ordinary," "extraordinary," "proficiency" *(título de suficiencia)*, and "professional." "Partial" examinations are usually of the written type; they last one hour and are limited to the material treated within the current school period. Two such examinations are permitted each year—before the short May and September vacations. "Ordinary" examinations, given at the close of school and comprising the work of the year, are either oral or written. Oral examinations are limited to twenty minutes, written examinations to two hours. "Extraordinary" examinations, administered by a committee of three faculty specialists in the subject matter to be covered, are both oral and written, and are given to those who received a mark of "5" or less in "ordinary" examinations, to those who were unable to take "ordinary" examinations, or to those who have failed in one of the "partial" examinations. "Proficiency" examinations are set for new students who have not studied at the National Preparatory School, for those who have received less than "5" in examinations in schools from which they came, for those who have failed "extraordinary" examinations, and for students whose class attendance credit was insufficient for "ordinary" examinations. The "professional" examination is the final test given just before the granting of the *bachillerato;* it comprises all the subject matter treated during the student's two-year preparatory course. The oral part of this examination is open to the public. Grading is recorded as either "pass" or "fail" in accordance with a majority vote of the examining committee.[9]

[9] *Anuario de la Escuela Nacional Preparatoria,* p. 49. Other universities and institutions of higher learning in Mexico maintain similar schools. The Preparatory School at Guadalajara is a school of the University of Guadalajara; it operates under arrangements similar to those of its sister institution in Mexico City. Requirements for entrance, examinations, courses of study, and the final bachillerato are equivalent to their counterparts in the nation's capital, except that in general the tendency has been to show greater leniency in the matter of academic background of the students and general course demands. See Universidad de Guadalajara, "Plan de estudios en vigor en las escuelas preparatoria de Jalisco y preparatoria nocturna, 1942-1943," MS.

So much for the bare program of the National Preparatory School. As for its general atmosphere and accomplishment, Francisco Larroyo joins educators of the more progressive type in revealing the "grave, complex and disheartening problem" still present at the preparatory school. Nor are matters noticeably improving; its decadence continues unchecked; the kind of education the students receive at present is actually of lower grade, even in its traditional verbalism, than that of a generation ago. Constructively, Francisco Larroyo urges that a new and modern structure be built, that new programs be initiated in accordance with new demands, and that the teaching corps be selected more carefully. More specifically, he recommends (1) that the present student body, congested in one structure, be distributed among several new buildings, each given over to a specific training for a specific *bachillerato;* (2) that the various courses of study be simplified and co-ordinated; (3) that activity methods be introduced in teaching, and the latest psychological findings be utilized to improve student selection and achievement; and (4) that a more adequate system of examinations be devised, based on modern pedagogical principles. "Only thus," warns Larroyo, "will education in the National Preparatory School raise its present level of attainment and respond to a resounding national clamor for reform."

While preparatory schools dependent on universities can hardly be termed public, since not all their income is derived from state funds, neither can they be classified as private. Private schools in Mexico must be entirely self-supporting; they must acquire their income mostly from student tuition fees. In the welter of private schools in Mexico, secular and nonsecular, foreign-language biased and otherwise, the American school in Mexico City occupies a place of sufficient importance and interest to the English speaking world to warrant discussion.

The American School Foundation is owned by Americans living in Mexico, who "operate on a non-profit basis an institution known as the American School." The school is coeducational and nonboarding, enrolling students from kindergarten through college, including selected phases of graduate work leading to the North American M.A. degree. All work is done in English, except for courses in the Spanish language and the history, geography, and civics of Mexico, required by Mexican law in the elementary school and taught by Mexican citizens. The kindergarten enrolls children of all nationalities who are five years old. Children may enter the elementary school when six years old.

The high school is a combination junior-senior high school, with grades from 7 through 12. The subjects offered in junior high school, grades 7 and 8, are English, general mathematics, general science, social science, Spanish, dramatics, art, music, speech, and physical training, with homemaking added in grade 8. According to a recent catalogue, the school offers the following units for graduation from high school: art (2), commercial studies (5), dramatics (1), English (5), French (3), history (4), homemaking (4), mathematics (5), music (2), science (4), Spanish (4). One unit of credit is given for courses requiring five recitations per week for ten months.

The school stipulates that a total of eighteen units must be acquired for graduation, attainable in four different types of curricula; college preparatory, commercial studies, general, and homemaking. A "major" is defined as three or more units in the same field. In Table 8 is an outline of the various courses of study.

It is evident from this brief sketch that the American School offers a program aimed to satisfy college entrance authorities both in Mexico and abroad. Many of the graduates find their way to colleges and universities in the United States, the diploma of the school being recognized by such accrediting agencies as the Southern Association of Colleges and Universities. Since Americans are settling in Mexico in constantly increasing numbers, it is manifest that a school of this type serves a vital purpose in offering the kind of training and preparation needed by young people who in most instances will return to their own country in later life. The atmosphere of the institution is more characteristic of the United States than of Mexico. However, in his personal observation the writer discerned a sincere attention to, and respect for, things Mexican.

TABLE 8

COURSES OF STUDY WITH REQUIRED NUMBER OF UNITS IN AMERICAN
HIGH SCHOOLS

COLLEGE PREPARATORY		COMMERCIAL	
SUBJECT	UNITS	SUBJECT	UNITS
English	4	English	3
Foreign language	2	Spanish	3
Algebra	2	Business arithmetic	1
Geometry	1	American history or civics	1
American history or civics	1	Biology	1
Other history	1	Commercial studies	4
Biological science	1	Electives	5
Physical science	1		18
Art			
Music	2 units from		
Dramatics	this group for		
Speech	all courses of		
Physical education	study 2		
Electives[a]	3		
	18		

GENERAL		HOMEMAKING	
SUBJECT	UNITS	SUBJECT	UNITS
English	3	English	4
Mathematics	1	American history	1
American history	1	Biology	1
Biology	1	Chemistry	1
Foreign language	2	Foreign language	2
Electives	8	Homemaking	3
	16	Electives	4
			16

[a] Electives include trigonometry, solid geometry, physics, chemistry, a second foreign language, mechanical drawing, etc.

VOCATIONAL AND TECHNICAL TRAINING

Snobbishness and disdain of work with hands and materials is at the root of our deficiency in technical achievement. People prefer academic forms and "liberal" professions; and for this our instruction is partly to blame for its inadequacy and insufficiency.—Manuel Avila Camacho.

Modern life would be inconceivable without a convenient and adequate social division of work; the secondary school is the stage for vocational exploration on the part of the student, and it cannot ignore its obligation.—La obra educativa, 1940-46.

*In order to avoid the pitfalls into which traditional secondary education
has fallen, our vocational schools will avoid stress on the theoretical, which
was originally basic to their instruction, and link their curriculum with the
National Polytechnic Institute.*—Jaime Torres Bodet.

*There exists in Mexico not only literary but also technical illiteracy—the
ABC's of productive skill.*—Manuel Gual Vidal.

No segment of Mexican education has been so much debated as
vocational and technical training. Long the unwanted, neglected
child of a secondary school system anxious above all things to
preserve the liberal arts tradition, vocational education has not
yet found its proper place in the general scheme of things. At first,
the influence of the secondary school was so strong that the theoretical methods used in academic training were transferred intact to
schools supposedly devoted to applied learnings. This was not
entirely due to a preference for theoretical teachings; it derived
in large measure from the lack of properly trained teachers and of
adequate equipment for the new schools. In Mexico more than
elsewhere, vocational teachers were likely to be those who "could
not or would not do." Even the most sanguine prophets could
hardly expect that the mere decreeing of vocational training would
bring about a sudden metamorphosis in the ability and character
of the teacher.

Then, too, teaching in a vocational school was considered a step
downward on the ladder of professional success. The vocational
schools thus became a haven for teachers who had failed to achieve
the superior intellectual standards required for regular academic
work. At present, however, vocational education is coming into
closer union with general secondary education, though it is still
dependent on the National Polytechnic Institute. For this reason
exception may be taken by Mexican educators to the method here
employed of isolating vocational education.[10] The author pleads
their indulgence both for purposes of better organization and in

[10] *Cf.* Angel Ceniceros, *El valor democrático de la enseñanza secundaria*, p. 30:
"Prevocational schools . . . should disappear in favor of the single secondary school,
so as to achieve the ideal of general education for all Mexican adolescents. Preparatory,
vocational, and normal schools should coordinate their programs with those of the
secondary schools as the necessary background of general education."

the personal conviction that the present official administrative arrangement may not be permanent.

With the possible exception of the Mining College and the School of Engineering, founded in the early 1790's, the first purely technical school in Mexico did not appear until 1868, followed by the School of Arts and Crafts for Women in 1871 and for Men in 1877. Oddly enough, for a period whose leaders gloried in the appellation *científico*, both the federal government and the state governments under Díaz showed little interest in the development of technical training, choosing to import the necessary experts from abroad rather than to train them at home. Previous to 1910 technical education was limited to certain arts and trades and practical administrative and commercial learnings, such as typing, accounting, and domestic science. These learnings were not profitably connected with the industrial and commercial life of the Republic.

Vocational and technical education on the secondary school level, including agricultural schools, dates from 1915 as a direct result of the demands of Mexico's laboring classes. The establishment of the Higher School of Mechanical and Electrical Engineering in that year brought the total number of technical schools in all Mexico to five. The re-establishment of the Ministry of Education in 1921 led to the creation of a Department of Technical, Industrial and Commercial Education in 1923, and two years later to the founding of the model Technical School of Tacubaya. Education Ministers Casauranc and Bassols in the early thirties advanced vocational education to such an extent that the new preparatory technical schools, founded 1932, practically excluded from their curricula all education in the humanities.

Modern provisions, derived from the Organic Law of 1942, Articles 84 through 88, stipulate that vocational education shall enable students to enter practical activities as qualified workers or technicians (Article 84). It is to be adapted to the inclination and aptitude of the student. Article 85 specifies that vocational, technical and agricultural education must be administered as separate and distinct units of instruction. The scope of this type of training is comprehensive, extending from early prevocational training, following elementary school, through the university schools, more specifically the National Polytechnic Institute.

The purpose of the prevocational school (the first three years of secondary education) is both terminal and preparatory. On completing this type of training, the student is awarded a certificate as a qualified worker, the exact title depending on the course of study pursued. He is then ready to enter a trade as a semi-skilled artisan above the apprentice stage, or continue in a vocational school for two or more additional years.[11]

There are about thirty prevocational schools in the Republic, nineteen of them devoted to industrial and commercial types of training. The total enrollment in recent years has averaged about 15,000. In marked contrast to enrollments in general secondary schools, where boys outnumber girls by at least three to one, vocational schools show a higher percentage of girls in attendance (60% to 40%). There are about four times as many students in general secondary education as in the trade schools, including agricultural schools. It is obvious that such an imbalance must be corrected if Mexico's life-needs are to be more properly served by her schools.

The curricula of all types of prevocational schools are basically the same in the first three years as for regular secondary education, except that shop work takes the place of some of the minor subjects offered in the general curriculum; also, there is a shift of emphasis to subjects most contributory to the vocations. The work is divided into three types of instruction: compulsory subject matter, practical activities, and practical electives. Three courses of study are offered: engineering, economics (business science), and biological sciences. The only determinant of these courses is to be found in the elective practical activities.[12]

[11] Secretaría de Educación Pública, *Resumen de los informes*, "Departamento de Enseñanza Industrial y Comercial," 1941-43, pp. 71 ff.

[12] "Horario de labores," MS, Escuela Prevocacional Nr. 3, Mexico City, 1944. Prevocational schools featuring domestic arts, dressmaking, costume and design, etc., employ approximately the same curriculum, with afternoons reserved for "practical activities." In the Industrial School of Dressmaking and Design for Girls (Escuela de Corte y Confección No. 2), courses are offered in millinery, glovemaking, lingerie, fashions, cooking and preserving. Another school for girls, "Miguel Lerdo de Tejada," prepares stenographers, archivists, and assistant bookkeepers. In boys' schools, automobile repairing has recently been added.

TABLE 9

CURRICULUM OF INDUSTRIAL AND COMMERCIAL PREVOCATIONAL SCHOOLS

COMPULSORY SUBJECTS	YEAR		
	1	*2*	*3*
Mathematics	6	6	3
Geography	3	3	–
English	3	3	3
Spanish	3	3	3
Botany	3	–	–
Zoology	–	3	–
Physics (one semester only)	–	–	5
Chemistry (one semester only)	–	–	5
Civics	2	2	–
Anatomy, physiology, and hygiene	–	–	3
History	–	3	3
Freehand drawing	3	–	–
Physical culture; military training	3	2	–
Mechanical drawing and projection	–	3	–
Applied drawing	–	–	3
Electives, maximum 9 hours	9	9	9
Totals	35	37	32
ELECTIVE "PRACTICAL ACTIVITIES"			
For engineering			
Modeling	3	–	–
Electricity	3	–	–
Couplings (*ajuste*)	3	–	–
Carpentry	–	3	–
Tin and lead plate	–	3	–
Iron work; the forge	–	3	–
	9	9	–
For economics (business science)			
Stenography	3	3	–
Machines	3	3	–
Commercial practice	3	3	–
	9	9	–
For biological sciences			
Modeling	3	–	–
Carpentry	–	3	–
Tin and lead plate	–	–	3
Electricity	–	–	3
Electives	6	6	3
	9	9	9

Prevocational schools go further than the general secondary institutions in classifying students by aptitudes. This procedure has been influenced by the limited number of higher vocational schools. The result is that only the most promising students con-

tinue to the higher levels. Teaching methods and course content
are similar to general secondary education, though here again the
heavy student program has been a matter of official concern for
many years.

Vocational schools equivalent to the second cycle of the general
secondary school were opened officially in 1932 and feature tech-
nical, industrial, commercial, and agricultural types of training.
There are fourteen of them in the Republic, officially listed as
Vocational Schools 1, 2, and 3; Vocational School 4 of Biological
Sciences; the Higher School of Mechanics and Electricity; the
Higher School of Engineering and Architecture; the Higher School
of Textile Engineering; the Higher School of Biological Sciences;
the National School of Homeopathic Medicine; and the Higher
School of Administration and Social and Economic Sciences, all
located in the Federal District. Some of these schools offer graduate
or professional work as well as regular vocational training. In the
provinces are the Federal School of Textile Industries (Río Blanco,
Veracruz) ; and three federal frontier preparatory schools at Nuevo
Laredo, Nogales, and Piedras Negras, respectively.

Vocational education functions in three departments: mathematics and physics, biological sciences, and socio-economic studies.
Vocational School No. 1, formerly the Technical-Industrial Institute, prepares students for the careers of master mechanic, master
electrician, and master auto mechanic. Completion of two years'
work entitles the student to the certificate of mechanical worker
(obrero mecánico). Three years' successful study results in the
certificate of mechanical official *(oficial mecánico)*. The satisfactory completion of four years' work leads to the diplomas of
master technical mechanic *(maestro mecánico técnico)*, master
technical electrician *(maestro electricista técnico)*, or master automobile technician *(maestro automovilista técnico)*. Vocational
School No. 2 for Physical and Mathematical Sciences leads to the
careers of architect, mechanical engineer, and so forth, in accordance with the courses of study given below. Vocational School
No. 3 for Social Science and Economics specializes in archivists,
secretaries, stenographers and bookkeepers. Vocational School
No. 4 offers courses in biological sciences preparatory to entrance

into the National School of Biological Sciences of the National Polytechnic Institute. Vocational courses in rural nursing and in pharmacy are also given under the auspices of the Polytechnic Institute.

The purpose of vocational schools is either terminal, graduates being awarded certificates of technical proficiency, or preparatory, for entrance into the National Polytechnic Institute. Vocational schools may thus be considered intermediate technical schools, or as links connecting prevocational training with later professional work. Two sample courses of study are given in Tables 10-11.

TABLE 10

COURSE OF STUDY IN VOCATIONAL SCHOOLS FOR ENGINEERING
AND ARCHITECTURE

FIRST YEAR	HOURS PER WEEK	SECOND YEAR	HOURS PER WEEK
Analytical geometry and differential calculus	4½	Integral calculus and higher algebra	6
General mechanics	4½	Elements of topography, plane drawing	4½
Descriptive geometry	4½	Resistance of metals and materials	4½
Physics	5		
Cosmography	3	Chemistry	5
Psychology	2	Numerical and descriptive calculus	3
Logic	2		
Etymology	3	Electricity and magnetism	5
Drawing	3	Perspective	3
Glassmaking and painting	3	Drawing	3
Total	34½	Total	34

In addition to the regular day courses there are evening schools *(escuelas nocturnas)* which combine prevocational with vocational training, omitting much academic subject matter because of the lack of time and because the students are usually engaged in industry. The course is three years in length. At the end of the second year, the student is entitled to a certificate, or diploma, as a worker in his special field *(certificado de obrero)*. If the course is completed, the student receives his diploma as a master technician *(diploma de maestro técnico)*. Evening courses are offered in mechanics, automobile mechanics, foundry work, and so forth.

Vocational concentration has perhaps been greatest in the field of agriculture, a circumstance scarcely to be wondered at in view of Mexico's economic demands. The agricultural program continues the work of the rural elementary school with training in making the land more productive. Under the new construction program for rural areas, no school may be opened without at least ten acres of garden space (called *parcelas escolares*) and a teacher trained in the rudiments of husbandry. The government is determined that the young farmer shall know how to get the most out of his land and bequeath his knowledge to his children. At the same time an effort is made to give the *campesinos* (peasants) a more

TABLE 11

COURSE OF STUDY IN THE VOCATIONAL SCHOOL FOR ECONOMIC, ADMINISTRATIVE, AND SOCIAL SCIENCES

FIRST YEAR	HOURS PER WEEK	SECOND YEAR	HOURS PER WEEK
Analytical geometry and differential calculus	4½	Integral calculus and higher algebra	5
Bookkeeping and accounting	5	Bookkeeping and accounting	3
Commercial arithmetic	4½	Economics	3
Economics	3	French or English	3
English	3	Civil and commercial law	5
French	3	Constitutional law	3
Etymology	3	Sociology	3
Archives	3	Psychology	2
Total	29	Office management	3
		Logic	2
		Total	32

rounded experience in order to counteract the increasing migration to urban centers, a sociological factor as prevalent in Mexico as elsewhere. Finally, upon the ministry devolves the task of providing constructive leisure-time activities and wholesome recreation for rural peoples.[13]

Agricultural schools were first established officially in 1925 under the Ministry of Agriculture, the plan being to provide at least one school for each of the several types of agricultural regions in

[13] No one expresses the social deficiencies of rural population in Mexico with more understanding than Guillermo Bonilla y Segura, *Report on Cultural Missions of Mexico, op. cit.*, p. 23: "Nowhere is life more monotonous, sad, and tiresome than in the country. Only the tourists, poets, or painters who live there for short periods of time can speak of rural life as a thing of beauty. People who live in the country see it in a different light. Eating, working, and sleeping are the only three links in the chain of rural life."

the country. These institutions came to be known as "regional agricultural schools" *(escuelas regionales campesinas)*. In 1932 the eight schools in this category were transferred to the Ministry of Education; but by 1943 they had lost their identity and were renamed in part "practical schools of agriculture" *(escuelas prácticas de agricultura)*. They are now under the control of the Ministry of Education.

The Mexican agricultural school on the preprofessional level is a combination rural secondary and vocational school. The length of the combined course, prevocational and vocational, averages four years. Students may specialize in the career of normal school teacher for rural areas, in crop cultivation, in rural industry, or in the organization of rural life.

In addition to these schools, the Ministry of Agriculture created in 1937 a system of vocational agricultural schools with their subject matter strictly confined to agricultural studies. In 1940 these schools, seven in number, were transferred to the Ministry of Education and co-ordinated with the existing institutions. In 1948 there were thirty agricultural schools in the Republic, divided into two groups: rural normal schools, of which there were eighteen, and the rest, practical schools of agriculture.

The curriculum of the agricultural schools is outlined in Table 12.

The character of the instruction given in agricultural schools is essentially practical—learning as the result of doing. An effort is made to provide all types of farm equipment and livestock, each school becoming a little agricultural industrial establishment in itself. Formal classwork is limited to the essentials prescribed by law for all secondary school training. Graduates of agricultural schools may pursue further education in the National School of Agriculture, the School of Forestry, or the Veterinary School. The Agricultural Education Law of 1946 also guarantees land and governmental aid in technical matters to all graduates.

Agricultural education thus brings to fruition peasant yearnings voiced as early as 1910. In the work of agricultural and educational ministries the *campesino* has concrete proof that his government has finally come to his aid. In consequence, his attitude toward Mexico's rural school system has changed. Originally apprehensive of "atheistic socialism," the native now shows more confidence in his new community school, for it teaches him and his children how to produce where production seemed no longer possible. He plows and plants and finds his harvest fuller because his government has sent him the seed-corn and he has learned how to plant in school. In no educational field has the cry "redemption through education" been answered as effectively; in no other area

TABLE 12

COURSE OF STUDY IN AGRICULTURE SCHOOLS

(Prevocational level)

SUBJECT MATTER	HOURS PER WEEK		
	1st Year	*2d Year*	*3d Year*
Arithmetic and geometry	5	4	3
Spanish	5	4	3
Geography, physical and human	3	2	..
History	3	..	3
Nature study	5	..	..
Drawing	2	2	2
Practical and industrial cattle raising	24	24	24
Elementary agriculture I and II	..	5	5
Animal husbandry	..	5	5
Rural industry	..	4	4
Elements of geology, botany, and zoology	..	3	..
Civics	..	2	..
Elements of physics and chemistry	..	..	3
Elements of rural economics and administration	..	..	3
Agricultural computation	..	..	3
Physical and premilitary education	3	3	3
Total	50	58	61

does the Mexican in return contribute more generously to the support and extension of his schools.

Schools of textile industries, first established in 1932 under private auspices, are now incorporated under federal control. Primarily for workers and the children of workers, these institutions prepare skilled artisans for Mexico's rapidly developing textile industry. Requirements for entrance, peculiarly enough, include a recommendation from the textile unions or guilds. This is evidence in the first degree of the influence of organized labor on school policy. Small in number and enrollments, these schools offer courses leading to the certificate of semi-skilled worker, spinning master, tackler, technical textile manager, and textile engineer. In the Federal School of Textile Industries No. 1, Río Blanco, Veracruz, the enrollment in 1945 was about one hundred. In the Federal School No. 2, Villa Obregón, Mexico City, the enrollment reached three hundred in the same year. These enrollments, while significant of progress, are nevertheless wholly inadequate for the needs of the country, and the necessity of drawing on foreign technical advice is still great.

Another vocational institution most essential to Mexican life is the School for Social Workers *(Escuela para Trabajadoras Sociales)*, formerly known as the School of Home Economics. Founded in 1940, this institution has recently become a branch of the Faculty of Law and Social Sciences of the University. The lower secondary school certificate is necessary for entrance. Classes meet in the evening for a total of four hours, the course of study being laid out for three years as shown in Table 13.

TABLE 13

COURSE OF STUDY FOR THE CAREER OF SOCIAL WORKER

FIRST YEAR	SECOND YEAR	THIRD YEAR
Theory of public welfare and social work	Mexican sociology	Nutrition and dietetics
Psychology	First aid and puericulture	Rural mental hygiene
Elements of biology, anthropology, and physiology	Recreational and cultural occupations	Practice in social work
Social economy	Pathological psychology	Labor, its legislation and problems
Fundamentals of law and civil law	Technique and practice of social work	General principles of social statistics
General sociology	Administration and organization	General criminology
Paidology	Fundamentals of penal law	

Formal class work is supplemented by practical experience in private and official labor agencies, such as the Ministries of Public Health and Welfare, Government, Education, the Department of Indian affairs, and the Department of Visiting Nurses. Yearly enrollments approximate three hundred, but comparatively few candidates ever finish the course, mostly because of marriage, since the enrollment is entirely female, but also because of low financial rewards and poor administrative co-ordination among the Ministries of Education and Public Health and Welfare. The first class, graduated in 1943, numbered sixty students, all of whom were immediately placed.

Fortunately, a goodly portion of the federal budgetary appropriation for the Ministry of National Defense is earmarked for strictly education purposes. Studies for a military career are obtainable at the Military College *(Colegio Militar)*, San Jacinto, D. F., officially termed a public boarding school on the vocational level. The Military College, founded in 1827, is administered by the Department of Military Education of the Ministry of National Defense, its academic program being derived from the programs set for this level by the Ministry of Education.[14] Requisites for entrance are much more rigid than for other vocational schools and are on a competitive basis: (1) The applicant must be a Mexican citizen from 15 to 20 years of age, at least 1.56 meters tall (about 5 ft., 1 in., and indicative of the average Mexican's small stature) and unmarried. (2) He must have completed the lower (three-year) secondary school. (3) He must submit to tests on military aptitude, natural bent, and physical fitness. (4) Oral or written examinations may be required in Spanish, trigonometry, geography, history, English, and elementary physics and chemistry. (5) In lieu of tuition, a bond of five hundred pesos is to be posted.

The main building of the Military College is a Díaz-inspired structure, imposingly situated in the immediate suburbs of Mexico City and surrounded by ample grounds, fields, and equipment for military maneuvers and games. The course of study is laid out for three years; during the last two years the students specialize in cavalry, infantry, artillery, or military administration. Some forty hours per week of classwork and "practical activities" constitute the body of the program, together with three hundred hours of fieldwork each year. Graduates are given the rank of second lieutenant *(subteniente)*. Six-year career courses in such fields as engineering and industry are also offered. Graduates may aspire to further training in the Higher Military School, created in 1932.

Special schools in Mexico are small in number and limited as to

[14] Secretaría de la Defense Nacional, Colegio Militar, *Instructivo de admisión*, p. 1. Larroyo, *Historia comparada*, gives the date of the Colegio's "humble origin" as 1833.

types. At present there exist a School for the Blind (founded 1870), a School for the Deaf and Dumb (1866), and a School for the Feeble-minded *(Débiles Mentales)*, all of which serve as practice schools for the Normal School for Special Education, described in the next chapter. Special schools, modest in achievement, are the joint concern of the Ministries of Education and Public Welfare.

Formerly a boarding school, the School for the Blind now prefers to house its pupils in private or collective homes in order that they may lead a more normal life. Its daily schedule is divided into two sessions: one in the morning for youngsters, another in the afternoon for adults over fourteen. Programs issue from the Ministry of Education and are especially adapted to the life and demands of blind people. Special attention is given to expressional activities, such as music; many graduates matriculate in professional music schools, especially the National Conservatory of Music. Courses are taught in such subjects as massaging, dressmaking, home economics, piano tuning, soap-making, and the manufacture of brooms and brushes. Much of the work is supported philanthropically and otherwise by the Junior League of Mexico City.

The School for the Feeble-minded, located in a former suburban manor house amid country-club surroundings, has about three hundred pupils between the ages of six and seventeen and operates under talented guidance and instruction. Acting as a central institute for the whole Republic, the school performs several functions, chief among which are the pedagogical and medical study of children and the orientation and direction of other centers ministering to similar types of children. At present the only institution of its kind in the country and an exemplary effort, mostly as a result of the competent labors of its director, Roberto Solís Quiroga, M.D., this school serves also as a valuable consulting agency for diagnosis and treatment on the request of parents.

The educational program of the School for the Feeble-minded includes arithmetic. language, nature study, activities demanding social co-operation, and lessons in observation. Formalized classwork is implemented by practical hygienic education; orthophonic gymnastics and organized sports, practice in sense perception, motor and neural co-ordination, orthology, orthopedics, and, most important of all, preoccupational and vocational activity. For all these purposes, the school is equipped with laboratories, workshops (especially in bookbinding), a swimming pool, outdoor playgrounds, and ample woods. Only children considered educable are admitted. The teaching is done by the staff and students of the Normal School for Special Education.

Secondary education thus embraces all fields of adolescent learning and seeks to respond in as full a measure as possible to the many demands of a varied and expectant youth. At the same time, it approaches more and more closely the unification sought by the Mexican government of the multifarious classifications of academic, general, vocational, technical, and specialized trainings. General schools give training in manual arts, while technical curricula provide for general studies. Nevertheless, classical training properly retains its position in the university preparatory and subpreparatory schools. Throughout the entire system, theory is being supplemented more and more by physical activity and first-hand observation. As popular secondary education grows in self-confidence, its appeal will be felt among ever-widening segments of the populace. Its influence, indeed, increasingly permeates all aspects of national life. The practical, popular training initiated in the elementary schools in the early twenties is steadily gathering force on the secondary level for a coming showdown with the traditions of higher education. As a terminal training, secondary schools send forth annually into Mexican life thousands of enlightened young men and women, more suitably equipped than their fathers for the struggle of life and more determined to win it.[15]

[15] Miguel Leal of the Department of Elementary Schools is impatient with progress in vocational education, particularly in the agricultural field: "It is useless to speak of the poverty of our peasants, the need for utilizing natural resources, the failure of students through poverty to continue their education, if we do not teach how to overcome poverty by taking advantage of natural resources. . . . Rural schools are not enough. . . . Specialized schools are needed, such as those concerned with resin and its derivatives, fish and fishing, shipbuilding, pottery, vineyards, milk production and distribution, floriculture, carpentry and cabinet-making from Mexico's fine woods, silver arts, etc." Leal concludes: "One of the most important characteristics of the Mexican rural school is that it is an integral part of community life, and not a reflection of the life proposed by contemporary pedagogy." *Nueva Era*, XIII (1944), 168-72.

VI. The Teacher

Mexico needs armies of teachers more than divisions of soldiers; for Mexico's future will be founded not so much on the might of arms as on the education of the masses.—Isidro Fabela, Governor, The State of Mexico.

The teacher is a priest; the real school always has the feature of a mission. The hands which touch the sacredness of a child's conscience must be clean and moved by a superior spirit, achievable only through love.—Octavio Véjar Vázquez.

We desire our teachers to be, first of all, persons, and not compendia of confused pedagogical formulas.—Jaime Torres Bodet.

We have no other aim than to obtain for the teacher a better position in our social life, and consequently greater consideration and fairer pay.—Manuel Gual Vidal.

ARMIES OF TEACHERS, like military divisions, are developed from raw recruits. Effective action in both cases presupposes the acquisition of basic skills, appropriate drill, synchronized operations, and above all ethical unity. The Mexican Constitution may prescribe mass education, but a healthy school system does not result automatically. The ministry may turn out well-meaning plans and worthy directives, but if the teaching corps is not properly trained, all efforts will fail.

On the occasion of the fiftieth anniversary of the Normal School of Coahuila, Minister Torres Bodet undertook an appraisal of Mexico's teaching staffs. Of the thirty thousand schoolteachers in the Republic in 1944, he observed, only one-half possessed degrees (a teacher with a degree or diploma is called a *maestro titulado*), and of these a quarter were concentrated in the Federal District. Rural schools, despite favoritism from the government, had failed dismally to attract better prepared teachers. Normal schools in

1944 had graduated 1,200 candidates, of whom only one-half were certified for rural schools. The Minister warned that unless production were accelerated, Mexico would never have enough trained teachers.[1]

In 1944, then, the ministry inaugurated a number of remedial measures, chief among them: a reform in normal school programs, an increase in enrollments, the establishment of new schools, a revision in teachers' salary and pension provisions, the continued federalization of normal schools, and the expansion of in-service training. The ministry also began two new publications, *Educación Nacional* and *El Maestro Mexicano*, devoted largely to methods and teaching aids. In 1946, despite these efforts, there were still more than seventeen thousand federal elementary schoolteachers without normal school diplomas—an actual increase in the number of unqualified teachers in the two-year period, due, of course, to a corresponding rise in school enrollments.[2]

Formal teacher training in independent Mexico dates from the founding of two normal schools, one for men and one for women, in 1833. Ideals and plans for a national system were promulgated by such leaders as Lucas Plemán, José María Luis Mora, and the renowned liberal Gómez Farías, but during the first troubled generation of independence few consistent results were attained.[3] "The ideals of the new school changed a great deal," Manuel Barranco recounts, referring to the new social pedagogy, but "the methods changed little, since there was the same lack of trained teachers and no official normal schools to educate such teachers."[4]

It was not until 1887 that a nationally controlled teacher-training institution was authorized by law, and a normal school exclusively for women opened three years later.[5] This institution combined in

---

[1] Jaime Torres Bodet, quoted in *Educación Nacional*, May 1944, pp. 291-92.

[2] Secretaría de Educación Pública, *La obra educativa en el sexenio 1940-1946*, pp. 22 and 291-92.

[3] Larroyo, *Historia comparada de la educación en México*, pp. 168-73. Especially notable in the later reform period was the pedagogy of Manuel Flores (pp. 213-315), a follower of John Stuart Mill and Spencer and a protagonist of "objective, concrete, natural" methods of instruction.

[4] Barranco, *Mexico, Its Educational Problems*, p. 50.

[5] Luis Hidalgo Monroy, "Formación del Profesorado en los Estados Unidos Mexicanos," in *Educación Nacional*, Secretaría de Educación Pública, Mexico City, July 1944, p. 48.

1925 with the Normal School for Men, to become the National School for Teachers *(Escuela Nacional de Maestros)*. Greatest impetus toward the nationwide establishment of government normal schools was given by President Calles, 1924-30, who extended radii of action to achieve the co-ordinated organization prevailing today.

The plight of the teacher in Mexico's political as well as educational history has been lamentable. As late as the thirties, conservative teachers, particularly in outlying communities, desperately resisted socialistic pedagogy. Defending what they considered their inalienable right to teach and worship as they chose, devoutly religious teachers clashed with their colleagues who had been sent out fresh from the ministry with new, strange, and quasi-atheistic ideas on education and cultural life. Orthodox Christian parents would have none of the new teaching; at the behest of the church authorities they withdrew their children from government schools and resorted to violence to root out the intruders and their works. The cost to the unfortunate teacher who obeyed the orders of the ministry was sometimes mutilation or death at the hands of those whom he would "save." Mexico has laid out a longer, harder, more frustrating road for her teaching corps to travel than have most nations; consequently, teachers have had more to think about than pedagogical principles and their pocketbooks. Bringing teaching staffs to a warmer understanding of community needs has been the most fundamental task, as has that of instilling a feeling for civic rather than academic or sectarian responsibility.[6]

Present authority for the establishment and administration of normal schools is derived from the Organic Law of 1942, Articles 78 through 89. All normal schools in Mexico are government controlled, with the exception of a few private institutions, which legally must submit to governmental regulations. Teacher training of whatever class or type has for its chief goal the formation of teachers to fulfill the educational needs of the country (Article 79). Plans, programs, studies, and methods are prescribed by the Ministry of Education in accordance with the necessities and characteristics of the environment in which the school is located (Article 80).

---

[6] *Cf.* Gática and Carrillo, *La educación normal en la post-guerra,* pp. 25-26 especially.

Upon the completion of their studies, students are expected to join teaching staffs in communities where they are most needed. They must also contribute to the education of illiterate adults and encourage the assimilation into the nation of all elements of the population. The law does not require full professional training of pre-school teachers (Article 55), but preference is given to those who have been prepared in teacher-training institutions. In practice, few teachers are hired for kindergarten work who have not pursued special professional studies. In the nursery schools, however, the need of personnel has been so great that until recently there has not been a sufficient supply of professionally trained people to fill all places.

Normal schools today are administered both by the newly created Department of Teacher Training *(Dirección General de Enseñanza Normal)* of the Ministry of Education and by the various states. They are of two main types: urban and rural, subdivided into kindergarten schools, urban and rural elementary teacher training, secondary, physical education, and special schools, the last named designed for the training of retarded and abnormal children.

The distribution of Mexico's thirty-odd normal schools is most uneven; two-thirds of them are located in only one-third of the states—those closest to the Federal District. The extreme southeastern states of Yucatán, Campeche, Tabasco, and Chiapas are served by only two schools, while the thinly populated northwestern states, including Chihuahua, can boast but three. Worse than this, fourteen of Mexico's thirty federated states have no normal school whatever within their boundaries. It should be clear to the ministry that an equitable distribution of teachers is scarcely possible if the normal schools themselves are not so situated as to condition candidates to localities in which they are expected to teach. For it happens that the regions most unpopular with the rank and file of teachers are just the ones that have few or no normal schools. Why, indeed, must teacher training be centered around the capital?

Urban normal schools specialize in the training of teachers for city kindergartens and elementary schools. The course of study is

TABLE 14

COMPOSITE COURSE OF STUDY FOR ALL REGULAR NORMAL SCHOOLS[a]

SUBJECT MATTER	YEAR OF STUDY					
	1	2	3	4	5	6
Mathematics	5	5	3	..	..	..
Botany	4	..	..	..	..	..
Zoology	..	4	..	..	..	..
Anatomy, physiology, and hygiene	..	..	3	..	..	..
Spanish	5	5	3	..	..	..
Geography	3	3	3	..	..	..
Civics (agrarian and labor legislation)	3	3	3	..	..	..
English (urban schools)	3	3	3	..	..	..
Physics	..	3	..	..	..	..
Chemistry	..	..	3	..	..	..
History	..	3	3	3	..	..
Drawing	2	2	..	2	..	..
Penmanship	3	..	..	..	..	..
Vocal and instrumental music	2	2	2	2	2	2
Home economics and trades (urban schools)	3	2	2	2	..	..
Home economics (rural schools)	3	2	2	2	..	..
Practical cattle raising (urban schools)	2	2	2	2	..	..
Agriculture, stock raising, rural industry, and trades (rural schools)	3½	3½	3½	2	..	..
Physical and military education	2	2	2	2	2	2
Modeling	..	..	1	..	..	..
School observation and criticism	..	..	3	..	..	..
Techniques of teaching with practice	..	..	..	6	6	6
Science of education	..	..	..	3	3	..
Biology applied to education	..	..	..	3	..	..
General psychology	..	..	..	3	..	..
General literature	..	..	..	3	..	..
Political economy	..	..	..	3	..	..
Etymology, Greek and Latin roots	..	..	..	3	..	..
Paidology (kindergarten specialty)	..	..	..	..	3	3
Psychology of learning	..	..	..	..	3	..
Educational measurements	..	..	..	..	3	..
Logic	..	..	..	..	3	..
General sociology; Mexican social problems	..	..	..	..	3	..
French (urban schools)	..	..	..	..	3	3
Dancing and the theater	..	..	..	..	2	..
School hygiene (including nursing for girls)	..	..	..	..	..	3
History of education	..	..	..	..	..	3
Philosophic problems	..	..	..	..	..	3
School administration, organization, and statistics	..	..	..	..	..	3
Elementary abnormal psychology and pedagogy	..	..	..	..	..	3
Ethics	..	..	..	..	..	3

[a] Compiled from various manuscripts of normal school schedules; from the printed schedules of the Escuela Normal para Maestros, Mexico City; and from the Secretaría de Educación Pública, "Plan de estudios para la carrera de profesor normalista urbana y rural," 1943. Additional courses available since 1946 are mineralogy, geology, cosmography, and optional specializations in such fields as indigenous languages, teaching techniques in drawing and music, adult education and biology.

set for six years, professional training commencing with the fourth year. Entrance into the urban normal school is dependent upon satisfactory completion of the elementary school. In other words, the future teacher takes his secondary school training in a normal school. Upon graduation, teachers become "certified" *(titulados)* for positions anywhere in the Republic. The fundamental course of study is the same for all regular normal schools, and is outlined in Table 14.

Attached to every normal school is a model or demonstration school, where future teachers may do their practice teaching and experimentation in pedagogical methods may be tried under professional guidance. Teachers are also scheduled to practice in regular schools during the professional cycle of their course of study. Specialized teachers at the nursery and kindergarten levels and physical educationists receive the same basic preparation during the first three years as do prospective elementary teachers. The second three years are given over to specialization.

The Normal School for Physical Education occupies buildings in a public park, Parque Balbuena, Mexico City. Formerly a part of the University, its present status was determined in 1936. It admits competitively only unmarried students from 18 to 25 years of age who have completed secondary education or rural normal school. Table 15 gives the academic material of the three-year course.

To these subjects must be added practical studies, which include all forms of physical exercise, military knowledge, calisthenics, and games. About 25 hours per week are devoted to this phase of the work. During the second year students are assigned to elementary schools for five hours per week of practice teaching, while in the third year the same amount of time is spent in secondary schools. The day school is open to both men and women; instruction and activities are coeducational only when administratively necessary. Women specialize in dancing, music, and rhythmic exercises, for which men substitute boxing, wrestling, baseball, and football. All students attend on a scholarship basis with additional subsidies available of about fifty pesos a month, paid by the government. The ministry expressly desires that no worthy candidate for the teaching of physical education shall be barred for financial reasons. As a result, the student body of this school is of unusually high caliber.

The Normal School for Special Education, enrolling about one hundred prospective teachers of specialized subjects, has been mentioned previously in connection with the School for the Feeble-minded. The curriculum of this institution is basically the same as that of the regular normal school, and provides for practical professional training on location. Mornings are spent in classwork and activities with the pupils; afternoons are devoted to instruction

TABLE 15

COURSE OF STUDY FOR THE NORMAL SCHOOL FOR PHYSICAL EDUCATION

SUBJECT MATTER	YEAR OF STUDY		
	1	2	3
Biology	2	..	..
Anatomy	2	..	..
Psychology	2	..	..
English	2	2	2
Music	2	2	..
Spanish	2	2	..
Physiology	..	2	..
Physical measurement	..	2	..
Sociology	..	2	..
Hygiene	..	1	..
Physical therapy	..	..	2
Techniques of teaching	..	..	2
Orientation, organization, and administration of physical education	..	..	2
First aid	..	..	2
Tests of physiological efficiency	..	..	2
History of physical education	..	..	2
Totals	12	13	14

under leaders in special education, especially medical advisers on abnormal psychology. The school is new and still in the experimental stage, having been founded in 1942. Its present merger with the School for the Feeble-minded dates from May, 1943, though other special schools are now under its direct guidance. Established on the grounds of a former luxurious and idyllic manor house, this institution, in contrast to the usual urban structure, has surroundings that are most elegant and conducive to learning.

Rural normal schools were established as a part of the federal school system in 1922. Until 1942, however, they were left largely to their own financial devices, the costs of administration being met by profits on livestock and agricultural produce derived from their own labors. This situation was finally recognized by the ministry as incompatible with the government program for the expansion of agricultural production and the development of rural citizenship, so that rural schools now receive greater budgetary allotments. Admission to rural normal schools, as in the case of other teacher-training institutions, follows the successful completion of elementary school education; but graduation from a rural normal school has been allowed after three, four, or five years of study instead of the regular six required. The reform of 1946, however, stipulates that students must pursue their course for six years. This goal must be attained, explains the ministry, not for purposes of symmetry, but because of the conviction that the vocation of rural teachers is a difficult one.

The need for teachers in rural areas and the scarcity of equipment have been responsible for the reduced requirements in rural normal schools. Actually, the Mexican Government has had considerable difficulty in keeping teachers in rural schools because of the low salaries, the hard work, and the attraction of city life. Socially and professionally, the rural teacher has always been on a low plane. This condition persists despite the ministry's declaration that the "elevation of rural normal training must be pursued as an inflexible charge."

To cope with the shortage of rural teachers and to counteract the tendency of students to drop out of school, the government has instituted boarding features, admitting students on full scholarships. In many instances it is the custom to grant students a small cash allowance *(pre)* of a few pesos per week. Others receive around fifty pesos monthly, a sum equivalent to that paid army conscripts. This measure has reduced the high ratio of premature withdrawals, and has tended to keep more men in training for longer periods.

The Ministry launched a drive in 1940 to improve the salaries of rural school teachers. Comparisons of rural salaries show that by 1946 they had increased 70-100 percent above the salaries of 1940; but these comparisons fail to take into account the higher cost of living and the lower value of the peso. Special increments are now offered to teachers in unhealthful climates, the total budget in 1946 for this purpose being 3,600,000 pesos. Bonuses for length of service have also been created to help retain experienced teachers. Likewise, recent pension laws have been far more generous than the original legislation of 1925. The new law permits a pension of 40 percent after fifteen years of service, progressively increasing to an allowance of full pay after thirty years' service. Though these efforts have increased the enrollment, results are far from satisfactory. Still larger sums will have to be allotted in future budgets to cover the construction and equipment of normal schools, salaries, and board before Mexico can obtain the number of certified rural school teachers it requires.

Improvement in the quality of future teachers, though a major objective, is only a part of the whole task. An equally important project is that of providing teachers in service with a means for acquiring their teaching certificates. In 1938 a School for In-Service Training was opened in Mexico City. This experiment was undertaken at first on a very informal scale by a few instructors, who donated their services in the interest of their profession. In 1941 the government formally assumed the administration of the project in accordance with Article 82 of the Organic Law, which provides for the professional improvement of teachers in service. The enrollment in 1941 was three hundred; today it is double that number. The program of this in-service training school is strenuous and bears witness to the eagerness of the teachers themselves to attain not only the salary and status which higher qualifications permit but also the personal development which goes with this type of study. In 1945, for example, classes met for a total of twenty-seven hours in three days—all consuming a precious week end.

For rural schoolteachers unable to attend the city normal schools the Ministry established in 1945 the Federal Institute for Teacher Training *(Instituto Federal de Capacitación del Magisterio)*, dedicated to "enlightenment and opportunity for rural teachers." This institution formalizes and extends the work of the cultural missions, which have proved inadequate for in-service training chiefly because of time limitations and the lack of continuity. The program of the Institute leads to government certification through basic courses administered both by correspondence and in discussion groups. The results have been productive. In 1946 alone, 2,610 teachers in thirteen widely scattered centers became fully certified.

Recognition of the need for training secondary-school teachers in pedagogical institutions gave impetus to the founding in 1910 of the School for Advanced Studies at the National University. In the middle twenties, under Education Minister Puig Casauranc, the Higher Normal School was created as a branch of the university's Faculty of Philosophy and Letters. This noble effort "had to disappear," as Larroyo puts it, "for inexplicable reasons." It was therefore not until 1936 that a school was founded specifically for the preparation of secondary-school teachers and designated as the Institute for Secondary Teacher Preparation. Under the Education Law of 1942 this institution was reorganized to become the Higher Normal School *(Escuela Normal Superior)*. In 1944 the enrollment totaled nearly six hundred men and women. In 1947 an imposing new modernistic structure was opened to a thousand prospective teachers and a girls' practice secondary school.

The Higher Normal School is often referred to as the "Graduate School of the Ministry of Education." It holds exclusively evening sessions from five to ten o'clock and gives courses leading to the Master's degree and the degree of Doctor of Education *(Doctorado en Educación)*. Subject matter is taught with a high degree of competence. Admission to the Higher Normal School requires an elementary school teaching certificate, and a minimum of five years' normal school preparation or the *bachillerato* (completion of secondary school, second cycle). Because of the school's limited capacity, preference is given to secondary school teachers already in service.

Professional studies in education and psychology are obligatory for all students. Courses include general psychology, the psychology of adolescence, mental measurement, vocational orientation techniques of teaching and class administration, and education and its relation to the social order. General cultural courses, likewise obligatory for all students, include philosophy, sociology, a foreign language, and the history of the student's major subject.

Specialties are limited to academic subjects, though some amount of vocational specialization is possible. The student's schedule consists of six or seven three-hour courses per week; he thus spends about twenty hours per week in the classroom.

Recognizing that the administration of teacher training would be subject to political and personal influences without the aid of fact-finding agencies, the ministry in 1936 founded the National Institute of Pedagogy *(Instituto Nacional de Pedagogía)*. This agency, entrusted at one time to the Division of Pedagogical Studies, was transferred in 1942-43 to the Office of the Subsecretary *(Subsecretaría)*; the internal administration of normal schools rests with the Division of Pedagogical Studies, which regulates such matters as entrance and final examinations, course content, student practice-teaching, the granting of degrees, and the general conduct of the school. The Institute of Pedagogy investigates pedagogical problems, controls psychological testing, organizes teaching faculties, and makes individual teacher assignments. Ten subsections conduct research and provide experimental and informational services. The Institute also possesses laboratories in pedagogy, psychology, anthropology, physiology, biochemistry, paidology, professional orientation, and mental hygiene; most of them are located in the Normal School for Women in Mexico City. A service of publications and exchange is maintained. Finally, the supervision of school programs, pedagogical methods and systems, tests, and experimental schools promotes the general advancement of Mexican education.

Mental testing is in its early stages in Mexico, though the psychological laboratory at the Normal School for Women uses materials and equipment of the latest type, some of it imported from the United States. North American psychological tests, such as the Otis Elementary and Secondary, the Detroit-Eagle, the Pintner-Cunningham Elementary, the Terman Mental Ability, the Kohlmann tests of mental development, and other tests in the fields of aptitude, personality, and achievement have been translated and adapted. The Mexicans themselves have developed tests, among which are the Herrera y Montes-Herrejón tests for reading comprehension and general achievement and the National Intelligence Tests.[7]

The outline of teacher training given above reveals visible growth. Institutions have increased in number, and invaluable experience has been gained relative to the professional advancement of teachers. Academic standards are on the upgrade. Enrollment in normal schools has increased, though it is still far below the goals of the ministry. These accomplishments have laid the foundation for future progress.

Suggestions for improvement in teacher training have originated mostly from the experience of the normal-school workers themselves. In 1944, at the National Congress of Normal School Education in Saltillo, a number of fundamental proposals were advanced, of which four are pertinent here: (1) the adoption of a universal selection system for the admission of students to normal schools, with emphasis on a combination of physical, intellectual, and moral development; (2) the employment throughout Mexico of methods and procedures in use at the national normal schools of the capital; (3) the elimination of the secondary-school cycle in normal schools, or at least its separation from the regular normal-school course, leaving the normal school an entity in itself; and (4) the establishment of increased material and professional rewards for teachers with a view toward attracting candidates from the most desirable elements of the population.

The elevation of professional standards today in Mexico is at once a financial, an administrative, and a social process. The certified teacher is first of all a public employee with civil service status, subject to all the regulations regarding retirement, pensions, social security, and general conduct issued by the ministry in cooperation with teachers' unions. These regulations include the following: (1) Teachers must attend normal school every five years for refresher courses in subject matter and method; (2) the first year of teaching is probational, tenure coming only after the first

---

[7] Sample materials have been placed by the author in the Library of the Office of Education, Washington, D. C. An excellent account of the development of Mexican measurement techniques may be found in two monographs by Tirado Benedí, *Psicotécnica de la educación pública,* and *Bases para una técnica de la educación,* 1944.

year; (3) teachers may be dismissed or suspended for one month or more for a wide variety of reasons, including ineptitude, immoral behavior, repeated or willful errors, insubordination, propagandizing religion, applying corporal punishment, bribery, fraud, general failure to perform duties, etc. Laws on teacher tenure, pensions, insurance, and retirement date from 1925, and the provisions—at least as far as Mexico City is concerned—are most favorable. But additional statutes are needed to regulate tenure, improve personnel relations, construct a uniform salary scale, and establish the profession on a more equitable basis throughout the country.

In the matter of salary schedules especially there is much injustice and confusion. Fixed scales are rare, the various municipalities determining their own standard of payment. The Federal District and other large communities have taken the lead by providing model schedules for the nation, but it is unlikely that the provinces can follow suit unless the ministry increases the allotments for institutional purposes. As things now stand, only the federal government is in a position to equalize salaries.

The salary schedules of the Federal District may set the pace for the nation, but they must be interpreted in terms of the cost of living. Thus, the 80 percent increase in teacher salaries in the capital over the last decade has been more than offset by enormous rises in living costs.[8] A certified preschool specialist in 1946 received 315.70 pesos per month (about $65) in comparison with 142 pesos per month (about $28.50) in 1940. Other salaries have been increased in proportion, ranging up to the comparatively munificent sum of 510.80 pesos ($105) for a teacher of special subjects in the elementary schools. Rural scales lag considerably, though they show improvement. A rural school principal received 236.90 pesos in 1946, in contrast to 136 in 1940. Certified principals could earn 300 pesos; regular teachers were paid 156.20 as against some 80 pesos six years earlier. Training beyond gov-

---

[8] *Compendio estadístico, 1947*, pp. 184-86, shows that the cost of living has tripled between 1936 and 1946 throughout Mexico, and has nearly quadrupled in the capital itself.

ernment requirements usually raises the individual in the salary scale. In 1949 the peso was devalued 35 percent and salaries were increased about 15 percent.

Secondary-school teachers currently receive from 7 to 10 pesos an hour. While the standard monthly salary in the capital is fixed at a minimum of about 500 pesos for full-time classroom teachers *(de planta)*, a teacher who has sufficient energy to give instruction to more than one school, day and evening, may augment his income to more than 750 pesos, plus a cost of living bonus. Some of Mexico's most industrious secondary-school teachers carry home pay checks totaling more than a thousand pesos monthly, including the cost-of-living bonus. At 8 pesos to the dollar, this amounts to about $125.

The practice of employing part-time teachers in secondary schools, though somewhat on the wane, is still too widespread. Chosen from the ranks of industry or the practicing professions, these individuals may bring much that is valuable from the working world, but their teaching methods by-and-large are faulty. They tend to impart information rather than to teach; they are influenced by material considerations, not the least of which is the supplementary income for themselves. By its very nature this practice is a makeshift; teaching should not be a side issue.

Another evil arises from the fact that teachers can earn more money by working on an hourly basis and traveling from school to school. Resident *(de planta)* teachers invariably receive less pay than their traveling colleagues. The ministry understands that if stability is to be attained and student development achieved in other than purely academic ways, instructors must remain with their charges during the entire day. Teachers who rush from one school to the next and peddle their wares to the highest bidder are usually more interested in a profitable market than in the essential business of helping young people to grow. The matter is not so easily remedied as might appear, since the best teachers are in demand by many schools and there are few persons qualified to teach certain special subjects. Nevertheless, the ministry should take the first bold step by adjusting salaries so as to encourage *de planta* teachers. The footloose should also be required to acquaint themselves with important educational practices in the field of student guidance, behavior, and all-round accomplishment— matters which they now prefer to ignore.

In Mexico the teacher's financial and social destinies are subject to the control of union organizations. Practically all Mexico's teachers belong to some union, the chief one being the Syndicate of Teachers of the Republic of Mexico, or STERM *(Sindicato de Trabajadores de la Enseñanza)*. Needless to say, these organizations exert a powerful influence over the policies of the ministry in regard to teacher welfare. In most cases a teacher must be recommended by the union; without union approval, it is difficult for teachers to hold their positions. The present trend is toward the centralization of the various unions into one National Syndicate of Educational Workers, pooling dues and resources for greater teacher benefits.

The Department of School Construction estimated in 1946 that 45,000 new classrooms were required to provide for the mass education which the Constitution guaranteed. "But 45,000 new lecture rooms," writes Torres Bodet, "even supposing that we had them, would be ineffective without a staff of 45,000 new teachers. Mexico can produce a staff of this size only by the establishment of new normal schools, by taking measures to reduce the large number of student withdrawals, and by provisions for higher salaries to make the teaching profession more attractive."

But growth in the professional standards and attainment of Mexico's teaching corps involves many factors, all intimately interdependent. It is estimated, for example, that it would cost 200,000,000 pesos a year to provide properly paid teachers in adequate numbers. It is obvious that this sum could not be advanced in the budget of a single year. Further, a mere flow of teachers is not enough. Forty-five thousand new classrooms call for worthy classroom leadership, an achievement that can come about only with time, conscientious effort, and a program of public orientation on the value of the teaching profession. Meanwhile, the ministry plods toward its goal: better qualified candidates, better training schools, and more adequate rewards—financial and professional.

VII. Higher Education

We know very little about the destiny of the human soul after bodily death; but we may assert that the destiny of man in this world is to yearn for knowledge about himself and about the universe, and to use all his physical and mental resources to harness the forces of nature, and to unveil the mystery of matter, life, and soul.—Rodulfo Brito Foucher, Rector, The National Autonomous University of Mexico, 1944.

In the advancement of culture, higher education holds the greatest responsibility. To broaden it and bring it close to the mass of the people is the duty of every man who has accepted the welfare of the human race as his highest purpose.—Roberto Moreno y García, 1945.

All universities are genuine sources of culture—not that self-styled brand of culture which, under political fetters, frequently finds itself used as a weapon of aggression and predatory domination—but true culture, that uplifts the spirit of man and leads it to the highest goals.—President Miguel Alemán Valdés, 1947.

THE HISTORY of higher education in Mexico is chiefly the history of the National Autonomous University, inspired by Bishop Zumárraga and founded in 1551 by Antonio de Mendoza, first viceroy of New Spain.[1] First known as the Royal Pontifical University, out of deference to the union of church and state, the new creation was predominantly medieval and ecclesiastic in spirit; its curriculum was constructed on those seven pillars of wisdom which constituted the university curricula of most of the Christianized world: the-

---

[1] Larroyo, *Historia comparada de la educación en México*, pp. 99-100. George Sánchez, *The Development of Higher Education in Mexico*, affectionately traces the history of the Colegio de San Nicolás, "the oldest institution of higher learning in the New World (founded 1540)," from which grew the University of Morelia (Michoacán). Larroyo differs from Sánchez in that the former considers the Colegio de Santa Cruz de Tlaltelolco to be the first institution of higher learning in America (p. 95). The latest publication presenting the Jesuit point of view is Mayagoitia's *Ambiente filosófico de la Nueva España*, pp. 57 ff.

ology, sacred scriptures, canon law, jurisprudence, the arts, rhetoric, and grammar. The teaching of these subjects was controlled by the Holy See; the level of scholarship was equivalent to that of other Spanish medieval universities.[2] The higher education of the early colonial era has received commendation as great as that bestowed on achievement in other realms of Mexico cultural progress. John Tate Lanning's favorable attitude, mentioned earlier, is shared by Mexico's outstanding medical historian, Ignacio Chávez, who asserts that at that time "Spain was at the head of civilization in humanities and behind no country in medicine." Dr. Chávez is appreciative of Spain's generous gift of medical knowledge to the New World, as exemplified by the large number of hospitals—ten in the capital and twenty in the provinces —which were established by order of the Spanish kings. Lanning, a neo-scholastic, strengthens his case by calling attention to the fact that the university's professors "recognized the limitations which were imposed on the authority of the Holy Father by the strict requirements of the physical universe." Later, he observes, Descartes' methodical doubting came to be recognized as accepted methodology, and by the end of the eighteenth century Locke's philosophy was guiding university thinking. Lanning therefore contends, along with David Mayagoitia, S.J., that the amount of critical thinking which took place in the *Pontificia* has not yet been given its due in educational literature.[3] All this and more is included in a manuscript entitled *La Real y Pontificia Universidad de México—Bosquejo Histórico*, by Don Pablo Martínez del Río, director of the Institute of History. In scholarly fashion Don Pablo seeks to combat any notion that the university was devoid of enterprise and blind to progress—at least in the sixteenth century. On

[2] Steck, *Education in Spanish North America during the Sixteenth Century*, p. 17, qualifies "higher education" previous to the arrival of the Jesuits, 1572: "During the first fifty years of Spain's rule in Mexico comparatively scant attention was given to what we would call popular higher education . . . until about the time that the first Jesuits reached Mexico, 1572 . . . and devoted themselves almost exclusively to boys of Spanish and creole families." *Cf.* Mayagoitia, *Ambiente filosófico de la Nueva España*, pp. 93-94.

[3] Lanning, *Academic Culture in the Spanish Colonies*, p. 85. Ignacio Chávez, *México en la cultura médica*, Chapter 1, *passim*. Lanning believes, incidentally, that Cartesianism and natural law are but advanced stages of scholasticism. Mayagoitia, *Ambiente filosófico de la Nueva España*, p. 111.

the contrary, he states, heterodoxy was prevalent; the writings of Erasmus were read (confessedly within limits), and religion was not the only study.[4]

Scientific progress in the same period and later is cited by Father Mayagoitia and Bishop Kelley on the authority of Baron von Humboldt:

No European government has sacrificed greater sums to advance the knowledge of the vegetable kingdom than the Spanish government. . . . The principles of the new chemistry, which is known . . . by the equivocal appellation of "new philosophy," are diffused more in Mexico than in many parts of the peninsula . . . The best mineralogical work was printed in Mexico (M. del Río's *Manual of Oryctognosy*).

Von Humboldt is also the leading authority for Lanning's conclusions and those of others who extol the scientific attainment of the period; while Irving Leonard reports an impressive amount of printing and book-trading in early colonial times.[5]

On the other hand, Mayagoitia clearly brings out a characteristic lack of originality, and Lanning himself speaks of the oppressive routine, rigid formality, and stifling rote-memory methods "likely to go hand in hand with superstition." Lanning condemns the decadent discipline of the higher learning of a century later as "not only immobilizing but paralyzing the arts." With regard to the specific field of medicine, C. H. Haring, of Harvard University, differs markedly from Chávez: "Medical science lagged behind that of Europe, and often included a good mixture of astrology and superstition." Native medicine, asserts Haring, was probably as efficacious as that of Spain; in fact, "the latter held it in consider-

---

[4] Don Pablo's authorities merit mention as outstanding commentators in the field: Cristóbal Bernardo de la Plaza y Jaén, *Crónica de la Real y Pontificia Universidad de México;* Lanning, and others, *Reales cédulas de la Real y Pontificia Universidad de México;* Marcel Bataillon, "Erasme au Mexique," *Deuxième Congrès National des Sciences Historiques,* Argel, 1932; Joaquín García Icazbalceta, "La Universidad de México," in *Obras* (Mexico City, Agüeros, 1905); Aurea Verla Martínez, "El Erasmismo Español," thesis, The Faculty of Philosophy and Letters, Mexico City, 1947; José Almoina, *Rumbos heterodoxos de México,* C. Trujillo, 1947; and Ignacio Carillo y Pérez, *La Universidad de México en 1800,* Mexico City, 1945.

[5] Kelley, *Blood-drenched Altars,* p. 104. John Tate Lanning in Whitaker, *Latin America and Enlightenment,* p. 81. Irving Leonard, *Romances of Chivalry in the Spanish West Indies.* Mayagoitia, *Ambiente filosófico de la Nueva España,* pp. 94 ff.

able respect."[6] Lewis Hanke, in a brief but conscientious study of the formidable sociological problems facing Spain in transferring the benefits of her culture to the New World, reluctantly concludes that the aims of the mother country were too high and that the result was mostly confusion. The Spaniards never could make up their minds, asserts Hanke, as to whether the Indian was, after all, a rational being and could respond to the Aristotelian concepts which guided Old World thought and activity; and this indecision interfered with every attempt to introduce Spanish culture.[7] Finally, the failure of most commentators to become enthusiastic about post-sixteenth-century achievement in higher education is at least suggestive of the fact that the university did little more than to perpetuate the scholastic principles on which it had been founded.

In addition to the Pontifical University, the sixteenth century brought to Mexico several institutions of higher learning: the Colegio de San José de Belén, Mexico City, founded in 1529 by Archbishop Zumárraga, and designed to give higher education to the Indians; San Nicolás Obispo, Pátzcuaro, founded in 1540 by Don Vasco de Quiroga primarily for the training of priests; San Juan Letrán, Mexico City, founded in 1547 by Archbishop Zumárraga and Viceroy Mendoza for mestizo boys, where, in Magner's words, "Indians became so proficient in the liberal arts as to arouse envy"; and the Colegio de San Gregorio, established in 1575 at the request of the Indians.[8] All these institutions have either fallen into oblivion or been transformed into state schools.

After the sixteenth century the history of higher education becomes tedious, confused, and not very rewarding.[9] The vicissitudes of the university comprise one more story of a type long familiar to students of Mexican education—a story of precious periods of enlightenment and solid contribution interrupted and frustrated by

[6] Haring, *The Spanish Empire in America*, p. 233. Martínez del Río, "Mexican-America Relations," cites the fact that doctors of medicine were not allowed to become rectors of the university.

[7] Hanke, *The First Social Experiment in America*, p. 40 especially.

[8] Apstein, *The Universities of Mexico*, p. 3. Magner, *Men of Mexico*, p. 156.

[9] For an intimate account of the personnel, development, and services of the university see Brito Foucher, "The National Autonomous University of Mexico," in *Mexico's Role in International Intellectual Cooperation*, pp. 31 ff.

sacerdotal restrictions, political caprice, and the heavy hand of tradition. Simpson observes that although an amount of robust literature was produced, inspired by the Conquest, the literary and intellectual life of New Spain during the Silver Age was completely dominated by clerical pedantry, centering in the university.

Bernal Díaz del Castillo's Homeric *True History of the Conquest of New Spain* is one of the greatest chronicles of all time, but it was written in a soldier's language by a soldier. His lack of Latin was his abiding sorrow. The elegant literature produced by the learned imitated only too successfully the wearisome obscurities then considered in good taste in Spain.

The one great exception, Simpson asserts, was the playwright Juan Ruíz de Alarcón. Concerning science, Martínez del Río humorously yet trenchantly comments: "The magnificent hurricane of science became a mere breeze" within the walls of the university.

Not that the *Pontificia* was different in its attitude and behavior from the other universities of the Christian world. Authorities such as Charles Jourdain and Louis Liard are highly critical of the intellectual stagnation and the general aversion to scientific progress prevalent in the period at the Sorbonne and the University of Paris. British writers, such as William S. Knickerbocker, C. Grant Robertson, Christopher Hobhouse, and Edward Gibbon, all comment on what the latter characterizes as the "intellectual decay and moral paralysis" afflicting British universities. And Martínez del Río is on solid ground when he cites for contempt the sterile curricula, the pointless doctrinaire examinations, and the indolent, routinized professors who, according to Gibbon, had "absolved their consciences of the necessity of having to read, think and write." But Don Pablo acutely observes that "educators in those days were as sure of their righteousness as twentieth-century democrats are of theirs."

Nevertheless, the university cannot be totally excused for its imitative conduct and lack of creativity. Actually, as Martínez brings out on the authority of Lanning, Mexico's higher education after the sixteenth century did not accept the more advanced findings of European philosophers and scientists until almost a century after their introduction into European educational circles. New

Spain did not countenance the teachings of Descartes, for example, until eighty-five years after his death, and there was a lag of fifty years before Newton's mathematical principles became part of the course of study. The responsibility for the university's deficiencies rests with those of its teachers who lived in the past and looked exclusively to Paris, Rome, and Madrid for inspiration. Like other educational institutions of the Christian world, the Pontifical University had become the higher educational representative of the church, which meant that scholasticism, hieratic symbolism, and neo-Thomism determined method.

Toward the end of the old regime [writes Simpson] timid these in bad Latin began to appear, discussing the revolutionary ideas which were to destroy the University and all it stood for, but it would be hazardous to assume that these feeble stirrings of the mind went much beyond the closed circle of the elect. The great mass of colonial society, white, Indian, and mestizo, remained untouched by foreign heresies, under the sheltering wing of the Mother Church and the Inquisition.

Even Mayagoitia frankly admits "decadence" in the scientific attitude from the beginning of the eighteenth century. Up to the period of the Revolution the university, then, remained a conservative, tradition-minded body, opposed to any change in the social order and hence to the whole idea of Mexican independence—political or educational. Little wonder that the various Mexican governments throughout the nineteenth century failed to find adequate justification for keeping open the doors of the institution.[10] While Mexico was struggling for her life, her university elected to join forces with the outside world, ever ready to discredit the new-born nation.

A departure from orthodoxy occurred in the nineteenth century as a result of French liberalistic influence. Samuel Ramos, anti-scholastic Francophile of the Mexican Cultural Relations Office

[10] Kelley, *Blood-drenched Altars*, pp. 97-98: "The University had, like most of its scattered sisters all over the world, its ups and downs. The worst of the latter was its closing by Vice-President Gómez Farías in 1833. This protégé of Poinsett evidently saw no common sense in higher education for Mexicans. President Santa Anna reopened it in 1834, but along came the revolutionist Comonfort who suppressed it in 1857. It was again reopened by President Zuloaga the year following. President Juárez shut its doors in 1861. Maximilian opened them again, but only to shut and bar them finally in 1865."

and university professor of comparative literature, interprets the influence as one which "accommodated itself easily to our tropical sensuality." Both Ramos and Northrop agree that not only the French spirit—in particular that of the Encyclopedists—but also French cultural and political preferences were exactly suited to Mexico as a nation striving for a modus operandi.[11] The teachings of Voltaire and Rousseau only tended to throw the old-line intellectuals into confusion, and to prepare them for the "orderly thought" of Auguste Comte and positivism.[12] Here at last was a code, a standard of values, a prescribed body of knowledge, to end once and for all the dreams of romantics, the muddled experimentalism of the new intellectuals, the jumbled ideals of economic futurists, and the atheistic vagaries of political revolutionaries.[13] So deeply did positivism become rooted in Mexican political and intellectual life that even the liberal Sierra failed to free himself completely from its influence. However, during the first three decades of the twentieth century the fate of positivism was sealed by José Vasconcelos and Antonio Caso, Mexico's outstanding philosopher, and its ultimate demise prepared the way for modern secular educational ideals bearing less the imprint of French intellectualism and more the materialist stamp of modern Russia and the English-speaking world.[14]

[11] Ramos, *El perfil del hombre y la cultura mexicana*, p. 28; Northrop, *The Meeting of East and West*, p. 28. Northrop quotes Ramos and Alfonso Reyes as his authorities.

[12] A useful definition of positivism from the Mexican side is to be obtained from Vasconcelos, *Historia del pensamiento filosófico*, p. 358: "Comte taught a very simple epistemology: It is useless, he said, following Kant, to pretend to know the ultimate causes of things. The noumenon is a phantasm which always succeeds in eluding us; but science does not have to concern itself with it. Science busies itself with the phenomenal. In the past, in order to explain phenomena, we have resorted to metaphysical causes, mysterious forces, divinities which exist only in the imagination. But (Comte tells us) we do not lack an explanation of the world. It can be explained in terms of its laws. These laws are given to us in our continuous experiences, the most valuable medium of which is the testimony of our senses."

[13] On the authority of Edmundo O'Gorman, *Fundamentos de la historia de América*, Northrop, *The Meeting of East and West*, pp. 56-57, explains that Mexicans, through the teachings of Las Casas "relegated" Aquinas "to oblivion" in favor of Cartesianism, "thereby opening up the whole of modern philosophy to the Mexican Catholics' mind and providing the humanistic and skeptical assumption of Voltaire and the French Encyclopaedists, which brought in the democratic revolution and led to the nationalization of all the Roman Church's property."

[14] On Caso see García Máynez, ed., *Antonio Caso* [selections from the works of Antonio Caso], p. vii: "Antonio Caso's doctrine is a philosophy of life, of intuition, and

Summarizing and assessing the achievement of the Pontificia to the end of the nineteenth century, Martínez del Río presents the most generous estimate that could, perhaps, be made within the bounds of objectivity. Confessing the university's lack of creative spirit and initiative, its artificial prestige and false brilliance, Martínez nevertheless defends the institution as a well-spring of great literary and cultural productivity, and for centuries "the principal organized center of culture in both the Americas." While the claim may be somewhat extravagant, there can be little refutation of the fact that in both Martínez's and Clavigero's terms, the Pontificia "did not fare badly in comparison with its companions in the Old World." At least it remained stanch and faithful to its great ideal of the oneness of truth and life, however much that loyalty may have blinded it to other ideals.

University affairs entered a new phase under President Díaz and Minister of Education Justo Sierra. In 1910 the Pontifical University officially became the National University, dependent on the Ministry of Education and, in Sierra's memorable words, "dedicated to the love of science and country, wherein lies the security of our people." Sierra, respectful above all of his country's cherished traditions, maintained that the university's primary function was to crown the endeavors of public education, yet remain free of political controls. So atrophied had higher learning in Mexico become, that this Minister elected to bury its memory: "The University has no history," he proclaimed. "The Pontifical University is not the antecedent; it is the past." Henceforth, higher learning was to desist from its ponderous verbalism and become investigative in its attitude; it was to "seek and love pure truth." At the same time it was expected to enter into the spirit of Mexican idealism: "He who has had university training must not limit his thinking to him-

---

of action; his criticism represents an uninterrupted and vigorous polemic against the excesses of intellectualism, and above all, of positivism." A sample of Caso's philosophy is found on pp. 180-81: "The antithesis between the individual and society cannot be resolved without a new synthesis; the individual is real; society is real. Ontologically, the individual cannot subordinate himself to society nor society to the individual. Only by culture, for axiological and not ontological reasons, is it possible to achieve synthesis; culture, as an end of the individual, implies society, and as an end of society, implies the individual . . . Law is the cultural creation which resolves the antithesis of individuals and society in productive harmony."

self alone. He must never forget either humanity or his nation." Finally, the university was to become the educational capstone of the country's rising national educational structure, and no longer a thing apart from it.

The revolutionary attitude of Sierra and his followers can be understood only by considering the total picture. The sudden influx of educational and ideological innovations, which reached Mexico a century or two later than most nations, could not help but inspire a more rugged resistance. Northrop observes that the acceptance of democracy was inevitably linked in the minds of the Mexicans with the repression of their religion. "It is by no means certain," he writes, "that modern science and philosophy and modern democracy would not have had the same extreme anti-religious consequence in the English-speaking world which they exhibit in Mexico." Institutions are assimilated slowly; a people has to grow into change. Even today, medieval beliefs, old-fashioned French influences, and antiquated ideas that have disappeared from North American institutions of higher learning survive in Mexico's university. The buildings themselves, essentially French and Spanish in design, preserve tradition in stoutest physical form; and it is certain that until a new university city, now projected, arises at a distance from the seventeenth-century structures, Mexico will not have a system of higher education that she can call her own.

In the last two decades, however, a genuine Mexican humanistic movement has arisen in university thought, headed by Alfonso Reyes, of the Colegio de México, and Manuel Toussaint, of the Institute of Aesthetic Investigation, and including such scholars as Pedro Enríquez Ureña, Eduardo Colín, and Enrique González Martínez. This movement believes in a healthy nation united for total social, economic and cultural progress.[15] But Mexican humanism, sound enough in its beginnings and carefully, though not

[15] Toussaint, "Mexico Today; Thought and Expression," *Annals of the American Academy of Political and Social Sciences*, p. 169, asserts that Germany in the 1920's set the style in Mexican philosophy, "but its influence has reached Mexico by way of Spain. José Ortega y Gasset, through his splendid magazine, *Revista del Occidente*, and still more through his translations of German works, has placed the great philosophical contributions of postwar Germany within the reach of all Mexicans. Among these should be mentioned Oswald Spengler's *The Decline of the West*, which is the *vade mecum* of many Mexican thinkers."

unskeptically, nourished by the higher learning, too soon dissipated its strength by exposing radical philosophies of social anarchy— philosophies which had thoroughly divested themselves of all ecclesiastic and aristocratic influences.

The impetus toward socialistic teaching was provided by President Calles during the late twenties and later by Cárdenas, who in 1935 placed all institutions of higher learning under government control. Their administration was in the hands of a National Council of Higher Education and Scientific Investigation, whose avowed purpose was to see that socialism became the recognized basis of instruction in all higher and professional courses. The aim, as the President put it, was to reorganize higher education in compliance with the social orientations of the Mexican Revolution and the desire of the Mexican government to reflect the interests and aspirations of the national proletariat. All ideas of a privileged educated class were to be eliminated.

Cárdenas' edict met violent opposition. University faculties and student bodies rushed to defend the church and academic freedom. Every university enterprise suffered from internal dissension, and productive scholarship was at a standstill. Student strikes made every university in Mexico a center of political intrigue.

Some semblance of order was restored in 1942, when Rodulfo Brito Foucher became rector. However, Brito's neo-Thomism was considered too "rightist" and too "reactionary" for a country governed by revolutionary principles, and his regime lasted but two years. He was succeeded for a brief interval by Alfonso Caso, formerly director of the Institute of Anthropology. Caso's appointment reflected a new and all-too-long-delayed interest in scientific studies—aesthetic, archeological, and anthropological—of Mexico's cultural past, but his abilities and temperament were not suited to the new task.

Under his successor, rector-physician Salvador Zubirán, the tendency was to preserve Caso's program and at the same time to bring the activity of the university closer to Mexican daily life, in accordance with the practical program of Education Minister Manuel Gual Vidal. The university has since become a more vital contributor to Mexican progress in every field. Conflict remains, however, between what Sánchez pertinently terms "the leftist educational goals of the Revolution, and the inherited rightist educational goals and standards." All of which is another way of saying that the university has, perhaps, become too embroiled in the social and political activity of the nation, a position somewhat in contrast to its former detachment.

The university's present organization dates from 1910, when a congressional decree provided for the establishment of the National Preparatory School and the various schools and faculties of law, engineering, fine arts, and advanced studies. Modifications occurred in 1929, 1933, and 1945 to provide the following faculties, schools, institutes, and other branches: Faculty of Philosophy and Letters, Faculty of Sciences, the National Schools of Jurisprudence (including the Institute of Comparative Law), Economics (including the Institute of Economic Research), Commerce and Administration, Medicine, Nursing and Obstetrics, Dentistry, Veterinary Medicine and Zootechnics, Engineering, Chemical Sciences, Architecture, Plastic Arts, Music, and the Institutes of Mathematics, Physics, Chemistry, Geology, Geography, Biology, Medical and Biological Studies, Social Research, Historical Research, Aesthetic Research, Center of Philosophic Studies, National Astronomic Observatory, National Library, Department of University Extension and Cultural Relations, and the National Preparatory School.[16]

Organizational and administrative authority is derived from the university statutes and is vested in five powers: the governing board *(junta de gobierno)*, the university council *(consejo)*, the rector, the directors of the various faculties, schools and institutes, and the technical councils. According to the Statutes of 1945, the highest administrative authority of the university is the governing board, a self-perpetuating body of fifteen, serving in somewhat the same capacity as an American board of trustees. The governing board appoints or removes the rector and, on recommendation of the rector, the directors of the various branches. It also has final authority in internal disputes among university authorities.

[16] Universidad Nacional Autónoma de México, *Ley constitutiva, leyes orgánicas y estatuto*, pp. 3-4.

The council passes on all matters of internal organization and practice. It includes not only the rector, the directors of the various schools, and certain professors, but also—strange as it seems—representatives from among the students and the university employees as well. In organization and administration the university displays a greater application of democratic practice than do most institutions of higher learning in the United States. MacFarland states that "the University is unique in that the student is admitted almost on an equal footing to the management of the institution."

The rector corresponds in position and in function to the president of a North American university; he is titular head of the university and its legal representative. There are, however, a number of differences. In Mexico, the rector is ranked second to the minister of education. The practical monopoly enjoyed by the university in the sphere of higher education bestows on its chief officer an importance exceeding that of college presidents in the United States. For election to office, the qualifications demanded of a candidate are correspondingly strict. He must be a Mexican by birth and be between the ages of 35 and 70 at the time of his election. He must have obtained a degree higher than the *baccalaureate* (that is, a university degree) and have served at least ten years on the university's teaching staff; during that time he must have distinguished himself as a teacher and a scientific investigator. Chosen by the governing board for a four-year term, he may be re-elected only once.

A still greater contrast lies in those nonprofessional factors which, though seldom if ever candidly set down in black and white, nevertheless play a leading part in determining the eligibility of a candidate. The rector is not selected, as are so many American college heads, in recognition of his proved ability as a businessman, a fund raiser, and a speaker at ceremonies and at meetings of social clubs. These qualifications are desirable, of course, but it is more essential that the rector's political beliefs accord with those of the national administration. In view of the conspicuous nature of the post, the government is usually careful to elect a man who has earned the respect and recognition of his colleagues by his educational leadership and his intellectual and scholarly attainments. But he must have the "right" political views.

The directors of the various university schools are appointed by the governing board for four years and may be reappointed once. Requirements for the directorship are similar to those for the rectorship, except that the candidate must at the time of his election have been for at least eight years a member of the faculty or the school of which he is elected director. According to Apstein, the directors of the faculties and schools are appointed by the governing board for four years and may be re-elected once. Their duties are to supervise all the activities of their respective departments, convene the technical councils, and recommend appointments to their teaching staff; also, they are expected to teach at least one course in their school or faculty. The technical council of a faculty or a school consists of one professor from each department and two students from the entire faculty or school. This body approves the courses of study to be submitted to the rector, formulates the regulations, studies new projects, appoints assistant and visiting professors, and passes upon the three candidates whom the rector suggests for the directorship.

University statutes designate professors as "ordinary" or "career" and "extraordinary," the first named holding full-time appointments after five years of successful service. Regulations regarding the professional staff of the university were revised in 1943 to provide for clearer definitions of requirements, duties, rank, and benefits of professors; but the situation remains unorganized. Efforts have been made since 1943 to stabilize faculties and their professional status by establishing a hierarchy similar to that of North American institutions and fixing a definite program of requirements, duties, and emoluments. Characteristic of these proposed definitions is the one concerning the requirements for a full professorship:[17]

(1) The candidate must be at least forty years of age.
(2) He must have served at least five years as a resident associate professor, demonstrating proof of punctuality, diligence, scholarly in-

[17] *Reglamento que crea la posición de profesor universitario de carrera*, pp. 3 ff.

terest and attainment as proved by the undertaking and publication of scientific investigation or works of literary or artistic value.

(3) During his university career previous to the full professorship, he must have published books, articles, or monographs of original and authentic nature.

The maximum teaching load of a full professor would be twelve hours per week, with provisions for sabbatical leave. Provision is also made for Mexicans who have distinguished themselves in intellectual pursuits to obtain permanent professorships without previous university experience. The same would apply to distinguished foreign professors, except that under no circumstances would they be allowed to participate in the government of the university. Financial difficulties have impeded the enactment of these proposals, but until some such program of professional advancement is enacted, Mexican educational leaders know that the university professorate will remain a relatively haphazard and insecure occupation.

Student life in the National University and in other Mexican schools of higher education is characterized by a lack of the sociability and conviviality which permeate college life in the United States. Social gatherings, dances, and entertainment are infrequent —a circumstance accounted for partly by the relative poverty of the students and partly by the greater seriousness and attention to studies demanded by the keener competition that Mexican students must face in later life. The relationship of faculty members to students is therefore inclined to be of a business and scholarly nature rather than of personal interest and friendship. Indeed, student association with faculty members is rare.

In the absence of dormitories, fraternities, or sororities at the university, what undergraduate organizations there are—athletic teams, music clubs, and so forth—have come into being chiefly on the responsibility and initiative of the students themselves. The university charter specifically recognizes the importance of these activities by providing funds and other assistance to student organizations whose purposes are deemed worthwhile, but the letter of the law unfortunately does not permit much university enterprise in this field. Intercollegiate and interuniversity athletic competition exists, but on a far smaller scale than in the United States.

The one field of extracurricular activity which consumes abundant student energy, interest, and time is politics. Political feeling runs high and reveals itself in the organization of countless clubs, associations, and pressure groups formed to influence not only university but also national administration and policy. Demonstrations and riots are frequent. At the slightest provocation students form ranks and parade with banners, placards, and streamers in protest against some phase of political policy which has aroused their antipathy. Though newspaper editors and public figures generally make light of such demonstrations, it cannot be denied that student political excursions have often been a potent force in steering national as well as educational policy. Students are free to organize clubs and recommend changes in university policy, but they may not enter into activity contravening the best interests of the university. Prospective students are in fact warned to acquaint themselves with university ideals and practices, and not to seek admission unless they are willing to respect them.

The campus of a typical North American university, with its "wide lawns and stately elms," is scarcely to be found in Mexico. University buildings are likely to be concentrated in business districts; often as not, the inner patio offers the only space available for sports and games. School spirit and student morale suffers in consequence. The recognition that students must be given a chance to expend their physical energy under helpful supervision has prompted a movement on the part of university administrators to found a university city in the environs of the capital.

The university is designated as a "public corporation . . . endowed with full juridical rights." By official definition its purposes are fourfold: (1) to provide for higher education; (2) to produce professional and technical specialists; (3) to provide for scientific investigation, principally concerning national [*sic*] conditions and problems; (4) to extend the benefits of Mexican culture as widely as possible. The university is statutorily dedicated to serve the country and humanity in accordance with the best ethical practice and with social service in mind. Private or particularist interests must be eliminated, when they come in conflict with university or national ideals.

The university year begins the first week in March and ends the last week in October, examinations lasting to December 15. The year is divided into two semesters, the first ending in June, the second beginning in July. Vacation courses, primarily for Mexican schoolteachers, are offered during the winter months, when Mexico's schools are customarily closed for their long vacation. The summer schedule is designed chiefly for foreign students and corresponds to the typical summer school in the United States, in extent, purpose, and scope.

Normally, the *bachillerato* with a general scholastic average of at least 75 percent from a Mexican preparatory school or its equivalent is the requisite for admission to any of the university schools. The student is expected to pursue the same course of study in the university that he did for his *bachillerato*. In exceptional cases the student may be required to pass a proficiency examination. Advanced standing is allowed only up to the fourth year of career courses requiring five or more years of study. Quotas are filled by students in accordance with the excellence of their previous scholastic achievement. Graduates from secondary schools in the United States enter the fourth year of the five-year National Preparatory School, assuming proficiency in Spanish. Because of the intrinsic specialized quality of Mexico's University schools, graduates of North American colleges are allowed to count only those credits obtained in their major fields.

Registration and tuition fees are many and varied, ranging from 200 to 400 pesos in toto per year, excluding special fees for degree examinations (about 150 pesos). Foreign students are liable to further assessments for the accreditation and revalidation of credentials. Since the university has no dormitories or official boarding houses, there are no fees for board. Scholarships, loans, and prizes are few. Student employment is as yet only on an informal, semi-official basis. It was not until 1944 that a beginning was made with the establishment of an office to assist indigent students to find work. No teaching positions or student assistantships are available to non-Mexicans except exchange professorships or lectureships, offered, on recommendation of the rector, to distinguished professors from foreign countries.

The designated examinations are, for the most part, similar to those of the National Preparatory School, with special provision for examinations taken in partial satisfaction of degree requirements. The final examination includes a thesis and an oral examination, open to the public. If the student fails the examination, he may try a second time, but must submit another thesis. Only two grade notations are recorded: pass or fail *(aprobado* or *reprobado).*

The lecture method of instruction prevails. The presentation of subject matter, methods of study, and general scholastic behavior resemble those of a French university. Textbooks and reference works, even in the science schools, are likely to be in French or in English. A great need exists at present for up-to-date text and reference books; of those which are available, the most modern are in English. Aside from the regular university school libraries, the National Library, the Ministry of Education Library, the Spanish-American Library, the Museum Library, and the Periodical Library *(Hemeroteca)* are all drawn upon. There is also the Benjamin Franklin Library, supported principally by North American interests.

Courses are termed "general," "monograph," or "seminar." In general courses, the material is studied comprehensively. Monograph courses are thematic in nature, limited to an intensive treatment of some phase of subject matter designated by the particular department of the school. Seminar courses are founded on a particular field of investigation, subject to approval by school administrative officers.[18] In this connection, a sketch of the course requirements of the Faculty of Philosophy and Letters and the Faculty of Sciences will serve to represent what is done in other schools.

The Faculty of Philosophy and Letters, whose present name dates from 1938, is one of the oldest and most important divisions

---

[18] The numbering of courses in many schools—the Faculty of Philosophy and Letters, for example—purposely follows the North American system, "in order to accommodate foreign students." Numbers from 1 to 20 indicate courses for students who have not obtained the North American B.A. degree or its equivalent. Courses numbered from 21 to 50 are primarily for those with two years' credit toward their B.A. degree; numbers from 51 to 100 designate courses for graduate students and advanced undergraduates. The first figure indicates the number of credits obtainable in the course, as a rule two credits for each class which meets two hours per week. The number 273, for instance, would indicate a course for undergraduates or graduates in which two credits were given.

of the university. It is situated at some distance from the main body of the university, on the Calle San Cosme, in a historic building which also houses the summer school. This faculty is composed of the following departments: philosophy, letters, history, geography, anthropology, education, and psychology (added in 1945). Under a course of study worked out originally in 1929, the degrees of Master and Doctor are awarded in the various branches of these departments. Requirements for the Master's degree include: (1) the *bachillerato* or its verified equivalent, (2) certain course re-

TABLE 16

COURSE OF STUDY (1946) FOR THE DEGREE OF MASTER OF PHILOSOPHY

(All courses meet two hours per week unless otherwise specified)

FIRST YEAR	SECOND YEAR	THIRD YEAR
Greek or Latin (2 or 4 hours)	Greek or Latin	Philosophy of history
Introduction to philosophy	Theory of knowledge (epistemology)	History of Mexican philosophy
Logic	Aesthetics	Metaphysics
Ethics	History of philosophy to the period of Enlightenment	Philosophy of law or philosophy of education
History of classical philosophy	Psychology	History of philosophy from Kant to the present
Two electives[a]	Two electives	Two electives

[a] Electives may be chosen as follows: (1) the Department of History: European history, history of Mexico, history of science, history of art, history of religion, etc., (2) the Department of Letters: monograph courses in ancient and modern literature, comparative literature, theory of literature, etc. Electives may be chosen only after consultation with heads of departments.

quirements specified by the particular department of study, and (3) an acceptable thesis. The Doctor's degree is awarded in recognition of similar attainments: (1) the Master's degree or its verified equivalent, (2) certain required courses, including at least six monograph courses and the seminar courses of his specialty, and (3) an acceptable thesis. The thesis must be written in one of the languages in which the faculty offers instruction, preferably Spanish. Strict rules control thesis format. A Doctoral candidate is required to present his thesis in printed form. To obtain the Master's degree, an average of sixteen class hours per week for three years are required, as illustrated in the sample course of study shown in Table 16.

The degree of Master of Education is awarded after successful completion of one year of study, but only to candidates who have previously obtained a Master's degree in another field. The course of study includes the philosophy of education, psychology of education, adolescent psychology, mental testing, techniques of instruction in secondary schools, history of education, educational sociology, teaching techniques of the subject matter specialty, and two semesters of electives. Electives are chosen from the following subject groupings: (1) exploratory physical anthropology concerned with attitudes, qualities, and physical defects of adolescents; (2) special psycho-techniques of the endowment and physical functions of adolescents; (3) educational sociology (socio-economic research); (4) exploratory techniques in individual adolescent education; (5) history of education (monograph course). All courses meet two hours per week, making a total of sixteen class hours.

The Faculty of Sciences was born as a branch of the School of Advanced Studies *(Altos Estudios)*, which was incorporated in 1910. Though the aim was officially "to assist in scientific investigation," cultural ends and the preparation of secondary-school teachers were given greatest attention.[19] This school became part of the Faculty of Philosophy and Letters in 1924 without any notable change in orientation. Sciences did not come into their own till 1929, when, under the university reorganization, a Science Department was created as part of the Faculty of Philosophy and Letters, and the degrees were granted of Master and Doctor of Physical or Biological Sciences.

The Faculty of Sciences was at first divided into seven departments: mathematics, physics, chemistry, biology, geology, geography, and astronomy. In 1942, however, the Department of Geology was transferred to the National School of Engineering, while the Department of Geography became a part of the Faculty of Philosophy and Letters. Geophysics and physical geography remain in the curriculum.

Among the aims of the Faculty of Sciences are the following: (1) to train teachers of the basic sciences which are taught in university and technical schools; (2) to produce scientific investi-

<hr>

[19] *Anuario de la Facultad de Ciencias*, 1943, p. 5.

gators on whose labors depend scientific progress and technical development; (3) to co-ordinate the work of all schools and institutes in scientific investigation. To these ends the Faculty of Sciences is divided into two cycles: the professional cycle and the cycle of advanced studies. The professional cycle prepares teachers of mathematics, physics, and biology and gives instruction in courses leading to the doctorate awarded in the cycle of advanced studies. Students completing the second year of the professional cycle are eligible for positions as instructors in the National Preparatory School. Four years of training enable the candidate to accept a professorship in his specialty in any university or technical school. After two or four years of study, students may become assistants in scientific investigation.

To the cycle of advanced studies may be admitted only those who have been graduated from the professional cycle or who have obtained their "title" in professional schools. The cycle of advanced studies awards the Doctor's degree and at the same time prepares students for posts as investigators in the various institutes of the university. Degrees of Master of Science and Doctor of Science are awarded in all departments.[20] In the departments of mathematics, physics, and geography, the title of "Preparatory and Secondary School Teacher" is also granted.

Course numberings are the same as for the Faculty of Letters, and all classes meet three hours per week, divided into four groups:

[20] Minimum requirements for the Master of Science degree are as follows: (1) a prescribed four-year course of study, two years of which may be granted as advanced standing to students with approved qualifications; (2) the successful demonstration through examinations of ability to use foreign languages in scientific reading (English is compulsory; and either French, German, or Italian may be chosen); (3) the presentation of an acceptable thesis; (4) a final examination, or "degree examination," based on the subject matter of the thesis (this is a two-hour public oral examination).

Minimum requirements for the Doctor of Science degree are as follows: (1) at least two years' residence; (2) the Master's degree, or professional title, or authorized equivalent in the student's specialty; (3) a "General Examination"—a comprehensive examination, oral or written, or oral and written. (Students obtaining their Master's degree, or students who have pursued professional courses in the National Autonomous University, may be exempt from this examination); (4) the doctoral thesis—an independent, original work showing that the candidate has achieved technical and scientific proficiency in his field. The thesis must be printed or mimeographed, and 100 copies deposited with the Director of the Faculty; (5) the final or "degree" examination—a public, oral defense of the thesis. It may also assume the form of a subject-matter examination at the discretion of the Examining Committee.

intermediate, advanced, doctoral, and seminar. The various curricula are, on the whole, inflexible, though with faculty approval some choice of subjects is permissible in the student's final year, as is illustrated in the sample course of study in Table 17. A seminar, meeting one hour a week, is required of all candidates

TABLE 17

Course of Study Leading to the Master's Degree in Mathematical Sciences

FIRST YEAR

Algebra
Geometry and trigonometry
Analytical geometry
Differential and integral calculus
Physics I (mechanics and heat)
Physics laboratory I

SECOND YEAR

Analytical geometry (conic sections)
Differential and integral calculus and
    differential equations
Practical calculus
Physics II (electricity and optics)
Physics laboratory II

THIRD YEAR

History of mathematics
Vector analysis
Introduction to mathematical analysis I
Higher algebra
Probability

FOURTH YEAR

Introduction to mathematical analysis II
Modern algebra
Five subjects from the following:
    Theory of analytical functions
    Differential geometry
    Introduction to theoretical progress I
    Algebraic geometry
    Projective geometry
    Differential equation

COURSES FOR THE DOCTORATE

General analysis
Foundations of analysis
Calculus of variations
Absolute differential calculus
Differential equations
Theory of real variable functions
Mathematical statistics
Theory of groups
Topology

for the Doctorate and all students enrolled in advanced courses of study.

University instruction in medicine did not begin until a generation after the founding of the National University, since in those days it was considered beneath the intellectual dignity of a learned institution to be concerned with such experimental trivia as physical healing. As late as 1621, instruction in medicine was given by only one teacher, but by the end of the seventeenth century surgery was granted a "certain prestige." At present the National School of Medicine has a large and distinguished faculty and, along with affiliated schools, is responsible for the training of the vastly great majority of Mexico's physicians and surgeons. (Dentists are prepared in the *Escuela de Odontología*.) The course of study leading to the degree of Doctor of Medicine is six years in length; all but the final half-year must be spent in classwork and clinical practice. Interneship lasts three years on a part-time basis. The last half of the sixth year must be dedicated to public service in whatever locality medical services are officially needed. For admission to the Medical School, the candidate must present his *bachillerato* or its equivalent in biological sciences or premedical subjects.

An outline of the courses of study for the year 1945 reveals that laboratory work and classwork are now on a unified basis, with instruction better adapted to immediate clinical practice. In the first year, for example, descriptive anatomy and dissections are taught jointly. Interneship begins in the third year.

The summer school of the National University, housed in the Faculty of Philosophy and Letters, has been in existence since 1921. The school offers graduate work leading to the degree of Master of Arts in Spanish; the prerequisites are given as follows: (1) a bachelor's degree from an approved institution in Europe or the United States; (2) a "perfect" knowledge of Spanish and a general acquaintance with two other languages, the student's own included; (3) the following undergraduate subjects: Latin, phonetics, Spanish history, Spanish literature, Spanish-American literature, Mexican literature, Mexican history, Spanish philology, Mexican art, Spanish art. Provision is made for candidates to pursue some of these courses while working for degrees, and they may also be considered for credit. Further requirements include the accumulation of 36 credits or semester hours, of which at least 12 must have been obtained in the summer school. One unit of credit represents one hour of class work per week for one semester. In the summer school, two credits are usually given for a course meeting five hours per week for six weeks. A transfer of 6 credits is allowed from any of the graduate schools of the National University. Not more than 8 credits may be secured in a single session of the summer school, and not more than 24 per year. Graduate work consists of one specialized course in each of the following fields: Spanish philology, Mexican literature, Spanish literature, Mexican art, and Spanish art.

The residence requirement may be satisfied by attending three summer school sessions, with the alternative of two summer school sessions and one semester in the Faculty of Philosophy and Letters, the over-all time in the latter case being at least fourteen months. Candidates must also submit a thesis, written in Spanish and at least 30,000 words in length, the subject of which has previously been approved by the director and an advisor. The examination for the Master's degree is administered by a board of five faculty members; it is based primarily on the thesis, but often includes questions of a general nature. The inclusive fee for the Master's degree is about $45, while that of the regular summer session is $50 (U. S. currency).

Burgeoning from the summer school is the Spanish Language Institute. Founded in 1944 by Francisco Villagrán Prado, formerly director of the National Preparatory School, its purpose is to foster international intellectual co-operation and provide intensive courses in Spanish and Mexican culture for teachers of Spanish abroad. The institute is a joint enterprise of the National University of Mexico, the Ministry of Education, the U. S. Office of Education, and the U. S. Department of State. Though operating under similar arrangements and in the same locale as the summer school, it nevertheless prefers to limit its enrollment to 100 students between the ages of 22 and 40. Up to 1947 the Office of Education, which assists in selecting the Americans in this group, made a grant of one hundred dollars to each successful candidate. Courses listed for 1946 include Mexican music, literature, and civilization, grammar, Spanish composition, and phonetics.

Higher education in the capital is obtainable at a number of other institutions, chief among which are the Colegio de México, the Women's University, the National School of Anthropology and History, the Workers' University, and Mexico City College. On the more purely vocational side, the National Polytechnic Institute, the National School of Agriculture (at Chapingo), and the School of Tropical Medicine and Health and Hygiene are most important. The Colegio de México is a research institute co-operatively maintained by the Federal Government, the National University, the Bank of Mexico, the Fondo de Cultura Económica (a nonprofit publishing firm), and La Casa de España. It originated in the Casa de España, a privately supported agency established in 1938 to assist refugee Spanish intellectuals. The members of the Colegio are relatively free from the usual political pressures and devote their time to creative research. During the period from May, 1943, to December, 1946, the ministry reported the completion of some sixty-six studies, half of which were in the scientific fields of engineering, medicine, biology, and nuclear physics.[21] The institute sponsors other research bodies, such as the Institute of Physiological Investigation, under the auspices of the Faculty of Medicine of the National University; the Institute of Chemistry, under the auspices of the School of Chemical Sciences at the Polytechnic Institute; and the Center of Historical Studies, which the Colegio operates independently. However, the classical bias of its director, Alfonso Reyes—probably Mexico's leading philosopher today— together with the heavily-weighted literary and linguistic predilections of a number of the senior members, has resulted in considerable disappointment among the more ardent advocates of technical studies.

Aristotle's reasonable hypothesis that no good democratic system can afford to neglect the education of its female members, "since women form one-half of the population," prefaces Mexican endeavor to provide in a systematic way for the higher education of women. The Women's University of Mexico (Universidad Femenina), located in Chapultepec Park, came into being early in 1943 as a branch of the National University, but it is now inde-

[21] Secretaría de Educación Pública, *La obra educativa en el sexenio 1940-1946*, p. 250. The ministry allocated a total of 521,000 pesos for the maintenance of the Colegio from May, 1943, to December, 1946. For these years the following partial membership is reported: Ezequiel Ordónez and Manuel Sandoval Vallarta, engineers; Ignacio González Guzmán, biologist; Ignacio Chávez, cardiologist; Isaac Ochoterena, physiologist; Diego Rivera and José Orozco, artists; Carlos Chávez, musician; Ezequiel Chávez, educationalist; Enrique González Martínez and the eminent novelist Mariano Azuela, literateurs; Antonio Caso and José Vasconcelos, philosophers; Manuel Toussaint, architectural aesthete, and the classicist Alfonso Reyes, director.

pendent. The first year's program was concentrated on the three secondary-school years of university initiation, the first year of the *bachillerato* in law and social sciences, the first year of the career course in administrative sciences and the "nonfaculty" *(no facultativa)* career in archival sciences. In 1944 career courses were added to the program for the various *bachilleratos*. Since then the university has slowly intensified its curriculum, though its academic achievement to date is below that of the National University.

Post-*bachillerato* courses were initiated in 1944 under the title "faculty careers" *(carreras facultativas)*, and were adapted to the standards of the Faculty of Philosophy and Letters of the National University. The offerings by departments were as follows: Spanish language, literature, and letters; administrative sciences; public administration; foreign service; archives and libraries; and sciences. Special courses, not requiring the *bachillerato* for admission, included journalism, nursing, music, art, and many others, mostly vocational in nature. For the most part the faculty of the Women's University is composed of women, particularly in the departments of philosophy and letters, but the regular staff of the National University is drawn upon heavily. Leaders in national life and professors and visiting scholars from other countries are also to be found on the faculty roster.

Beyond its educational purposes, the Women's University is significant as evidence of the increased participation of women in national and cultural affairs. The Association of University Women *(Asociación Universitaria)*, organized recently and including the leading women educators of Mexico, is a joint endeavor toward the same goal. Women's organizations in the last few years have had a definite humanizing influence on Mexican educational policy, a benefit that has been too long delayed.

The Workers' University *(Universidad Obrera de México)* was founded early in 1936, during the high tide of Mexican socialism. It aims to diffuse among manual and intellectual workers of Mexico and Latin America information concerning the impact of the times on the working classes. Study centers deal with socioeconomic problems in the United States and in Soviet Russia and their implications for Mexico. Seminars concentrate on investigations in Latin-American and Mexican socio-economic problems. In the field of artistic expression two branches are sponsored: the People's School of Dancing and the School of Popular Choral Singing.[22]

The procedures of the Workers' University are manifestedly based on class consciousness. The subdivisions of the School are entitled: School of the Problems of Mexico; School of Political Preparation for Workers; School of Labor Law; School of Union Organization; School of Modern Languages; Seminar in the History of Mexico; Journalism Seminar; Research Seminar; Cultural Activities, and so forth. Socialist, Marxist and liberal teachers predominate on the faculty, which contains a number of young and ambitious professors once on the staff of the National University. Though termed a university, the school does not, of course, enjoy the same professional rank as the National University. The courses are of a political rather than of a professional or technical nature. The institution has, however, contributed notable service to the country by co-operating with the Ministry of Education in such endeavors as the illiteracy program. There are no entrance requirements, no fees, no degrees, and no diplomas; and only certificates of attendance and progress are granted.

Under the direction of two American educators, Henry L. Cain and Paul V. Murray, the American School Foundation in 1940 extended its endeavors to provide for the Mexico City College. The purpose of the college is to offer a type of college training identical with that given in the United States. To date, the college has not been recognized by educational accreditation agencies in the United States, though its course credits are honored by many American universities. Entrance requirements and academic standards approximate those of the average North American college, the B.A. and B.S. degrees being granted after four years of acceptable study. In addition to the usual college offerings, courses include business administration, education, and engineering drawing. Graduate training with specialties in Latin American affairs lead-

[22] Universidad Obrera de México, "Programa para 1944," pp. 5 ff.

ing to the degrees of M.A. and M.S. was inaugurated in 1946.
The school year begins July 1 and operates on a quarterly basis.
With the partial exception of the National University and the
semi-independent institutions mentioned above, Mexico's higher
education today is controlled and administered by the Division
of Higher Education and Scientific Investigation of the Ministry of
Education. Provision for this type of training is made in Articles
89 through 101 of the Organic Law, special directions for scientific
investigation being embodied in Articles 99 through 101. Higher
education is officially designated as a training for technical and
professional excellence through scientific study directly applicable
to life (Article 89). The state is obliged to provide higher education in those specialties which are necessary for national progress
and in the light of the particularized demands of the various
regions of the country (Article 94). Plans, programs, and methods
are to be used which will enable the student to gain sufficient technical proficiency for his life work, with the thought always present
that he may be compelled for economic or other reasons to leave
school before terminating his entire course (Article 95). This accounts in part for the three stages of vocational education: prevocational, vocational, and higher vocational (Article 98), and the
provision for terminal education implicit in their offerings. The
state is also obliged to provide for postgraduate work, so as to
raise the level of national culture and enhance the possibilities of
individual specialization (Article 96). Only specialists chosen by
the schools themselves are allowed on faculties of higher education
(Article 97). Freedom of investigation is stipulated by law (Articles 99-100). The state is bound to establish and maintain the
necessary schools, laboratories, and institutes especially designed
for scientific investigation, and to support all persons or institutions dedicated to approved productive research and investigation
(Article 101).

Administration is handled by the Division of Higher Education
and Scientific Investigation *(Dirección General de Enseñanza Superior e Investigación Científica)*, whose prescribed duties are: to
regulate and administer higher education and scientific investigation throughout Mexico, whether public or private; to unite univer-

sity systems; and to design pedagogical norms and programs, practical and experimental, with direct application to instruction. It is also within the province of this office to steer scientific research toward the betterment of Mexican society in accordance with "Mexican biophysic proclivities"; and to see to it that the orientation of all higher education is at once theoretical and practical.

Of the many higher schools and institutes which the Division supervises, one of the most outstanding is the National Institute of Anthropology and History, created in 1939, with subdivisions including the Office of Prehispanic Monuments, the Office of Colonial and Republic Monuments, the National Museum of Anthropology, and the National Museum of History (at Chapultepec). Other institutions are the School of Mechanical and Electrical Engineering, the Higher School of Engineering and Architecture, the Federal School of Textile Industries, the Higher School of Engineering, the National School of Biological Sciences, the National School of Homeopathic Medicine, and the Higher School of Administrative, Social, and Economic Sciences. Aided by an income of more than half a million pesos annually from the Rockefeller and Viking Foundations, the institute's activities include: the care and conservation of the archeological zones entrusted to the Ministry of Education; the exploration and restoration of monuments; the promotion of historical investigation; the classification and cataloguing of museum collections; ethnographic investigations and studies on indigenous languages, physical anthropology, and folklore. Finally, the institute is responsible for the administration of the National School of Anthropology.

The latter school has until recently concerned itself exclusively with anthropological and historical studies. In 1944 new professional courses were added in library science, archives, and museum science.[23] The academic rank of this school corresponds to that of the National Autonomous University and all official professional schools. In 1939 an agreement was made with the university whereby the Department of Anthropology of the Faculty of Philosophy and Letters unified its curriculum with that of the School of

---

[23] Escuela Nacional de Antropología, *Anuario para 1944*, pp. 5 ff.

Anthropology, thus combining the courses of both schools into a single study schedule. Classes are held in the National Museum of Anthropology. The School also has an arrangement with the Colegio de México for the use of its Center of Historical Studies and for the unification of its curriculum with the professional instruction given by the Colegio. The laboratories of the National School of Biological Sciences of the National Polytechnic Institute are used for the school's courses in physical anthropology.

The director of the National Institute of Anthropology and History is the chief administrator of the School of Anthropology, but the school has its own director. The head of the Department of Anthropology of the University Faculty of Philosophy and Letters and the secretary of the Colegio de México join with the two directors to form the Administrative Committee of the school. A College of Professors, a Scholarship Committee, and an Honorary Committee complete the administrative personnel. The school gives some 70 courses, taught by 48 professors, including several visiting professors from the United States, notably in linguistics and library science. Titles and the degrees of Master and Doctor are awarded for work of the same quality as in the university.

The types of study pursued give evidence of a trend toward practical technical studies. When this goal was first proposed in the Organic Law, skeptics condemned it as impossible of attainment. But so determined have Mexico's leaders been to establish higher technical and vocational training, especially in response to increased industrialization, that these studies have received attention, favor, and financial support to the very limit of educational budgets.[24] Three great institutions—the National Polytechnic In-

---

[24] Industrial employment, according to official statistics, nearly doubled between 1930 and 1944. Assuming that the 1930 occupational classifications were correct, there would be a proportionate increase in engineering positions to around 11,000 by 1943. The 1940 census reported 4,384 men and women who had received university training in engineering and physical and mathematical sciences. From 1939 to 1943 less than 1,000 degrees were granted in all fields of engineering, the number for 1943, however, being more than double that of any previous year. This means that the preponderance of industrial leadership in technical fields is drawn from the technical schools, whose programs necessarily emphasize applied studies at the expense of theoretical and humanistic general education. *Cf. Compendio estadístico 1947.* According to this census, an additional 9,000 men were reported to have received technical training, but no distinction was made as to specific fields.

stitute, the National School of Agriculture, and the National School of Health and Hygiene—have been the chief beneficiaries of this program.

At the pinnacle of technical and vocational education in Mexico stands the National Polytechnic Institute, a huge institution containing approximately 20,000 students in all its schools and branches. Situated in an ideally spacious spot, within the limits of Mexico City yet removed from the overcrowded central area, the Institute since 1944 has enjoyed a large amount of autonomy under a director with full powers. The institute comprises seven professional schools, all of university rank. These include the higher schools of Biological Sciences; Engineering and Architecture; Textile Engineering; Homeopathic Medicine; Rural Medicine; Economic, Administrative, and Social Sciences; and Mechanical and Electrical Engineering. The institute also houses and supervises six prevocational schools and four vocational schools and oversees several other establishments throughout the nation. Among all these dependencies the administration strives for coordination in all matters relating to general discipline, a unified curriculum, and student activity. The institute is equipped with up-to-date laboratories and workshops, dental and medical clinics, an infirmary, a radio station, a stadium, a swimming pool, an indoor gymnasium, a library, and many playing courts and fields. Provision is made for about 250 boarding students. The total budget of the institute in 1947 was 11,500,000 pesos. In 1941 the per-student cost was 550 pesos; in 1947, 1,788 pesos.

For entrance into the technical and professional higher schools of the Polytechnic Institute, the requirements are: (1) the successful completion of a vocational school; (2) the *bachillerato* of the preparatory school; or (3) the equivalent, determined by entrance examinations.

The main purpose of the institute is "to prepare a new type of professional man," well-equipped technically and with sufficient cultural background to become a constructive force toward national progress. The plan of studies, the methods, and the programs are laid out in order of progressive difficulty, "based on scientific theories, directly applicable to practice." These theories concern the social and ethical obligations of the student to society with specific reference to his professional rights and duties, "interpreting them in a social-service sense."

The Higher School of Engineering and Architecture *(Escuela Superior de Ingeniería y Arquitectura)* is characteristic of the schools that make up the institute. This school awards titles in such fields as metallurgical engineering, geology, mining engineering, petroleum geology, petroleum chemistry, petroleum engineering,

TABLE 18

COURSE OF STUDY LEADING TO THE PROFESSIONAL CAREER OF
CIVIL ENGINEERING

FIRST YEAR		SECOND YEAR	
Applied mechanics	3	Steel constructions	4½
Topography	3	Stability II	4½
Stability I	4½	Systems of construction II	3
Systems of construction	3	Reinforced concrete	3
Reinforced concrete I	4½	Geology II	3
Hydraulics	4½	Machines I	3
Geology I	3	Hydraulics	4½
Practical topography	4½	Sanitary engineering	3
Topographical drawing	3	Architectural drawing I	4½
	33		33

THIRD YEAR		FOURTH YEAR	
Systems of construction III	3	Highways and railroads II	3
Organization, legislation, and budget estimates	3	Technology, analysis and specification of materials	4½
Applied engineering	4½	Paving	3
Highways and railroads I	3	Mechanics of soils	3
Bridges	3	Highways and railroad projects	4½
Practical photogrammetry	4½	Bridge projects and building	4½
Machines II	3	Structural design III	9
Furniture drawing II	4½		31½
Models	3		
	31½		

civil and architectural engineering, civil engineering on roads and railroads, civil hydraulic engineering, and topographical and hydrographical engineering. A sample course of study in civil engineering is outlined in Table 18.

Field work, theses, and final examinations are obligatory. Provision is made for terminal certificates on completion of each year of study.

Situated at Chapingo, an hour and a half by road from the capital, is a sister institution to the Polytechnic Institute, the National School of Agriculture. First established in 1853 in Mexico City, its present location dates from 1923, when the government purchased an old hacienda in a country town well adapted to agricultural training.[25] Funds from the Rockefeller Foundation have assisted in the erection of several attractive new buildings. The school's collection of murals by Diego Rivera is probably still the chief source of tourist interest. These murals—probably Diego's best—depict the struggle of Mexico's leaders to overcome "three negative forces: the military, the wealthy, and the church." They portray peace and prosperity through land development.

The purpose of the National School of Agriculture is to teach students the care and breeding of animals and the most profitable way to raise crops. The school also endeavors to create a sympathetic understanding of the social and economic conditions of those who till the soil. Much work is done in corn hybrids, new varieties of wheat, and methods of improving low yields. The students raise oats and barley, chiefly for the school livestock.

The school is administered by the Ministry of Agriculture rather than the Ministry of Education. There are at present about four hundred students in residence, an enrollment less than one-tenth of what Mexico should be supporting. The course of study takes them seven years beyond the lower secondary or prevocational school training. Preference is given first to children of owners of *ejidos* who work their land unassisted, and secondly to the economically underprivileged. Age limits on entrance are from 15 to 20 years. Scholarships and government allowances eliminate tuition fees almost entirely.

The first three years of study are general and preparatory; the

[25] On Chapingo, Mabel F. Knight, "Farming Looks Up in Mexico," *Christian Science Monitor*, January 19, 1946, has this to say: "Chapingo . . . the pride of Marte Gómez' heart. The college occupies what was once the estate of ex-President Manuel González. . . . The 400 or more students in attendance are all holders of scholarships, which cover the cost of uniforms, board, room, and tuition, besides a weekly sum for stamps, bus fare, and an occasional movie. . . . Each student must work somewhere in Mexico in his special field before his receives his degree of Agricultural Engineer and his diploma, and goes forth to hold some responsible agricultural position in the Republic of Mexico."

final four concentrate on such fields as irrigation, forestry, plant feeding, dairying, bee-raising, parasitology, and agricultural economics. Much reliance is placed on methods used in the United States, and most of the textbooks are in English. After graduation students must donate three years to government enterprise in return for their education.

Of all the schools one might wish to visit in Mexico, the School of Agriculture is among the most rewarding. Here one finds purposeful activity at its best, intelligently directed toward preparing young people for their life pursuits. The school boasts a hospital, a laundry, and a whole aggregation of hatcheries, poultry pens, dairies, carpentery shops, stables, hog-pens, and garden patches. The students study health and first aid, clothes-cleaning, turkey-breeding, poultry vaccination, incubation, steam-washing, homogenization, pasteurization, dehydration, dairy-products processing, and general machine overhauling, which may come in handy when hundreds of kilometers away from expert assistance. About the school's "campus" strut all breeds of domestic poultry—Rhode Island reds, minorcas, leghorns, white and barred Plymouth rocks, red and silver wyandottes, feather-legged brahmins, and "Henry Wallace" turkeys. As for the livestock, one may distinguish many breeds of cows and horses, Rambouillet sheep, Caracul and Angora goats, Hampshire and Jersey hogs, and a cross between the two called, appropriately enough, "Chapingo." All these and many others are gathered here in a veritable farmer's paradise of healthy productivity. Not all Mexicans want to be farmers, of course, but the school at Chapingo is of the type best fitted to cope with the country's economic needs. As such, it is the long-awaited answer to the driving distress of rural peoples and a fine example of the new Mexican educational program in action.

Not to be outdone by the Ministries of Education and Agriculture, the Ministry of Public Health in 1938 created the present School of Health and Hygiene. While not so dramatic and extensive as its agricultural and technical counterparts, this school's program is a sound and solid effort, created through the labors of health organizations in the United States and Mexico, to give scientific training in preventive medicine, personal hygiene, and social sanitation. The personnel attending this school must be registered physicians, nurses, or engineers, not older than thirty-five years. There is no tuition fee, and government subsidies are provided. The school grants the Diploma of Sanitary Physician, awarded since 1938 to over five hundred specialists. A sister institution is the School of Tropical Medicine reported to be among the best in the Western Hemisphere.[26]

In sum, these higher schools, the Polytechnic Institute, the National School of Agriculture, and the schools of Tropical Medicine and of Health and Hygiene, have joined with the Colegio de México and the National School of Anthropology to create and carry out for Mexico within a period of a few brief years a program of national rehabilitation through education in realms chiefly outside of the academic. It is difficult to imagine what would have happened to the industrial and technical advancement of the nation if an enlightened foresight had not prevailed in governmental circles. One may be charitable and grant that scientific research would have progressed equally well in the university, if given adequate support. However, the temper of the university scholars was not such as to respond to the repeated appeals of a people in economic need. The cries for help from Mexico's vast wilderness were heard and, for the most part, heeded by her government, not by her university, whose scholars still listened to voices from a distant past and of a different world.

[26] How far Mexico has come in the last decade is readily discernible when one rereads the plea of Manuel Gamio and José Vasconcelos, uttered twenty-five years ago in *Aspects of Mexico Civilization*, pp. 124-25: "This ignorance of the Indian's physical mechanism has carried over into Mexican medicine and even into hygienic legislation the same error which has characterized education, that is, the use of methods of foreign origin which, if applicable to the white minorities, are not so successful when applied to the indigenous and half-breed majorities. That is why, contrary to expectations, there are not among us schools of medicine for tropical diseases; nor, in those which we have, is there any special attention given to noteworthy phenomena, such as local or practically local diseases. One of these diseases is the *mal del pinto,* which causes a polychromatic pigmentation of the skin and which affects the inhabitants of an extensive southern area of the country, where is also found *afilaria* (choroiditis), a disease which causes blindness and which has recently been identified and studied by an eminent Guatemaltecan doctor. The *bocio* (goiter), an exaggerated glandular development in the neck, affects numerous inhabitants of central and southern Mexico; a peculiar dark coloring appears upon the teeth of the people of Durango; certain mental derangements are caused by the peyote cactus among Indians of Durango, Chihuahua, and other northern states."

Higher learning exists, of course, outside the precincts of the national capital, but its quality is debatable. There is, for example, the University of Guadalajara. Established on the eve of the War of Independence, it was redeemed from the sloth and corruption for which it was notorious throughout the nineteenth century only when the state of Jalisco undertook its rehabilitation in 1925. There is also the quaint Autonomous University of Guadalajara, a pocket edition of the National University, whose faculty enjoy the unique distinction of teaching without pay, so minute is the university budget; but who, for ideological reasons, stolidly refuse to join forces with their neighbor, the State University. Both these institutions publish the same requirements for entrance and graduation as the National University, though few Mexican educators take them seriously.

The University of Michoacán, in idyllic Morelia, is on a par scholastically with the University of Guadalajara, but its chief claim to educational fame lies in its history and its picturesque environment. More than four hundred years ago, Don Vasco de Quiroga founded the Colegio de San Nicolás in the inland fishing village of Pátzcuaro, famous for its butterfly nets. Morelia, now a brief hour's ride from Pátzcuaro, became the seat of the Colegio in 1580. Father Hidalgo was not only an alumnus of this school, but served also as its rector. Like most Mexican higher educational establishments, it was closed during the greater part of the nineteenth century, to be reopened in 1917 and placed under state control in 1939. The University of Michoacán, still revering the spirit of Father Hidalgo, preserves the ideals of Independence and the Revolution to a greater extent than do its sister institutions.

The enterprising city of Monterrey, confident as always of its superiority over the nation's capital, attempts to prove its claim by housing, in the manner of its rival, two institutions of higher learning: the University of the State of Nuevo León and the city's own Institute of Technology and Advanced Studies. The latter, established in 1943, is intended to serve a large industrial center by providing technicians and facilities for research on location. The University of Nuevo León advertises standards and requirements equivalent to those of the National University, but the Institute recognizes its academic inferiority by a more modest program. Nevertheless, the Institute may be cited for providing the capital with an example of what a great university campus can be. Still under construction, its model campus contains an open-air theater, a library, a stadium, a gymnasium, tennis and *jai-alai* courts, and a dormitory for three hundred students—all within a stone's throw of the Pan American Highway.

The University of Puebla, which originated in 1578 as the Colegio de San Jerónimo, is distinguished for its Jesuit influence. The Colegio functioned on and off till 1820; and it was not until 1937 that the state of Puebla finally decided to underwrite a state program of higher education and incorporate the Colegio for that purpose. The University of Puebla boasts only one building, in which an attempt is made to train students for all the professions, including those of the business and industrial world. For this purpose even the old catacombs have been turned into classrooms.

The curve of academic achievement in higher education then settles on a comparatively low but well-meaning plane. The remaining institutions deserve at least a roll call: The universities of Guanajuato, San Luis Potosí, Sinaloa, Sonora, Veracruz, and Yucatán, and the institutes of Science and Arts of Oaxaca, Chiapas, and Zacatecas.

It is evident from the above that higher education is excessively concentrated in the capital, where enrollments have doubled in the last ten years.[27] Clearly this trend is unhealthy. Professor Eduardo García Máynez of the National University sees injurious effects to the provinces if they must constantly look to Mexico City for inspiration. He therefore advocates a national system of universities in the five widely distributed centers which already support some form of higher learning. While it is impossible of realization for a considerable time to come, García's plan is indicative of a

[27] Martínez D., "Fracaso universitario," *Excelsior*, August 7, 1943; "Student population has increased 228 percent from 1931 to 1943. . . . Growth averages 1091 students per year." Per pupil costs for the achievement of degrees ranged in 1943 from 1,393 pesos for the law degree to 91,000 for the music degree. The medical degree cost 2,687 pesos. Martínez explains this great spread in costs, and the peculiarity of low costs for the medical, dental, and law degrees "not because the schools are better but because they produce more graduates. The most lamentable thing about it is that these schools are really the worst."

worthy tendency toward university construction under national auspices and is certainly one solution to a university program now decidedly top-heavy.

The overclassical bias of Mexican higher learning and its tendency to impart codified knowledge has naturally inhibited the growth of creative research. Laboratories and facilities for research have not been developed through the years, and the burden on current administrations to provide equipment which should have been the accumulation of years of effort is well nigh insupportable. If only for this reason, the creation, through direct government aid, of Mexico's present system of institutes of higher learning becomes a more readily understandable phenomenon. A pathetic and anomalous situation therefore exists, in that the university still clings to the idea of autonomy and of learning per se, and still subjects itself to extraneous influences, yet depends more and more on direct government subsidy for its very existence. Only recently, in one of his last generous gestures, President Avila Camacho induced his government to pass a direct supplementary grant of one million pesos to pull the institution out of its financial difficulties.

However, lest this study be accused of leveling unreasoned criticism against the university, certain extenuating circumstances need explanation. In the first place, Mexico's higher institutions have not been so fortunate as those of other countries in obtaining the benefits of private financial support; grants, endowed chairs, and other forms of philanthropy are for all practical purposes alien to the Mexican scene. Roberto Moreno y García, specialist in higher education, is correct in laying part of the blame for the dearth of scientific investigation on the failure of Latin American capitalists to provide the material help needed. He is somewhat bitter as he refers to Mexico:

Our centers of higher education do not yet consider research as a fundamental task, regardless of the voices we hear on every side praising it. . . . It is not a question of a hypertrophy of scientific investigation. On the contrary, research does not exist in our universities, primarily because industrial and mining companies have little or no interest in supporting laboratories capable of extending scientific knowledge.

Moreno y García finds much to laud in the attitude of American capitalists toward financing education, and recommends imitation by Mexicans.[28]

Deficiency in creative research does not in Mexico result solely from lack of physical equipment and financial means. Administrative practices have also tended to hamper professional advancement. As in the secondary school, the custom still prevails of hiring university teachers on a piecework basis from among the specialists whose major interests lie in the business world. Moreover, since the rates of payment are low, only an excessively heavy teaching load will provide the full-time professor with an adequate salary. With time and energy depleted by a taxing schedule, teachers on full time cannot be expected to indulge in much research. And part-time faculty members have shown themselves more interested in the prestige and extra pin money they derive from presiding over a class or two than in contributing their full energy to ferreting out new knowledge.

More insidious and detrimental to the advancement of higher learning has been the invasion into the academic field of political appointees devoid of sincere educational interest. Though Mexico's governments have in general paved the way to new learnings, they have too often assigned administrative and faculty positions as rewards for favorable political activity or for distinction in fields which do not necessarily prepare for the discharge of specific educational functions. Education as a professional career, let alone education as a dignified goal in itself, has been too far from the minds of many who have been responsible for Mexico's higher education.

Finally, university creativity and leadership has suffered for very lack of challenge, of comprehensive appeal, and the restrictive quality of faculties and student bodies. A well-known American educational pundit has facetiously remarked that higher education has been mostly for the "higher-ups." This has certainly

---

[28] Moreno y García, *Desarrollo y orientaciones de la educación superior*, pp. 439, 474. On pp. 367-421 Moreno analyzes the influence of the financial and moral support of industrialists upon the development of scientific research in universities of advanced industrial nations and the reciprocal effect of the "pure" studies upon applied development. He emerges with a strong case for private financial subsidy.

been the case in Mexico. "Higher education," Apstein confirms, "was reserved for the privileged classes, and was seldom open to Indians or mestizos." While this fact is far less true than formerly, its attendant attitudes remain with many faculty members, who shy away from extending the curriculum into more practical learnings and deplore throwing the doors of the university open to all segments of society. These men tend to preserve the inherited principle that learning is its own sufficient reward, that there should be no essential concentration on studies with visible vocational outlets, that students are a necessary evil, and that any attempt to create something Mexican out of the university vulgarizes the ideal of true universal learning. On the other hand, President Miguel Aleman in his address at the University of Kansas City, May 7, 1947, cited the need for universality: "In a measure never reached in the past, our educators are called upon to interest themselves not only in the way of life and the peculiarities of their own people but also in those of the other peoples of the world. And classrooms, laboratories, and libraries must open wide their doors—as Victor Hugo expressed it—to the 'four winds of the spirit.' " The overproduction of intellectuals in the capital today is evidenced in the shortsightedness of the academic-minded. Too many university professors are ignorant of, or indifferent to, the present imbalance in the vocations and unfortunately prefer to transfer their responsibilities to "vocational" schools.

The successful welding of new aims and old ways is not, of course, the work of only one generation. Painful steps must first be taken toward achieving a level of mechanical competence and interpreting human values in terms of new technical accomplishments. It is not a question of giving up treasured values, but of learning their place in a new pattern. George Sánchez is bold in his advice to Mexican higher educators: school administration is not incompatible with the observance of religious beliefs; the church-state question "is no more relevant to the basic forms of higher learning than any other political issue"; Catholicism "does not imply indifference to human welfare." Sánchez also comments on the original drives for education: "zest for accomplishment transcended the dictates of religious doctrine." He concludes that modern educators must not imitate the Jesuits. They may have rendered valuable service, but they "handicapped the evolution of the new, the Mexican, culture" by refusing to change the content of their teaching as environmental circumstances changed. Modern sciences demand not so much an extension of traditional liberal studies as a broadening of the scope, method, and tenor of higher curricula. Prerequisite, of course, is a redefinition of objectives, accompanied by increased professionalization and more effective continuity in university administrative procedures.

Higher education is not a thing apart from general mass education in elementary and secondary schools; it is the logical extension and climax of it. For within the walls of a university are trained not only scholars in restricted fields but also the leaders of a nation. Until the fusion of vocational, scientific, and liberal studies already begun in the secondary schools is achieved also in the higher schools of Mexico, educational leadership will remain out of contact with the vital growth of the country. Technical advancement in Mexico must no longer continue along the dead-end road of the erroneous, artificial dualism of academic and vocational education traveled by the educational systems of so many other nations. Against this President Avila Camacho and his successor have clearly posted the warning sign.[29]

[29] Rector Salvador Zubirán, reviewing university needs during the period 1946-48 in his *Ideario, realizaciones y proyectos*, pp. 54 ff., cites the following: The university must become authentically Mexican and incorporate the Latin spirit; It must educate men who are not only technically well-equipped, but who bear a moral responsibility toward their country; It must become a vital and intrinsic part of the entire cultural and educational makeup of the country and not a separate entity; Specialization must not usurp an active interest in the total realm of culture and learning; The inner life of the university must aim for greater unity, coordination, and collective responsibility for the common good; There must be a greater respect of university regulations and procedures; Extraneous influences on university life must be eliminated; The university must assume a greater responsibility for the guidance and education of the entire Republic.

VIII. Education in a Total Culture

THE ARTS IN EDUCATION

When Europe lived in medieval bleakness, Teotihuacán, the holy and ancient city on the fringe of the Valley of Mexico, had already been a warm, busy metropolis of brightly colored walls. Every inch of wall space in the sumptuous homes and temples of that city was decorated with red, pink, green, yellow, orange, and blue figures and landscapes. Huge, expertly done mural representations of their multitudinous gods are being discovered today by the hundreds.—Arturo César Castillo.

Teachers are not alone in bringing education to the people. The artist teaches with his music and painting. The scholar teaches with his unselfish investigations. The poet teaches with his message of poetry and song. And, with his visible example, the man of action, the artisan, also teacher. —Manuel Avila Camacho.

In Mexico the school must lead, direct, and inspire not only its pupils, but the other powerful moral agencies. . . . It must show the parents the folly of their conduct toward their children; it must educate them too.—Manuel Barranco.

So FAR, this treatment of education has been restricted to schools of the more academic or vocational-technical type. Some indication has also been given that other educational media should be enlisted in the service of national enlightenment. In the early twenties, Education Minister José Vasconcelos and his supporters daringly seized upon a simpler and more appealing medium than daily drill in the three R's. Philosophically conceived as "aesthetic monism," the Minister's methods bore the stamp of an educational campaign, in which all cultural agencies—art, music, museums, and literature—contributed to the formation and communication of educational ideals.[1]

[1] Aesthetic monism unites current scientific understanding with the "inescapable intuitive, aesthetic, and emotional components of the Indian and the Spanish spirit." Northrop, *The Meeting of East and West*, p. 39.

Mexican art is as ancient as the Indian tribes. Throughout the centuries the natives have utilized the rich color pigments of their soil and clay and have been in unbroken contact with every type of art—at home, in their places of assembly and worship, in their markets, and at their daily work. The Mexican is intuitively an artist, and his creations abound everywhere—from the bawdy walls of *pulquerías* to the sublime interiors of cathedrals; from public placards to private residences.

Art has also been a cultural, educational, and communicative necessity. In the absence or ignorance of the printed word, illiterate peasants have learned through pictures. Artistic expression and art education have reflected the vagaries of national development in forms that are varied, bold, grotesque, individualistic, even chaotic.[2]

It was this communicative necessity that led Vasconcelos to foster art in all its forms and to bring to its propagation every available material resource. Public-school art received a tremendous impetus when Mexico's great painters became teachers in the schools and universities and beneficiaries of government subsidies for other types of educational activity. Diego Rivera returned from Paris to champion revolution and to join David Siqueiros, José Clemente Orozco, and others in a movement which brought Mexico into unprecedented artistic leadership. No more was the Academy to dominate art for the edification of the "idle elegant." Painting only a step ahead of revolutionary salvos, Mexico's artists satirized, synthesized, and strove to find principles of inner harmony in the politico-economic chaos of Mexico's history and of their own times. Their production was characterized by fiery *élan* and straightforward conviction.

[2] Schmeckebier, *Modern Mexican Art,* p. 13, analyzes: "Practically all ancient art had a religious, symbolic content, told by means of the frescoes and reliefs that ornamented both architectural and sculptural monuments. That content was overwhelmingly impressed upon the mind and heart of the beholder of the realism of the representation and the massiveness of the block form itself. This strong monumental impressiveness of form can be seen in architecture like the Pyramid of the Sun at San Juan Teotihuacán; in sculpture like the terrifying figure of Mictlanteuctli, God of Death; and even in representational scenes in relief like the Mayan Votive Scene from the Temple of the Sun at Palenque." See also Arturo César Castillo, *One Thousand Years of Murals in Mexico,* a most useful and authoritative pamphlet issued by the Pemex Travel Club, Mexico City, 1945.

The enthusiasm of the artists and their strong missionary sense were expressed in the neo-Marxian manifesto of the Syndicate of Technical Workers, Painters, and Sculptors, organized through the efforts of David Siqueiros in 1922. "We repudiate the so-called easel art," proclaimed the syndicate, "and all such art which springs from ultra-intellectual circles, for it is essentially aristocratic. . . . We hail the monumental expression of art because such art is public property." It was an era of social transition, the artists decided, from a "decrepit" to a "new" order; and it was the duty of the creators of beauty to direct their efforts toward materializing art for the benefit of the people: "Our supreme objective in art, which today is an expression for individual pleasure, is to create beauty for all—beauty that enlightens and stirs to struggle." Perhaps nowhere else have the fundamental issues of a scientific world and the industrial revolution been faced with more intuitive honesty, though not exactly objectivity, than in Mexican art.

Throughout the twenties the countryside burgeoned with pictorial messages anatomizing progress. The Indian was represented everywhere as a victim of oppression; the church was publicly defiled, the corruption of former regimes excoriated, and education idealized. Far-flung upon the walls of public buildings—the National Preparatory School, the Ministry of Education, the National Agricultural School, the House of Tiles, and many others—the creative intelligence of individual artists spread the compelling picture of Mexico's historic struggles. The Revolution became an ineradicable element in the very aesthetic and cultural architecture of the country. As a catalyst effects unity within a chemical field and molds chaotic elements to a new form, so Mexico's artists gave expression to the cherished aspirations of their nation.

Through the years of fluctuation in politics and ideology leaders in Mexican art have displayed marked individualism and singleness of purpose. Rivera's figures, serene and almost classical, portray a fundamental faith in the beneficence of science and technology. Glorification of the worker and the co-operative spirit constitutes his central theme. In the Ministry of Education, Diego's weavers, dyers, industrial workers, and miners tell their story of the reward of work and applied intelligence. The ultimate triumph of science as the leading source of human values, a concept accentuated by Mexico's problem of inadequate supply, is an ever-recurrent theme. Rivera's anger is virulently displayed against those who misuse natural resources.

Orozco's paintings—violent, passionately intense, mystic—reflect a powerful insight into the contradictions of the creativity, destruction, and consequent suffering which beset our age. The theme of a disillusioned Christ chopping down his cross—once suppressed in the National Preparatory School—recurs in Dartmouth College, more disillusioned, more terrifying than before. The magnificent figure of Prometheus in the Frary Hall mural at Pomona College, in California, separates benign users from condemned misusers of the precious gift of fire. The tragic death of creativity itself is displayed at Dartmouth College in "Modern Education," which portrays a ghoulish array of complacent skeletons decked in academic robes—a theme which appears at the University of Guadalajara under the title "False Teaching and the Human Problem." Bearded savants, shown at their books, point to specious doctrines they know to be false, but force their students to believe. One pedagogue has a knife in his hand, symbolic of the force used to make people accept inherited, outworn dogma. Luminous power transfigures the scenes of Orozco's staircase murals "Thirsting Men and the Engineers" and "Youth," at the National Preparatory School. Here the artist urges the youth who tread that stairway to undertake the arduous creative effort necessary for personal fulfillment and universal human betterment.

While Diego Rivera speaks directly and simply to the people and is more expressive of the educational spirit desired by the ministry, Orozco more passionately reaches toward a synthesis of spiritual contradictions. His message, broader in scope, transcends the bounds of national unification and enters the realm of universal humanism. "For Orozco, scientific technology, by mechanizing man's life, destroys his soul," writes Professor Northrop. On the other hand, "Rivera tells us with equal certainty and appeal that scientific knowledge through universal democratic education is one of the highest and most perfect human values." The psychological freedom and aesthetic passion of Orozco are felt to be equally essential, Professor Northrop argues, with the scientific and economic values of Rivera. He concludes: "The most telling evidence to this end comes from the second generation of contemporary Mexican painters. They have studied the works and grasped the messages of both Rivera and Orozco. They follow Rivera in portraying science applied to man's mind and nature's resources as a human value."

Training in the arts has been supported by the federal government since 1923 in a series of laws providing for special schools. Legal bases for this and all other extra-school cultural activity are to be found in Articles 102 and 103 of the Organic Law of 1942. Article 102 stipulates that elementary cultural knowledge shall be spread to illiterate adults and the underprivileged. The many and varied indigenous and social groups are to be assimilated into national life through the extension of rudimentary cultural knowledge to localities not at present favored by other forms of special education. The Article further prescribes that education shall foster cultural presentations; it shall employ the press, the radio, the cinema, the theater, the arts, lectures, and cultural associations and clubs. According to Article 103 the state is expected to solicit private aid for extra-school services and grant funds and subsidies for the extension of these services.

In practice, extra-school services are considered primarily aesthetic in nature; as such, they are administered by the Division of Extra-School and Aesthetic Education of the Ministry of Education *(Dirección General de la Educación Extraescolar y Estética)*. Artistic education, embodied in the regular school curricula and taught in special schools or academies, is controlled by the Department of Fine Arts *(Departmento de Bellas Artes)*, which administers and controls all types of art education in its dependent schools, museums, and institutes. Among these types are (1) music (the Evening School of Music and the National Conservatory of Music); (2) the theater (the Academy of Cinematographic Arts and Sciences); (3) dancing (the School of Dancing); (4) plastic arts (the School of the Plastic Arts); and (5) the arts (the Schools of Artistic Initiation; the School of the Art of Bookmaking; the San

Carlos Museum of Popular Arts and other art galleries). In the capital alone there are at present some twenty-five schools of the arts with a total enrollment exceeding ten thousand students. Among these institutions are the School of Painting and Sculpture, which participates in Mexico's annual Book Fair and assists in the construction and modeling of national monuments, and the Schools of Artistic Initiation *(Iniciación Artística)*—free schools, operating mostly in the evening and open to children and adults without prerequisites. In addition, two advanced schools of fine arts enroll four hundred specialized students.[3]

Art thus becomes practical for the government as well as for the individual. It provides a medium of mutual understanding and creative expression. Likewise, the application of crafts to life activities as taught in the schools enables the Mexican to live richly amid the beautiful treasures that spring from his environment. He is able to create for himself the accoutrements of the good life, which are the major sources of national welfare everywhere. More materially, the simple, functional attractiveness of articles so created—*sarapes, rebozos, huaraches,* for example—has made for Mexicans a place in the markets of the world which could have been gained in no other way.

From the initial emphasis upon mural expression, aesthetic monism has spread into other fields, inspiring administrative support of music, drama, and the dance, not only in the public schools but also in the Republic at large. The ministry's Division of Aesthetic Culture has collected folkdances and folksongs from all parts of the country, and collated every available shred of knowledge concerning them.

Music and dancing are especially integral in the program of the cultural missions, which in their twenty-five years of life have seized upon every variety of mass activity, from drama and sports events to dances and fiestas, in an effort to compensate for the isolation of the peasant and catch him up in the tide of national growth. The choral music and festival dances staged by the cultural missions perform a double function: they provide the people

[3] Secretaría de Educación Pública, *La obra educativa en el sexenio 1940-1946,* pp. 198-99.

with entertainment in which the whole community may participate, and win them over to the less appealing ministrations of teachers of agriculture, skills, and hygiene. Recent bulletins illustrate the function of the music teachers of these missions:

You are responsible not only for the teaching of the technical aspects of music . . . but also for the important task of getting the people of all ages to participate in artistic activities. . . . One of the most important functions of the music teacher in the cultural mission is to guide and develop the creative spirit of the people.

The music teacher is further expected to foster the "ingenuous" and the "simple," as against commercialized, synthetic arts and "foreign perversions, such as rumbas, congas, and tangos, which are so popular in the cities and which the radio is spreading everywhere."

Until the early days of the Revolution, Mexican music folklore had been regarded as exotic material which might be treated in the Italian or French manner, but thirty-five years ago Manuel Ponce introduced it as an individual and natural form of art.[4] The years of the Revolution produced much partisan music in the tradition of the *corrido*—a type of romantic folk ballad. Powerful propaganda emerged from *corrido* singing in verses which, for example, extolled and memorialized Zapata and his struggle. "La Cucaracha"—perhaps the most popular revolutionary *corrido*—characterized Carranza, Villa's antagonist, as a "cockroach," to the liveliest and most abandoned of tunes. The *corrido* on Zapata runs thus:

Harken, educated public, to the song about our martyr,
Verses telling you the story of Emiliano Zapata,
Of his taking up of arms, and to fight then like a hero,
To defend the noble cause of Francisco I. Madero.

On the twentieth of November when the war blazed up in terror,
Was Madero in San Luis, and Zapata in his tierra;
And Zapata helped Madero, helped him to achieve a victory,
Feeling that the plans of each contained nothing contradictory.

[4] Mayer-Serra, *Panorama de la música mexicana,* dates the modern phase of Mexican national music from 1912, when Manuel Ponce gave a concert of his compositions which included works purely national in content.

But, no land was being given; "And if now Madero fail us,
We'll fight on," declared Zapata, "we the people of Morelos,
We, the suffering campesinos, who have lived till now in squalor,"
And he thereupon proclaims revolt—the Plan of Villa Ayala.

As with art, the twenties brought increased interest in music folklore, and popular music traditions. Musicologists and paleographers sponsored by the Ministry of Education studied and published indigenous themes, which serious musicians, such as Julián Carrillo, Manuel Ponce, and Carlos Chávez, adapted to their own compositions. Carrillo, a romantic nationalist, gave special attention to revolutionary musical developments of the scale. Ponce, more closely interested in native themes for their own sake, developed Indian dances far beyond the folk level. In "Ferial," a symphonic divertissement which appeared in 1940, Ponce exploited the theme of a typical Mexican fiesta from its beginning at the church door. Except for one old folk tune, however, all the themes were original. Carlos Chávez, probably Mexico's leading composer and orchestra conductor, early essayed a number of musical compositions on scientific themes, culminating in 1931 with a ballet entitled "H. P." (horsepower), which treated of the clash between human and machine values.

Music occupies a prominent place in school curricula. Singing is the chief medium of training, though many schools boast classes in instrumental music, along with fairly well-developed instrumental groups of the more popular type. Rhythm bands, organized especially for purposes of marching, dancing, and military training, are a specialty. As a rule, music is taught by special teachers. In the absence of printed scores, instruction is chiefly by ear and through imitation, but some theory and techniques of music reading are also presented. Courses in music appreciation are available in some city schools through phonograph records. While most schools own a piano, even in remote districts, they usually own little else in the way of musical equipment.

The trend in music teaching follows the rule "every teacher a music teacher." General teacher training in the normal schools now features courses which enable all future teachers to handle music instruction as complementary to their chosen field of work. To that end a special Institute for Musical Preparation has been established in the capital.

The Advanced School of Music is an active, productive institution giving instruction to over eight hundred students. Its staff of some fifty instructors offer courses over a nine-year period leading to certificates of Professor of Instrumental Music, Professor of Singing, and Professor of Composition. As is the case with most schools of music and the arts, admission to and progress in this school is based on individual talent and artistic achievement more than on definitely prescribed regulations.

The National Conservatory of Music *(Conservatorio Nacional de Música)*, founded in 1866, is likewise under the aegis of the Ministry of Education. The leading music school in the country, it enrolls about 1,500 students annually. The conservatory not only gives instruction in all musical and related forms, such as the theater and dancing, but also provides facilities for investigation in all these fields and supervises and administers programs for their general diffusion throughout the nation.

Courses of study in music on the prevocational and vocational levels are limited to young people between the ages of seven and thirteen and comprise introduction to music and music appreciation, choral singing, rhythmic gymnastics, history of music, history of art, musical improvisation, and instrumental music—a choice of piano, violin, cello, flute, saxophone, trumpet, or clarinet. The basic course in music—three years in length and on the vocational school level—is called the "selective course" *(curso selectivo)*. Students receiving a minimum average of 70 percent in this course are permitted to enter professional courses by passing a qualifying examination. Those who have averaged 80 percent or better are exempt from this examination.

For entrance into the vocational and advanced courses, the elementary school certificate is required. In addition, three years of basic training are prerequisite to courses leading to specialized "careers" or "titles." In recent years the following professional courses were offered, with additional years beyond the three-year basic course listed in parentheses: Professor of Elementary Music (1); Professor of Music with Specialty in Choral Singing and

Solfege (2); Piano Accompanist (3); Teacher *(Maestro)* of Music Theory (3); Professor of Instrumental Music (4); Professor of Organ Music (5); Professor of Composition (7); Teacher of Singing (2); Professor of Singing (3).

As a center for elementary and advanced instruction in dancing and the theater, the conservatory also offers three-year courses leading to the title of Professor of Dancing and Professor of the Theater. In dancing the general arrangement of courses is somewhat similar, in that the selective course, here called the "selective school" *(escuela selectiva)*, is also a preliminary for the later professional courses. The program for the selective school differs from its counterpart in the music department, in that the history, technique, and practice of the dance are substituted for similar forms in music.

The theater section of the conservatory, called the School of Theatrical Art, also has a children's course, followed by a selective course and two professional courses leading to the certificates of Professor of Theatrical Art and Professor of Operatic Singing. These three course levels are each three years in length.

Attached to the conservatory are three research academies: the Academy of Popular Music, the Academy of New Musical Forms, and the Academy of History and Bibliography—all functioning as research institutes, in which teachers and advanced students, particularly those in their final year at the conservatory, are expected to participate.

As a practical means of fulfilling one of its prime purposes, that of bringing music and related arts to the masses, the conservatory also trains and supports its own full symphony orchestra and chorus. The concerts of the conservatory, highlighted by annual presentations in Mexico City's sumptuous Theater of Fine Arts *(Palacio de Bellas Artes)*, form a regular and important part of the artistic endeavor of contemporary Mexican culture.

Finally, to co-ordinate and advance the work of related fields of art, President Miguel Alemán, in 1947, founded the National Institute of Fine Arts, the prime objective of which was to judge the aesthetic value of Mexican folklore as it contributes to the enlightenment of the people. In the interpretation of Francisco Larroyo, the Institute is to become the "jealous guardian and permanent judge of what is purely Mexican *(mexicanidad)* throughout the coming generations."

Literary masters have been no less interested in the state of the nation than have the artists and musicians. Mariano Azuela, noted especially for his novel *Los de abajo* (translated as *The Underdogs*), Martín Luis Guzmán, novelist of revolution, Gregorio López y Fuentes, and others have contributed to the literary heritage of the Western Hemisphere as artists grappling with their world and seeking to interpret, perhaps to right—its contradictions and injustices.

Mexican poetry has traditionally tended to remain aloof from national struggles and preferred to contain itself within its own timeless literary sphere. José Luis Martínez dates the beginning of contemporary modes as 1910, when the *Ateneo de la juventud* first protested against the spiritual oppression of the Díaz dictatorship. Under the leadership of Pedro Henríquez Ureña, this group included such contemporary leaders as José Vasconcelos, Alfonso Reyes, and Enrique González Martínez. Traditionally, too, Mexican poetry had been personal, intimate, melancholy. The Revolution, however, changed this subjective mood just as it did a similar feeling on the part of the academic artists. The *Contemporáneos*, a more recent group, enrolling Carlos Pellicer, Gorostiza, Villarrutia, Ortíz de Montellano, and Torres Bodet, have devoted themselves to a rather formal art dedicated to a cultivated minority. The representative periodical, *Taller* (originally *Taller Poético*), published the works of Octavio Paz, whom Martínez considers a major poet of Mexico, if only for the richness of his expression and his genuine lyrical feeling. Closer to the expression of the people themselves is the work of the poets associated with the *Tierra Nueva* (New Land), a periodical founded by Alfonso Reyes. This organ has published the work of Alí Chumacero and Jorge González Durán, who inherited the fugitive Sevillian line of Becquer and Juan Ramón Jiménez. Martínez laments the use of poetry for the promotion of political ideals, but concludes: "A social conscience and a literary career are not incompatible; the only condition for their coexistence—and it is a necessary condition—is respect for the inner nature of each."[5]

It is clear that Mexico's artists in every aesthetic realm have in the past twenty years become increasingly influential in exposing the infirmities of Mexican life. They have provided and are providing spiritual leadership in reconciling aesthetic with ethical values and resolving existing contradictions between human and machine-age values. In the realm of poetry, for example, Jiménez describes his ideal:

For me, the poet of the near future will be a free poet, isolated and clear, with a style which, like that of the four major influences, is personal; of magic but transcendent realism; more sensual than Unamuno; more introspective than Darío; more general than Antonio Machado; not so popular as Lugones; more of an optimist than myself; more simple than Gabriela Mistral; less tense than Guillén; more complete than García Lorca; more sane than Neruda; more of a piece than Alberti. And this poet, crown of the century of modernism, must be born in Spanish America, and on the Pacific side, which is waiting for him.

The Education Ministry's Commission for Intellectual Cooperation *(Comisión Mexicana de Cooperación Intelectual)* unites with the National Autonomous University to contribute new cultural syntheses on an international basis by fostering a program of exchanges of ideas and ideals. Originally the program of the commission concentrated on cultural relations within and among the various states of the Republic, but it has recently extended its services to embrace educational and cultural relations of Mexico with other nations. As such, the commission recommends and arranges for fellowships, scholarships, and study grants. Lecturers, visiting teachers, investigators, and guests of the Mexican Government in cultural fields make contact with the commission and operate under its suggested guidance. In addition to its numerous contributions to Mexican cultural publications, this agency publishes a quarterly entitled *La Cultura en México*, in which contemporary and historical thought are interpreted in the realms of philosophy,

[5] José Luis Martínez, "La poesía mexicana contemporánea," *Revista de Guatemala,* III (first quarter, 1946).

education, science, poetry, music, the theater, the arts, architecture, and social sciences.

In 1942 a group of North Americans and Mexican nationals, in co-operation with the commission, created the Mexican-North American Institute of Cultural Relations *(Instituto Mexicano-Norteamericano de Relaciones Culturales)* to co-ordinate and extend intellectual and cultural relations among the peoples of the Western Hemisphere, especially between the United States and Mexico. At first a private enterprise, the institute in its North American phases is now under the jurisdiction of the Cultural Relations Division of the United States Department of State; it has thus taken on an official international aspect.

The National Autonomous University of Mexico functions as the leading private intercultural center, especially for nations in the Western Hemisphere. Co-operation with such agencies as the Guggenheim, Carnegie, and Rockefeller foundations, and the Institute of International Education results in the promotion of scientific research and the exchange of scholars and teachers. The university has also participated in institutes and discussion panels held in various universities of Latin America and the United States.[6]

Economic leadership in international affairs has been demonstrated by the National University on a number of occasions. During 1943 its School of Economics organized a co-operative lecture series entitled "Economic Problems of the American Hemisphere," in which diplomatic and financial authorities from a number of American nations participated. During the War, economic surveys were conducted by members of the Geological Institute in co-operation with the Mexican Department of Economics and the United States Geological Survey.

The recognition that language differences constitute a major

[6] For example: Boston University, 1943; the Universities of Texas and New Mexico, 1944; the University of Kansas City, 1947. A praiseworthy development of recent years has been the movement of American university groups to Mexico, directly or indirectly in co-operation with the National University and the Mexican Government. In June, 1944, the University of Houston, Texas, conducted a summer session in Mexico City under the sponsorship of both schools. Brito Foucher, "The National Autonomous University of Mexico," in *Mexico's Role in International Intellectual Cooperation.*

barrier among North and South American nations has led to the opening, under university auspices, of English and Spanish language institutes. In 1944 the Spanish Language Institute was created; its chief purpose is to give intensive instruction to teachers of Spanish and Mexican affairs in the United States. The institute's course of study concentrates on three fields: advanced Spanish (five hours weekly of class work and five hours of semi-private tutoring); Mexican literature (seven hours weekly); and Mexican culture (three hours weekly). In 1944 the following topics were treated in the course in Mexican literature: Alarcón, *Las Paredes Oyen*; Inés de la Cruz and Poetry; Fernández de Lizardi, *El Periquillo Sarniento* and *El Pensador Mexicano*; Altamirano, *Aires de México* and *La Navidad en las Montañas*; Gutiérrez Nájera and Modernism; and Castro Leal, *Las Cien Mejores Poesías Mexicanas Modernas.*

Less spectacular, but essential to the promotion of national cultural autonomy, have been the processes whereby literary materials are disseminated to Mexico's scattered people. Within the past twenty-five years, the vital Library Section of the Ministry of Education has expanded the number of libraries from a scant seventy-odd to an impressive total of over five thousand. The Library Section assumes responsibility for the distribution of books, bibliographies, and printed materials to schools, libraries, and other educational agencies. It reaches isolated communities by means of traveling libraries, which employ several trucks and a railroad car. In 1943 this department supervised ninety school libraries with a total of over 800,000 readers.

The leading library in Mexico is, of course, the National Library, located in the capital; its collection amounts to more than one million volumes, dealing mostly with religion, literature, language, and history and including rare manuscripts of Spanish historians of the early sixteenth century. Aside from the library of the Ministry of Education, noted above, others are the Library of Congress, the Library of Social Sciences, the Library of the Hacienda, the Spanish-American Library, the National Museum Library, the Benjamin Franklin Library, supported by North American interests, and the Periodical Library *(Hemeroteca),* opened March 28, 1944. The National Periodical Library, located in the old Church of St. Peter and St. Paul, contains three thousand collections assembled in thirty-one volumes, including many old and rare periodicals. There is space for two hundred readers. It has a distribution agency and a Department of Braille. Unfortunately, Mexican libraries rarely permit books to be circulated. They must be used on the premises.

As music and the arts are supervised by the government, so the supplying of books and the training of librarians have become more and more a government responsibility. In 1944 the President of the Republic authorized an initial budget item of some 200,000 pesos to purchase new library books. Aided by a grant of $35,000 from the Rockefeller Foundation, a four-year course of study was initiated in that year leading to the degree of Master of Library Science and the title "librarian" *(bibliotecario)*. Personnel, facilities, and equipment were provided by the Ministry of Education under technical guidance from the United States.

All this cultural effort would have been of little avail, of course, if attention had been paid only to the literate and to the youth attending school. Adult education received an impetus in the early twenties not only as a means for combatting illiteracy but also as the outgrowth of a national need to train older people for better production in their life work. At the same time, the program was designed to enable people of all ages to participate in general cultural progress. It was properly felt that unless a continued program of education were provided, the future adult would stagnate mentally; he would not progress beyond the habits and standards of living of his indigenous ancestors.

In most communities adult education of considerable variety has been inaugurated in elementary schools, while night secondary schools function in all large cities. Night schools for workers were initiated in the capital in 1937. For a more socialized program of adult education and enlightenment, "cultural centers" *(centros culturales)* were opened in the thirties, along with adult evening schools. At present there are about ten thousand night schools for adults in the Republic.

Parent-teacher associations, fostered by the Ministry and its

Parents' Bureau *(Oficina de Padres de Familia)*, are found in practically all schools. Their orientation is, however, somewhat different from that of their North American counterpart. Many parents are actually students in the school attended by their children; they participate in the school's program of adult education. Parental interest in schools is also likely to assume more concrete forms, such as actual school building, carpentry, and dressmaking. There is less participation by parents in the management of the school and the handling of their children; the Mexican parent, as a rule, takes no part in school administration. He places more confidence in school authorities, and is more interested in learning from them how he may better bring up his children.

Mexico's socialized education has also penetrated the courts of justice, at least with regard to juvenile offenders under eighteen years of age. There are at least two courts in Mexico City which use the social welfare approach. Staffed with a lawyer, a psychiatrist, a doctor, and a teacher appointed by the Department of Social Security *(Prevención Social)*, they aim to assist juvenile delinquents to become socially useful citizens by removing them from a harmful environment and providing for them the proper type of education. Special courts have been created with less strict and less formal procedures than those of the ordinary courts. In localities where a district judge resides, the juvenile court is usually composed of the district judge, a federal health officer or the highest ranking local health officer, and a federal education officer or the highest ranking local education officer.

No aspect of social welfare has been more controversial than the status of women. Recent cultural and industrial demands have brought about the need for their education, where once tradition dictated ignorance. The plight of women a century ago is well brought out by Irma Wilson, who states that the education of women was practically nonexistent at the time of the French intervention: "The only book that the Countess Kollonitz, a lady-in-waiting to the Empress Charlotte, acknowledges having seen in the hands of a lady is a prayer book. She does no handwork, either. She writes letters, but with an unpractised hand." Their ignorance, observes Professor Wilson, was complete. "Europe to them consists of Spain, from whence they sprang; Rome, where the Pope rules; and Paris, from whence come their clothes."

Noticeable changes in attitude were first revealed in the 1880's, when Díaz' ministers of education endeavored to promote the education of women. But it was not until coeducation was legalized under the revolutionary administrations that any general program of female education became feasible.

Up to the advent of the socialist school, it had been the accepted custom to separate the sexes throughout their entire schooling. The socialist government of the 1930's, however, as a matter not only of preferred doctrine but also of compelling economy, advocated coeducation even in the boarding schools. While this policy may have been advisable ideologically and practically, it encountered insurmountable obstacles created by centuries of Spanish and Indian tradition. Public opinion, acting under the slogan "Man the more manly, woman the more womanly," forced President Avila Camacho to acquiesce. In December, 1941, the Chief Executive stated that educating boys and girls together was contrary to national inclination and without laudable results during its trial period. Accordingly, coeducation was officially abrogated, except in elementary schools in small communities. Coeducation below the university level is now legally permitted only in kindergartens.

The segregation of the sexes has naturally led to a demand for more school buildings, thus further complicating Mexico's school building program, though many schools have solved the problem by separating girls from boys as far as possible within the same school plant. While yielding on the matter of segregation, the law nevertheless declares that "the education of boys and girls shall be subjected to the same plans, programs, and methods." The spirit, if not the form, of the original program is therefore reserved. The law recognizes no essential educational differences between the sexes, except in so far as motherhood and special women's trades dictate deviation.

The segregation of the sexes was not only an acknowledgment of the weight of public opinion; it was also an indication to the world that Mexico was building her school system more and more to suit the intrinsic desires and characteristics of her people. Actually, coeducation was abolished over the strong protests of sincere educationalists and others, who felt, for one thing, that the country could not advance its school program efficiently if a dual system had to be supported. García Ruíz, for example, defended coeducation because (1) it represented a gain in the social status of women; (2) the Revolution advocated the equality of the sexes; (3) it reduced sexual abnormality; (4) the school was a working society and had to behave accordingly. There were, however, larger issues at stake, and compromise on this matter helped bring about reforms in social education which otherwise would have been impeded—improvements in sex education and the education of mothers, for example.

Of the comprehensive social and cultural progress evident in extra-school education there is no doubt. In the words of Education Minister Manuel Gual Vidal, the Mexican school is a "social emanation"; its structure and purpose are indissolubly bound to social progress. And all related agencies, acting with the school as a core, contribute under government direction to the enlightenment of Mexicans both with respect to inherited culture and the general progress of the country in all realms.

EDUCATION FOR AN EMERGING CULTURE

Mexico's struggle to educate her population, to better the standards of living of her people, to develop her own manufactures, and to impede the abusive and wasteful extraction of her natural resources, has often taken the appearance of a fight against foreign capital.—Ramón Beteta.

But if our old "gods" are dead, our God is alive. The spirit of Christianity is too deep in our hearts and too dear to our souls to fade away. How are we going to reorganize our beliefs? Protestantism perhaps? Oh, no! The missionaries that go to Mexico might keep this in mind. Mexico as a nation will be Protestant only when the New Englanders have bull-fights every Sunday!—Manuel Barranco, 1932.

Absolute and uncompromising non-intervention—national, collective, individual—in each other's internal affairs must be considered the cornerstone of friendly relations which we are now endeavoring to establish on a lasting basis.—Pablo Martínez del Río.

The dust of battle clears. The conflicting hopes and dreams of the contestants become reconciled in a brighter vision for tomorrow. What remains of Mexico's peculiar educational pattern? What are the gains from her long struggle to overcome a stubborn environment and unite her varied peoples by means of education?

We have witnessed the historic interplay of forces, indigenous and alien, which have brought about the present configuration. The early dawn of spiritual enlightenment which accompanied the first *conquistadores* inevitably faded before the material demands of colonization, leaving later generations to cope with the ensuing maladjustments and to train citizens for a modern world. In the march of Mexico's masses toward their present educational achievement, the years 1810, 1857, 1910, and 1921 are rock-hewn landmarks.

Though professedly democratic, education before 1910 was a luxury reserved for the privileged. There were exceptions, of course, but on the whole, the making of political engineers and intellectual aristocrats constituted the acme of educational achievement. Mexico emerged in the twentieth century with a modicum of industrial and educational productivity, thanks to Diaz' positivism, but there was a deplorable lack of national creativity, and few hands were trained in the new technology. The cry for land and schools which heralded the Revolution expressed the people's faint but firm understanding of the nature of their dilemma. And revolutionary leaders turned this spirit to account in the awakening of a new national political allegiance.

The Constitution of 1917 made sweeping promises and declarations concerning the educational rights of the people, and with the program of President Obrégon, in 1921, the longings of generations seemed at last to be on their way toward fulfillment. As had Juárez generations earlier, the educational planners of the twenties saw that the fundamental need was for elementary education for all Mexicans. A nationwide project was formulated to awaken all classes—white, mestizo, and Indian; rich and poor; *hacendado* and peon—to the powers latent in themselves, their country, and their culture. Revolutionary enthusiasts soon became aware that school buildings alone would not constitute an educa-

tional system. This led to a concentration on all fields related to
public enlightenment and to an extra-school education closer to
the demands of native environment than that given in regular academic courses. Today elementary education has been extended
throughout the Republic. Few communities of any size are without
a school or an educational center. The chief deficiency lies in the
number and availability of properly qualified teachers, though
expanding enrollments in teacher-training institutions attest to
healthy progress.

The years have brought shifts in educational orientation. Previous to 1910 education was based on particularist preferences;
training was channeled along lines of special interest groups. The
control of the state over education, which developed after the
Revolution, has tended more and more to replace these preferences
with unified educational aims and methods. This policy reached
its peak in the socialistic legislation of the twenties and early
thirties, by which the state assumed total responsibility for the
training of youth.

In the last decade government directives have combatted ideological excesses and have adapted themselves to the maturer demands of a nation at work. For instance, it has been more generally
recognized that the native church supplied spiritual values indispensable to the happiness and moral welfare of large segments of
the people. The fight against the church is now recognized as but
one aspect of Mexico's struggle to escape foreign influences, and
the gradual transformation of and *rapprochement* with Mexican
Catholicism has been one of the outcomes of this struggle. Characteristic of this attitude is the recent statement of Manuel Barranco:

We are not irreligious; "gods" are not immortals, but religious spirit is
eternal. The Catholic Church has refused to come up with us into the
modern world and civilization, and we have been left alone. We are now
too grown up to believe in "fairy tales" and this is the method by which
our Church has endeavored hopelessly to keep in our hearts the most beautiful and dearest thing in a soul, faith. Mexico needs a religious readjust-
ment. We need a renaissance in our faith and beliefs.

That this transformation is as yet incomplete and that the Mexican government still has far to go if it wishes total reconciliation with the church is as true today as it was in the thirties. At that time Charles MacFarland observed: "The Government rules out any right of the Church or priest to criticise the government, or any law, or to advocate any law." But considerable progress has been made since the same author chastised both church and state for doing each other injustice, "neither willing to take the other at its best."[7] James Magner, a friend of Catholicism, writes optimistically on conciliatory trends, stating that many churches which had been closed for years are open again:

There is everywhere a desire to clean and restore those which had been abandoned, and everywhere one finds a sentiment of warmth and security in Catholic worship. In Mexico City, the Archbishop takes an active part in social and civic affairs and enjoys the good natured gibes of the journalists and cartoonists who are obviously pleased with his democratic spirit and are glad to count him among the outstanding personalities of the country.

For its part, there is much that the church can do, as Magner continues:

It is of the utmost importance for the future of the Church in Mexico that it enlarge its outlook and activities from devotion and worship to include instruction and social work. The difficulties in the way are enormous. But the fact remains that the Church in Mexico is largely a woman's church. Moreover, the sociological aspects of the Church's mission and the intellectual aspects of faith have been obscured to a considerable extent by an exclusively mystical piety on the one hand and by a fear born of persecution on the other. The failure of the Church in Mexico to grasp the importance of practical moral as well as doctrinal instruction from the pulpit, as a regular program, may also be noted. As a result, the influence of the Church among business and professional men, as well as mong political elements, is comparatively small. Until this chasm has been bridged, the probability of liquidating the old sectarian Liberalism and of revising the anti-Catholic laws will remain remote.[8]

While a certain amount of realism has been brought to bear in the relations of the Mexican government with the church, there has been a strange but characteristic reluctance to exact the nec-

[7] MacFarland, *Chaos in Mexico*, pp. 263-64, 278.
[8] Magner, "Mexico on the Move," *The Commonweal*, XLVII (October 31, 1947), 63-64.

essary wherewithal for the support of education from those in position to provide it. The difficulties encountered by all cultural agencies in promoting education, health, aesthetics, and public improvements are attributable mostly to a lack of material means, traceable, in turn, to an inadequate system of taxation. As long as the artists and educators are victimized by an irrational economy, so long will they find themselves struggling with well-meaning but unattainable programs. The successive imported intellectualisms, from deism to positivism, succeeded in effecting only a superficial solution to Mexico's educational dilemmas because they did not face the economic determinants involved. Ideologies are of little use if separated from the roots of a national economy.

Of late, however, a note of economic realism has been sounded. Mexicans, along with other Latin Americans, have finally realized that economic imbalance cannot be righted until administrators and national leaders develop a statistical mentality capable of assessing the needs of the country and its economic capacity to implement educational and other projects. In other words, Mexico's leaders are becoming aware that educational programs must be based on a realistic appraisal of the economic resources available for their implementation. The ministry realizes that these programs should be based not merely on wishful thinking but on the understanding that Mexico's wealth and resources, both private and public, will have to be drawn on more and more to provide the necessary revenue.

But why should Americans be interested in Mexico's educational welfare? What profit may be derived from the study of a system born of a different culture? Mexican education is important because it fosters human values within the framework of all the educational endeavors that are operative in the Western Hemisphere. If for no other reason than that Mexico and the United States are contiguous, Mexico's educational successes and failures are significant; they cannot be limited to the boundaries of that nation, but will bring educational hope or despair to all the Americas. The differences between cultures which lead to different educational ideologies are not inimical to interhemispheric understanding. Indeed, Mexico's peculiar cultural heritage—her artistic, scientific, technical, literary, educational, and spiritual individuality—can be profitable for all and can enrich the cultures of other nations. History and geography have decreed that Mexico and the United States must live side by side; between the two there can be no isolation of knowledge or of ignorance; no quarantine of beauty or of ugliness. As the philosopher Rodó teaches, the two eagles of North and South America have much to learn from each other, not by "unilateral imitation but by the reciprocity of influences and by a combined understanding of those attributes on which the glory of both nations is founded." In other words, international enlightenment is not likely to prosper if communications are routed in only one direction. Rare indeed is the educator who fails to capture a new idea when he is abroad.

This volume has shown that as a result of education, mutually demanded and received by Mexico's government and her peoples, an indigenous, heterogeneous culture, once conquered, repressed, and rejected, finally has asserted itself, and the result is Mexico's present educational status. Like waves which with the incoming tide gather power, thrust forth, dash upon the rocks, and recede, only to gather more power, Mexico's masses have surged ahead to prevail over those who would deny them cultural strength.

Assessing the more tangible results of this development in the specific field of education and the schools, the North American investigator emerges with the following observations.

1. Mexican education is striving to reach the masses and endeavoring to establish cultural norms on a basis of education for Mexican citizenship.

2. The trend is toward learnings designed to render the student a more contented, self-provident individual.

3. Trades and technical training for Mexico's growing industrialization are receiving closer attention, along with new forms of agricultural education and training in the arts.

4. The school-building program is being concentrated chiefly on the erection of elementary schools, so that within the shortest time possible all children may receive at least an elementary school education.

5. The co-ordination and standardization of school procedures, aims, and accomplishments are enhancing the prestige of the public school in comparison with the private school.

6. Curricular changes show a slight tendency to substitute highly varied and formalized subject matter for activity more closely related to Mexican life and some amount of subject matter integration has been effected; but in general compartmentalization of subject matter persists.

7. Within the classroom formalized procedures are slowly giving way to pupil self-expression and participation, but large classes especially perpetuate the traditional teacher-dominated relationships.

8. In answer to a lamentable deficiency of classroom materials, a program for a more adequate distribution of textbooks and school reference materials has recently been inaugurated by standardizing minimum requirements on the basis of increased production, decreased cost.

9. Mexico's education with respect to school attendance, school construction, increased financial and material allotments, shows constant progress.

On the other hand, deficiencies still exist:

1. The relation of pupil to teacher tends to be distant and marred by lack of interest. Student guidance and personal counseling are casual, not an integral part of the school program.

2. There is a tendency on the part of many school administrators to look to the Ministry of Education for services and equipment beyond the resources of the ministry to provide. The ministry is too readily blamed for shortcomings and deficiencies by school administrators, whereas individual initiative and resourcefulness are what is needed.

3. A premium is still placed on artificial forms of competition and competitive types of learning at the expense of co-operative effort.

4. There is a tendency for school officials to be distrustful of students, as evidenced by the ubiquitous lock and key. Instead of accepting this situation as irremediable, authorities should encourage training in school loyalty, respect for property, and mutual trustfulness between teacher and pupil.

5. From the investigator's point of view the lack of adequate and sufficient statistics is deplorable, and there is little orderliness in statistical presentation. The failure of statistics to tally and the wide-open gaps in what is officially supposed to be comprehensive and detailed information render accurate deductions a practical impossibility.

6. There is also need for better planned and more efficient procedures, co-ordinated methods throughout all the administrative staffs of the ministry, and general simplification of the present overinvolved and uneconomical organization.

The rest of the story of Mexican education is a story of personalities. The Mexican school system is a highly vital human institution, constructed and kept going at great personal sacrifice. Many an absorbing saga could be told of individual effort, personal devotion, and unselfish group participation in founding and establishing Mexican schools. In countless communities civic-minded citizens have not waited for government subsidies; the local shoe-maker, carpenter, lawyer, physician have banded together not only to build a school but to teach in it as well. While some doubts as to the advisability of such an educational procedure might be raised, nevertheless it exemplifies the typical Mexican attitude—willingness to contribute to popular enlightenment without thought of personal reward.

Today there is throughout Mexico a desire to establish an educational system that will reflect the Mexican way and also compare favorably with that of the most advanced nation. When on the main-traveled highways the visitor to Mexico discerns new buildings prominently labeled "Escuela," let him not judge, as some do, that they are designed merely to impress foreigners. Schools also exist where the traveler is not so likely to journey. They are founded on real and basic aspirations. The education of Mexicans is a matter of sincere and sacred concern to Mexico's national leaders. It is unmistakable that the school is paramount and supreme in Mexican life today.

Bibliography

In 1941 the Mexican Ministry of Education suspended the annual publication of its *Memorias* and substituted a plan for their publication as a unit every six years to correspond with the six-year presidential term of office. The first volume appeared in 1947 and covered education during the administration of President Avila Camacho, 1940-46. Meantime, the various departments of the ministry have been required to submit typewritten reports annually. These reports, now on file in the ministry's Office of Statistics, were made available to the author, and permission was granted to have most of them copied for later use in this country. These manuscripts form the bulk of primary source material used in Chapters IV-VII.

Mexicans customarily use the surnames of both father and mother. For example, Manuel Avila Camacho bears his father's name, Avila, and his mother's, Camacho. He is therefore listed here under Avila, not under Camacho. Jaime Torres Bodet in similar fashion is listed under Torres, not Bodet.

PRIMARY SOURCE MATERIALS

(Unless otherwise indicated, place of publication or source is México, D. F.)

Chapingo, Escuela Nacional de Agricultura, "Requisitos." MS, June, 1944.

Escuela Normal de Educación Física, "Plan de estudios del año escolar, 1944." MS, 1944.

Escuela Normal Superior, "Planes de estudios." MS, June, 1944.

Escuela Prevocacional Nr. 3, "Horario de labores." MS, 1944.

Guadalajara, Universidad de, Anales, 1942. "Plan de estudios en vigor en las escuelas preparatorias de Jalisco y preparatoria nocturna, 1942-43." MS, 1943.

Instituto Politécnico Nacional, "Disposiciones reglamentarias para las escuelas." MS, 1944.

Jalisco, Estado de, Ley orgánica de los servicios culturales del estado de Jalisco. Guadalajara, 1940.

Monterrey, N. L., Instituto Tecnológico y de Estudios Superiores, Escuela de Estudios Contables, 1943-44. 1944.

Secretaría de la Defensa Nacional, Colegio Militar, Instructivo de admisión, 1944.

—— "Plan de estudios para la carrera de ingeniero constructor." MS, 1944.

—— "Plan de estudios para la carrera de ingeniero industrial." MS, 1944.

—— "Planes de estudios del curso de caballería, infantería y artillería." MS, 1944.

Secretaría de la Economía Nacional, Compendio estadístico, 1940.
—— Atlas estadístico. 1934.
Secretaría de Educación Pública. The following manuscripts:
"Datos estadísticos," 1943.
"Enseñanza normalista," 1943.
"Escuelas normales en el país," 1943.
"Escuelas normales rurales, sus orígenes y evolución," 1943.
"Estadística escolar—escuelas primarias en el D. F.," 1943.
"Formación del profesorado técnico," 1943.
"Guía para la interpretación y desarrollo de los programas de geografía," 1943.
"Orientaciones didácticas; la base del trabajo en escuela rural," 1943.
"Plan de estudios de las escuelas secundarias federales," 1944.
"Plan de estudios para la carrera de profesor normalista urbana y rural," 1943.
"Planes de estudios de la enseñanza agricola," 1943.
"Presupuestos de la educación en México, 1935-1943," 1943.
"Programa de cultura cívica," 1944.
"Programa de la historia de México," 1944.
"Programa minimo de los jardines de niños," 1944.
"Programas de dibujo," 1942.
"Programas del curso de historia universal para el primer grado de segunda enseñanza," 1943.
"Programas de matemáticas," 1943.
"Programas de segunda enseñanza, 1942-43," 1943.
"Puede considerarse la escuela rural como el eje de las comunidades campesinas," 1943.
"Resumen de los informes de la labor realizada por las distintas dependencias durante el período de 1941 a 1943 y planes de trabajo para 1943-44." 1943.
"Supresión de la coeducación," 1944.
Secretaría de Educación Pública. Comisión Mexicana de Cooperación Intelectual, Organización y trabajo. 1937.
—— Educación pública en México, La, 1934-40, 3 vols. 1941.
—— Escuela Madero, La. 1943.
—— Estudio acerca de la educación fundamental en México, 1947.
—— Instituto federal de capacitación del magisterio. Reglamento de la escuela rural (Dirección de Enseñanza Superior). 1946.
——Instituto Nacional de Pedagogía, Servicio de Orientación Profesional. Posibilidades educativas (para los alumnos que terminan su instrucción primaria). 1941.
—— Juegos deportivos nacionales, Los. 1941.
—— Ley orgánica de la educación pública. 1942.
—— Obra educativa en el sexenio 1940-46. 1947.

Secretaría de Educación Pública. Primeros anales del Conservatorio Nacional de Música, 1941.

—— Programas para las escuelas primarias de República Mexicana. 1944.

Secretaría de Gobernación, Comite Ejecutivo Nacional. Plan sexenal del Partido Nacional Revolucionario. 1935.

—— Segundo plan sexenal, 1941-46. 1941.

—— Seis años de gobierno al servicio de México, 1934-40. 1940.

United States Tariff Commission, Economic Controls and Commercial Policy in Mexico. Washington, D. C., Gov't Print. Off., 1946.

Universidad, Femenina de México, "Planes de estudios para el curso de 1944." MS, 1944.

Universidad Nacional Autónoma de México, Biblioteca Nacional, Inauguración del nuevo local del Departamento de Hemeroteca. 1943.

Universidad Nacional Autónoma de México, Calendario escolar para el año de 1948.

—— Ley constitutiva, leyes orgánicas y estatuto. 1945.

—— Planes de estudios aprobados por el H. Consejo Universitario para los bachilleratos de ciencias y letras en cinco años. 1943.

—— Reglamento que crea la posición de profesor universitario de carrera. 1944.

—— Summer School Catalogue. 1945.

Universidad Nacional Autónoma de México, Escuela Nacional de Antropología, Anuario, 1944.

Universidad Nacional Autónoma de México, Escuela Nacional de Ciencias Químicas, Anuario, 1940. 1945.

Universidad Nacional Autónoma de México, Escuela Nacional Preparatoria, Anuario, 1940.

—— "Plan de estudios." MS, 1946.

Universidad Nacional Autónoma de México, Facultad de Ciencias, Anuario, 1943.

Universidad Nacional Autónoma de México, Facultad de Filosofía y Letras, Catedras que se impartarán en el año de 1944.

—— Historia, constitución, guía del estudiante, 1944.

Universidad Nacional Autónoma de México, Facultad de Medicina, Anuario, 1945. 1947.

Universidad Nacional Autónoma de México, Instituto de la Lengua Española, "Curso intensivo expecial para profesores norteamericanos de Español." MS, 1944.

Universidad Obrera de México, Programa para 1944. 1945.

GENERAL SOURCE MATERIALS

Alba, Pedro de, Del nuevo humanismo y otros ensayos. Mexico City, 1937.

Alemán, Miguel, Address. The University of Kansas City, May 7, 1947. Mimeographed.

Angel Ceniceros, José, El valor democrático de la enseñanza secundaria. Mexico City, 1944.

Apstein, Theodore, The Universities of Mexico. Washington, D. C., Pan-American Union, 1946.

Avila Camacho, Manuel, A la juventud de América. Mexico City, 1943.

—— Ideario. Mexico City, 1943.

—— Speeches. Mexico City, Secretaría de Gobernación, 1941-46.

Avila Garibay, José, La Escuela Francisco I. Madero y la educación mexicana. Mexico City, 1945.

Azuela, Mariano, Los de abajo. Madrid, Espasa-Calpe, 1930.

Bach, Federico, "The Distribution of Wealth in Mexico," *Annals of the American Academy of Political and Social Sciences* (Philadelphia), CCVIII (March, 1940), 70-77.

Barranco, Manuel, "Mexico," in *Educational Yearbook*, New York, Teachers College, Columbia University, 1932.

—— Mexico: Its Educational Problems. New York, Teachers College, Columbia University, 1915. Teachers College Contributions to Education, 73.

Barreda, Gabino, Estudios. Mexico City, 1941.

Basauri, Carlos, La población indígena de México. 3 vols. Mexico City, Ministry of Education, 1940.

—— "La población negroide mexicana," *Estadística* (Mexico City), December, 1943.

Beals, Carleton, Mexican Maze. Philadelphia, Lippincott, 1931.

Benjamin, Harold, "Education in Mexico's Six-Year Plan," *School and Society*, XI (November 17, 1934), 666-68.

Betancourt Pérez, Antonio, Interrogatorio al C. Lic. Octavio Véjar Vázquez. Mexico City, 1942.

Beteta, Ramón, "Mexico's Foreign Relations," *Annals of the American Academy of Political and Social Sciences* (Philadelphia), CCVIII (March, 1940), 170-80.

Blair, Evelyn, Educational Movements in Mexico, 1821-1836. Austin, University of Texas, 1941.

Blasio, José Luis, Maximilian, Emperor of Mexico; tr. by R. H. Murray. New Haven, Yale University Press, 1934.

Bonilla y Segura, Guillermo, Report on the Cultural Missions of Mexico. Washington, D. C., Gov't Print. Off., 1945. U. S. Office of Education, Bulletin 1945, II.

Booth, George C., Mexico's School-Made Society. Palo Alto, Calif., Stanford University Press, 1941.

Brenner, Anita, Idols behind Altars. New York, Harcourt, 1929.

—— Mexican Holiday. New York, Putnam, 1941.

—— The Wind That Swept Mexico. New York, Harper, 1943.

Brito Foucher, Rodulfo, "The National Autonomous University of Mexico," in Mexico's Role in International Intellectual Cooperation (Albuquerque, University of New Mexico, 1945).

Brubacher, John S., A History of the Problems of Education. New York, McGraw-Hill, 1947.

Burbank, Addison, Mexican Frieze. New York, Cowan McCann, 1940.

Bustamente, Miguel, "Public Health and Medical Care," *Annals of the American Academy of Political and Social Sciences* (Philadelphia), CCVIII (March, 1940), 153-61.

Callcott, Wilfred Hardy, The History of Liberalism in Mexico. Durham, Duke University Press, 1926.

Caso, Alfonso, "The Indigenous Cultures of Central America," in Mexico's Role in International Intellectual Cooperation (Albuquerque, University of New Mexico, 1945).

—— "Richest Archeological Find in America," *National Geographic Magazine*, LXII (October, 1932), 487-512.

—— "What Has the American Indian Contributed to World Economy?" *Butrava* (Newton, Mass.), VI (February, 1942).

Caso, Antonio, Discursos a la Nación Mexicana. Mexico City, 1922.

Castillo, Arturo César, One Thousand Years of Murals in Mexico. Mexico City, Pemex Travel Club, 1945.

Céspedes, Francisco S., Education in the Latin American Countries, *Nineteenth Educational Yearbook of the International Institute*. New York, Teachers College, Columbia University, 1942.

—— Educational Trends in Latin America. New York, Bulletin No. 3, Division of Intellectual Cooperation, Pan-American Union. Washington, D. C., 1942.

Chandos, Dane, Village in the Sun. New York, Putnam, 1945.

Charlot, Jean, Art from the Mayans to Disney. New York and London, Sheed and Ward, 1939.

Chase, Stuart, Mexico; a Study of Two Americas. New York, Macmillan, 1931.

Chávez, Ezequiel A., "La educación nacional," in México; su evolución social. Mexico City, 1900.

—— Las cuatro grandes crisis de la educación de México a través de los siglos. Mexico City, 1942.

Chávez, Ignacio, México en la cultura médica. Mexico City, Colegio Nacional, 1947.

Ciro, César Gallardo, El maestro rural. Mexico City, 1945.

Clark, Sydney A., Mexico—Magnetic Southland. New York, Dodd, 1944.

Cook, Katherine M., The House of the People. Washington, D. C., U. S. Office of Education Bulletin, 1932, No. 11.

Covarrubias, Miguel, Mexico South: the Isthmus of Tehuantepec. New York, Knopf, 1946.

Diamant, Gertrude, The Days of Ofelia. Boston, Houghton, 1942.

Díaz del Castillo, Bernal, A True History of the Conquest of Mexico. New York, 1938.

Dossick, John Jesse, "Education among the Ancient Aztecs," MS, Cambridge, Harvard University, 1941.

Downing, Todd, The Mexican Earth. New York, Doubleday, 1940.

Ebaugh, Cameron Duncan, "Mexico Studies Sex Education," *Social Forces*, XV, (October, 1936), 81-83.

—— The National System of Education in Mexico. Baltimore, Johns Hopkins Press, 1931.

Fabela, Isidro, "Address to the Youth of Mexico," *Excelsior*, May 1, 1944.

Gallardo, Ciro César, El maestro rural en México. Mexico City, Ministry of Education, 1945.

Galván, Rafael Ramos, El problema alimenticio en México. Montevideo, 1943. *Boletín del Instituto Internacional Americano de Protección a la Infancia*, July 18, 1950.

Gamio, Manuel, "Geographic and Social Handicaps," *Annals of the American Academy of Political and Social Sciences* (Philadelphia), CCVIII (March, 1940), 1-11.

—— Hacia un Mexico nuevo. Mexico City, 1935.

Gamio, Manuel and José Vasconcelos, Aspects of Mexican Civilization. Chicago, University of Chicago Press, 1926.

García, Arnuldo N., and Rolando Uribe, La escuela social; foreword by Rafael Ramírez. Orizaba and Veracruz, 1934.

García Icazbalceta, Joaquín, Don Fray de Zumárraga. Mexico City, Porrua, 1947.

García Maynez, Eduardo, Antonio Caso. Mexico City, Ministry of Education, 1943.

García Ruíz, Ramón "Coeducation in Mexico," *World Education*, July, 1944, pp. 352-54.

—— Agenda del supervisor escolar. Mexico City, 1943.

—— Principios y técnica de la supervisión escolar. Mexico City, 1943.

Gardner, Helen, Art through the Ages. New York, Harcourt, 1936.

Gática, Crisólogo, and José Carrillo, La educación normal en la postguerra. Mexico City, Confederation of Teachers, 1946.

Gerwin, Herbert, These Are the Mexicans. New York, Reynal and Hitchcock, 1947.

Gessler, Clifford, Patterns of Mexico. New York, Appleton-Century, 1941.

Goertz, Arthemis, South of the Border. New York, Macmillan, 1940.

González Garza, Federico, El problema fundamental de México. Mexico City, Ministry of Education, 1943.

González, Jiménez, Epifanio, La verdad de España en América. Madrid, Talleres Perman, 1946.

González Peña, Carlos, History of Mexican Literature. Dallas, Southern Methodist University Press, 1945.

Goodspeed, Bernice, Mexican Tales. Mexico City, American Book and Printing Co., 1946.

—— Paracutín. Mexico City, American Book and Printing Co., 1945.

Green, Otis H., and Irving A. Leonard, "On the Mexican Booktrade in 1600," *Hispanic Review*, IX (January 1, 1941), 1.

Griffin, Charles C., ed., Concerning Latin American Culture. New York, Columbia University Press, 1941.

Gruening, Ernest, Mexico and Its Heritage. New York, Appleton-Century, 1928.

Gual Vidal, Manuel, Diez discursos sobre educación. Mexico City, Ministry of Education, 1947.

Gunther, John, Inside Latin America. New York, Harper, 1941.

Hagen, Victor W. von, Maya Explorer. Norman, University of Oklahoma Press, 1947.

Hanke, Lewis, The First Social Experiment in America. Cambridge, Mass., Harvard University Press, 1935.

Haring, C. H., The Spanish Empire in America. New York, Oxford University Press, 1947.

Herring, Hubert C., "Education in Mexico," in Twenty-sixth Annual Schoolmen's Week Proceedings (Philadelphia, University of Pennsylvania, School of Education), March, 1939.

—— Good neighbors. New Haven, Yale University Press, 1941.

—— Mexico: the Making of a Nation. New York, Foreign Policy Association Inc., 1942.

Herring, Hubert C., and Herbert Weinstock, Renascent Mexico. New York, Covici, 1935.

Hidalgo, Monroy, Luis, "Formación del profesorado en los Estados Unidos de México," *Educación Nacional* (Mexico City), II (July, 1944), 6, 48-51.

Hobart, Alice, The Peacock Sheds His Tail. Garden City, N. Y., Sundial Press, 1946.

Holmes, Olive, Latin America: Land of Golden Legend. New York, 1947. Headline Series, Foreign Policy Association, No. 65, September-October, 1947.

Humboldt, Baron de, Selections from the Works of, ed. by John Taylor. London, Longmans, 1824.

Icazbalceta, J. G., Don Fray Juan de Zumárraga. Mexico City, Porrua, 1947.

Jackson, J. H., Mexican Interlude. New York, Macmillan, 1938.

Jacobsen, Jerome v., Educational Foundations of the Jesuits in Sixteenth Century New Spain. Berkeley, University of California Press, 1938.

James, Concha Romero, "Spanish American Literature and Art," in C. C. Griffin, ed., Concerning Latin America Culture (New York, Columbia University Press, 1941).

James, Neill, Dust on My Heart. New York, Scribner, 1946.

Jones, Chester Lloyd, "The Production of Wealth in Mexico," *Annals of the American Academy of Political and Social Sciences* (Philadelphia), CCVIII (March, 1940), 55-69.

Joyce, T. A., Mexican Archeology. New York, Oxford University Press, 1934.

Kelley, Francis Clement, Blood-drenched Altars. Milwaukee, Bruce, 1935.

Kimelman, Juan, "Algunos problemas de educación y enseñanza estadística," *Estadística* (Mexico City), September, 1943.

Knight, Mabel F. "Farming Looks Up in Mexico," *Christian Science Monitor*, January 19, 1946.

La Farge, Oliver, "Scientists Are Lonely Men," in A Treasure of Science, ed. by Harlow Shapley and others. New York, Harper, 1943.

Lanning, John Tate, Academic Culture in the Spanish Colonies. New York, Oxford University Press, 1940.

Lanning, John Tate, and others, Reales cédulas de la Real y Pontificia universidad. Mexico City, 1946.

Lansing, Marion, Liberators and Heroes of Mexico and Central America. Boston, Page, 1941.

Lanz Duret, Miguel, Derecho constitucional mexicano. Mexico City, 1936.

Larrea, Julio, "Spirit, Trends and Problems in Latin American Education," *Nueva Era* (Mexico City), December, 1943.

Larroyo, Francisco, Cuadros de la historia de la pedagogía. Mexico City, 1943.

—— Historia comparada de la educación en México. Mexico City, Porrua, 1947.

Lawrence, D. H. The Plumed Serpent. London, Secker, 1926.

Lea, Henry Charles, The Inquisition in the Spanish Dependencies. New York, Macmillan, 1908.

Leal, Miguel, "The Need for Special Studies," *Nueva Era* (Mexico City, 1944), p. 168.

Leonard, Irving A., Romances of Chivalry in the Spanish Indies. Berkeley, University of California Press, 1933.

López y Fuentes, Gregorio, El Indio. Mexico City, Botas, 1935.

Lummis, Charles, The Spanish Pioneers. Chicago, McClurg, 1893.

MacFarland, Charles S., Chaos in Mexico. New York, Harper, 1935.

Magdaleno, Mauricio, El respandor. Mexico City, Botas, 1937.

Magner, James A., Men of Mexico. Milwaukee, Bruce, 1943.

Magner, James A., "Mexico on the Move," *The Commonweal*, XLVII (October 31, 1947), 62-64.

Manrique de Lara, Juana, Manual de bibliotecario. Mexico City, 1942.

Martínez, José Luis, "La poesía mexicana contemporánea," *Revista de Guatemala*, III (1st quarter, 1946), 63-78.

Martínez D., Guillermo, "Fracaso universitario," *Excelsior*, August 7, 1943.

Martínez del Río, Pablo, "Mexican-American Relations," in Ortega, J., ed., Mexico's Role in International Intellectual Cooperation (Albuquerque, University of New Mexico Press, 1945).

Mayagoitia, David, Ambiente filosófico de la Nueva España. Mexico City, 1947.

Mayer-Serra, Otto, Panorama de la música mexicana. Mexico City, El Colegio de México, 1941.

Mecham, J. Lloyd, "Mexican Federalism—Fact or Fiction," *Annals of the American Academy of Political and Social Sciences* (Philadelphia), CCVIII (March, 1940), 23-28.

Mendieta y Núñez, Lucio, "The Balance of Agrarian Reform," *Annals of the American Academy of Political and Social Sciences* (Philadelphia), CCVIII (March, 1940), 121-31.

Millan, Verna C., Mexico Reborn. Boston, Houghton, 1939.

Miller, Max, Mexico around Me. New York, Reynal and Hitchcock, 1937.

Miñano García, Max N., La Educación rural en México. Mexico City, 1945.

Moreno y García, Roberto, Desarrollo y orientaciones de la educación superior. Mexico City, Secretaría de Educación Pública, 1945.

Morley, Sylvanus G., The Ancient Maya. Palo Alto, Stanford University Press, 1946.

Navas Macedonio, Historia de América. Mexico City, 1944. Textbook for the 5th grade in Mexican schools.

Northrop, F. S. C., The Meeting of East and West. New York, Macmillan, 1946.

O'Gorman, Edmundo, Fundamentos de la historia de la América. Mexico City, Imprenta Universitaria, 1942.

Olave, Francisco, "The Instituto Politécnico Nacional—Its Cultural and Social Function," in A Brief Survey of the Federal System of Public Education in Mexico. Mexico City, 1942.

Ortega, J., ed., Mexico's Role in International Intellectual Cooperation. School of Inter-American Affairs, Albuquerque, University of New Mexico, 1945.

Padilla, Ezequiel, Memoria que indica el estado que guarda el ramo de educación pública. Mexico City, Ministry of Education, 1929.

Palacios, Manuel R., "El significado de la educación socialista," *Progressive Education*, XII (February, 1936), 21.

Parkes, Henry B., A History of Mexico. Boston, Houghton, 1938.

Parsons, M. C., Mitla, Town of Souls. Chicago, University of Chicago Press, 1936.

Parsons, Wilfred, Mexican Martyrdom. New York, Macmillan, 1936.

Pereyra, Carlos, Historia de la América española. Madrid, Editorial Saturnino Calleja, 1920-26. 8 vols.

Plaza y Jaén, Cristóbal Bernardo de la, Crónica de la Real y Pontificia Universidad. Mexico City, Rangel, 1931.

Plenn, J. H., Mexico Marches. New York, Bobbs, 1939.

Prescott, W. H., History of the Conquest of Mexico. New York, Collier, 1902.

Prewett, Virginia, Report on Mexico. New York, Dutton, 1941.

Puig Casauranc, José M., Mirando la vida. Mexico City, 1933.

Ramírez, Rafael, La enseñanza por la acción dentro de la escuela rural. Mexico City, 1942.

—— "Mexico," in Nineteenth Educational Yearbook and The International Institute of Teachers College, Columbia University, New York, 1942.

Ramos, Samuel, El perfil del hombre y la cultura mexicana. Mexico City, 1938.

Redfield, Robert, "The Material Culture of Spanish-Indian Mexico," *American Anthropologist*, XXXI (October, 1929), 602-18.

—— The Folk Culture of Yucatán. Chicago, University of Chicago Press, 1941.

—— "The Indian in Mexico," in *Annals of the American Academy of Political and Social Sciences* (Philadelphia), CCVIII (March, 1940), 132-43.

Reyes, Victor M., Pedagogía del dibujo: teoría y práctica en la escuela primaria. Mexico City, 1943.

Ricard, Robert, La "conquête spirituelle" du Mexique. Paris, Institute of Ethnology, 1933.

Ríos, Fernando de los, "Action of Spain in America," in Griffin, C. C., ed., Concerning Latin American Culture, New York, Columbia University Press, 1941.

Robles, Antonio, De la cultura infantil. Mexico City, 1942.

Roeder, Ralph, Juárez and His Mexico. New York, Viking, 1947.

Romero de Terreros, Manuel, La Universidad de México en 1800. Mexico City, Instituto de Investigaciones Estéticas, 1947.

Romero James, Concha, see James, Concha Romero.

Sahagún, Bernadino de, History of Ancient Mexico. Nashville, Fisk University Press, 1932.

Salazar, Juan B., Bases of the Socialist Secondard School. Mexico City, 1936.

Salazar, Mallén Rubén, El secretario de educación pública en la camara de diputados. Mexico City, 1943.

Sánchez, George I., "Education," *Annals of the American Academy of Political and Social Sciences* (Philadelphia), CCVIII (March, 1940), 144-52.

—— The Development of Higher Education in Mexico. King's Crown Press, New York, 1944.

—— "The Problem of Education in Mexico," *Educational Forum*, VII (May, 1943), 321-27.

—— Mexico; a Revolution by Education. New York, Viking, 1936.

Sánchez Mejorada, Javier, "Communications and Transportation," *Annals of the American Academy of Political and Social Sciences* (Philadelphia), CCVIII (March, 1940), 78-93.

Sánchez Pontón, Luis, Hacia la escuela socialista. Mexico City, 1935.

Sanford, Trent E., The Story of Architecture in Mexico. New York, Norton, 1947.

Sapia M., Raúl, Mexico. Mexico City, Secretaría de Gobernación, 1942.

Schmeckebier, Laurence E., Modern Mexican Art. Minneapolis, University of Minnesota Press, 1939.

Senior, Clarence, Mexico in Transition. New York, League for Industrial Democracy Series, VI, No. 9, 1939.

Simpson, Eyler, The ejido; Mexico's Way Out. Chapel Hill, University of North Carolina, 1937.

Simpson, Lesley Byrd, Many Mexicos. New York, Putnam's, 1941.

Slonimsky, Nicolas, Music of Latin America. New York, Crowell, 1945.

Smith, Henry Lester, Education in Mexico. Bloomington, School of Education, Indiana University, July, 1942.

Solís Quiroga, Roberto, El debil mental; cartilla para los médicos escolares. Mexico City, Secretaría de Educación Pública, 1942.

Spinden, Hubert J., Ancient Civilizations of Middle and Central America. New York, 1928.

Steck, Francis Borgia, Education in Spanish North America during the Sixteenth Century. Washington, D. C., National Catholic Welfare Conference, 1943.

Strode, Hudson, Timeless Mexico. New York, Harcourt, 1944.

—— Now Is Mexico, New York, Harcourt, 1947.

Thompson, John Eric, The Civilization of the Mayas. Chicago, Field Museum of National History, Anthropology Leaflet 25, 1932.

Tirado Benedí, Domingo, Bases para una técnica de la educación. Mexico City, Secretaría de Educación Pública, 1944.

—— "Panorama educativo de México," *Nueva Era*, 1944.

Tirado Benedí, Domingo, Psicotécnica de la educación pública. Mexico City, 1946.

Toor, Francis, Guide to Mexico. New York, McBride, 1945.

—— Mexican Popular Arts. Mexico City, Toor Studios, 1939.

—— New Guide to Mexico. Mexico City, Toor Studios, 1944.

Toro, Alfonso, Compendio de la historia de México. Mexico City, 1933.

Torres Bodet, Jaime, Educación mexicana. Mexico City, Ministry of Education, 1944.

—— La escuela mexicana: discursos, documentos y entrevistas. Mexico City, Ministry of Education, 1944.

—— "Relations between Mexico and the United States," in Mexico's Role in International Intellectual Cooperation. Albuquerque (University of New Mexico, 1945).

Toussaint, Manuel, "Mexico Today: Thought and Expression," in *Annals of the American Academy of Political and Social Sciences* (Philadelphia), CCVIII (March, 1940), 162-69.

Ugarte, Jose Bravo, Historia de México. Mexico City, 1946.

Vaillant, George C., The Aztecs of Mexico. New York, Doubleday, 1941.

Vasconcelos, José, Historia del pensamiento filosófico. Mexico City, Universidad Nacional de México, 1937.

Vasconcelos, José, and Manuel Gamio, Aspects of Mexican Civilization. Chicago, University of Chicago Press, 1926.

Véjar Vázquez, Octavio, Carta a la madre y al maestro. Mexico City, Ministry of Education, 1942.

—— Hacia una escuela de unidad nacional. Mexico City, Ministry of Education, 1944.

—— Mensaje a la nación mexicana. Mexico City, Ministry of Education, 1942.

—— Orientaciones para una escuela del porvenir. Mexico City, Ministry of Education, 1943.

Vera, María, Luisa, "Mexico," in Educational Yearbook (New York, Teachers College, Columbia University, 1940.

Vera Estañol, Jorge, "Education," in Essays on the Reconstruction of Mexico, New York, 1920.

Villagrán Prado, Francisco, "The Importance of the Study of English and Spanish," in Mexico's Role in International Intellectual Cooperation. Albuquerque, University of Mexico, 1945.

Watson, Goodwin B., Education and Social Welfare in Mexico. New York, Council Pan-American Democracy, 1940.

Webb, James Henry, "A Study of Certain Social and Nationalistic Attitudes as Revealed in a Group of Mexican Textbooks." Master's thesis, MS, George Washington University, 1943.

Whitaker, Arthur P., ed., Latin America and Enlightenment. New York, Appleton, 1942.

Wilcox, Marian, article in the Americana (New York, 1941), XI, 691-92.

Williams, Ronald I., "Art in Mexico." MS, New York University, School of Education, 1941.

Wilson, Irma, Mexico: a Century of Educational Thought. New York, Hispanic Institute of the United States, 1941.

Wolfe, Bertram, Diego Rivera; His Life and Time. New York, Knopf, 1937.

Zavala, Silvio, "Síntesis de la historia del pueblo mexicano," in *Mexico y la Cultura* (Mexico City, 1945).

Zollinger, Edwin, Enrique Rébsamen. Mexico City, 1935.

Zubirán, Salvador, *Ideario, realizaciones y projectos*. Mexico City, Imprenta Universitaria, 1948.

SELECTED NEWSPAPERS AND PERIODICALS

Annals of the American Academy of Political and Social Sciences (The), (Philadelphia), CCVIII and CCIX (March, 1940, and May, 1940).

Departamento de Salubridad Pública, *Boletín*. Mexico City, April, 1943.

Estadística, journal of the Inter-American Statistical Institute, Mexico City, December, 1943.

Excelsior; Mexico City daily.

Monterrey, N. L., Consejo de Cultura Superior, *Universidad*. September, 1943.

Nacional, El; Mexico City daily.

Nueva Era; revista interamericana de cultura (Mexico City), XIII, 1944.

Revista de América (Bogotá), March, 1946.

Revista nacional de cultura (Caracas, Venezuela), December, 1938.

Secretaría de Educación Pública, Comisión Mexicana de Cooperación Intelectual, *Anales culturales de México* (continuation and supplements to *La cultura en México*, Nr. 1, Año II), Mexico City, 1943.

—— *Educación nacional;* monthly periodical, 1944.

—— *La cultura en México*, Vols. I-IV, 1942-43.

—— *Información pedagógica;* monthly.

—— *Maestro mexicano, El;* monthly.

Tiempo; weekly.

Universal, El; Mexico City daily.

Index

school aims assumed by, 115; forced to acquiesce in abrogating coeducation, 220
Aztec Indians, 9f., 17, 27
Azuela, Mariano, 187n, 214

Baccalaureate, certificate, 127, 128
Bakunin, Mikhail, 65
Bank of Mexico, 187
Banks, agricultural credit, 52, 57
Baranda, Joaquín, 41
Baranda, Manuel, 36
Barranco, Manuel, 13, 37, 38, 150; quoted, 30, 43, 59n, 74, 97, 204, 221; on the Catholic church, 223
Barreda, Gabino, 32, 125
Bases Orgánicas, 35
Bassols, Narciso, 51, 137
Becquer, poet, 214
Benjamin Franklin Library, 180, 217
Best-Maugard, 49
Beteta, Ramón, quoted, 221
Biological sciences, 122
Boarding schools, government: 86; importance, 107; functional specialties, 108; Military College, 146; boarding features in rural normal schools, 156
Bonilla y Segura, Guillermo, 18, 19n; quoted, 105, 142n
Book Fair, 209
Booktrade, colonial, 28, 166
Booth, George C., quoted, 33n
Boston University, 216n
Brenner, Anita, 48
Brito Foucher, Rodulfo, 173; quoted, 164
Budgets, *see* Funds
Buildings, requirements, 89; restrictions upon acquisition, 96; number of new classrooms needed, 163; university, 172, 178; demand for more, following segregation of the sexes, 220
Business interests, means of compelling provision of educational facilities for workers, 19, 53; employer-owned schools, 44, 106f.; balance values of education against cheap labor, 45; purpose of donations to schools, 82; employment by, and training for, industry, statistics, 192n; failure to aid universities financially, 200; effect of such aids to foreign universities, 201n
Bustamente, Miguel, 17

Cain, Henry L., 189
"Calendarios del Maestro," 18
Callcott, W. H., quoted, 38
Calles, Plutarco Elias, 15, 33n; administration, 49f.; impetus given normal schools, 151; and socialistic teaching, 173
Campus, few in Mexico, 178; model, in Monterrey, 199
Cárdenas, Lázaro, land redistributed, 6; administration, 51-55, 56; Six-Year Plan, 52ff.; "socialist school," 53ff., 63ff.; scale for allotments, 82; placed higher education under government control, 173
Carnegie Foundation, 216
Carranza, Venustiano, 210; quoted, 43; regime, 44, 45n, 47
Carrillo, Carlos A., elementary education, 41n
Carrillo, Julián, 211
Casa de España, 187
Caso, Alfonso, 12, 173; quoted, 8, 13
Caso, Antonio, 35n, 37, 187n; quoted, 59; outstanding philosopher, 170; doctrine, 170n
Castañeda, Estefanía, 93
Castillo, Arturo César, quoted, 204
Catholic, *see* Roman Catholic
Center of Historical Studies, 187
Centralism vs. federalism, 35; a triumph of practical circumstance; whether an evil in itself, 77
Central Plateau, 4, 9
Céspedes, Francisco, 77
Charles V, 25
Charlotte, Empress, 219
Chase, Stuart, 5
Chávez, Carlos, 187n, 211
Chávez, Ezequiel, 36, 187n
Chávez, Ignacio, 165, 187n
Chiapas, Institute of Science and Arts, 199
Children, characteristics, 90
Children's Educational Army, 18
Children's Theater, 96
Child Welfare Bureau, 92
Christianity, conversion of Indians to, 27f.
Chumacero, Alí, 214
Cien Mejores Poesías Mexicanas Modernas, Las, 217
Cities, five largest; populations, 8
Citizenship and voting right, 76

of government-controlled, 151; administrative bodies: distribution, 152; course of study, *tab.*, 153; rural, 155ff.; advanced study, 158; mental testing, 159; growth: suggestions for future improvement, 160; *see also* Teachers
Northrop, F. S. C., 2, 170; quoted, 172, 204*n*, 207f.
Novelists, 214
Nuevo León, University of the State of, 198
Nursery schools, 84, 92

Oaxaca, Institute of Science and Arts, 199
Obispo, San Nicolás, 167
Obregón, Alvaro, 43; remedial measures during administration, 46-49, 79, 222
Ochoterena, Isaac, 187*n*
Office of Colonial and Republic Monuments, 191
Office of Education, U.S.; mental-test material in Library, 160
Office of Prehispanic Monuments, 191
O'Gorman, Edmundo, 170*n*
Oil, 7
Open-air classes, 5
Ordónez, Ezequiel, 187*n*
Organic Law, 63, 106, 119; the *Bases Orgánicas* of 1843, 35; provision re elementary education, 37; government programs took official form in First, 42; Law of 1942 a main contribution of Véjar Vázquez, 56; prescriptions re rights to education and re government's obligations, 99; goal of "equal opportunity" set by, 110; basis for all secondary education, 123; provisions re vocational education, 137, 192; authority re normal schools, 151, 157; provision for higher education and scientific investigation, 190; legal basis for training in the arts and other extraschool cultural activity, 208
Orozco, José Clemente, 43, 48, 187*n*, 205-8 *passim*
Ortega y Gasset, José, 172*n*
Otis Elementary and Secondary tests, 159
Otomí language, 10

Painting and painters, 205-8; beneficiaries of government subsidies, 205
Pan American Highway, 4, 199

Paredes Oyen, Las, 217
Parental assistance to kindergartens, 93, 96
Parents' Bureau, 219
Parent-teacher associations, 218
Parsons, Wilfred, 12, 50, 52, 74
Party of the Mexican Revolution (PRM), 77
Paz, Octavio, 214
Pedro de Gante (Peter of Ghent), 28
Pellicer, Carlos, 214
Pensador Mexicano, El, 217
Pensions, 157
Peonage, 33
People's School of Dancing, 189
Periodical Library, 180, 217
Periquillo Sarniento, El, 217
Pestalozzi, Johann H., 28
"Pestalozzi," kindergarten, 93
Petroleum, 7
Philosopher, leading, 187
Philosophic concepts underlying educational system, 59-75, 98; influence of modern, upon university, 172
Philosophy, influences upon colonial university thinking, 165-71 *passim*
Philosophy and Letters, Faculty of, 180ff.
Physical Education, Normal School for, 154
Physical resources, 4
Physical sciences, 123, 126
Pintner-Cunningham Elementary test, 159
Plan de Acción de la Escuela Primaria Socialista, excerpt, 59
Plemán, Lucas, 150
Plenn, J. H., 13
Poetry and poets, 214
Poinsett, protégé of, 169*n*
Political appointees in academic field, 201
Political history, force and violence, 76; controlling parties, 77
Politics, student interest and influence, 178
Polytechnic Institute, *see* National Polytechnic Institute
Pomona College, 207
Ponce, Manuel, 210, 211
Pontifical University, Royal, 32*n*, 164-71; officially became National University (*q.v.*), 171
Population, largest cities, 8; estimated: distribution by race, 16

of campus life, 178; National Polytechnic Institute, 193f.; state universities, 198f.; institutes and discussion panels in U.S., 216*n; see also* Higher education, *and names,* e.g., National University
Ureña, Pedro Enríquez, 214

Vasconcelos, José, 170, 187*n*, 197*n*, 214; quoted, 4, 21; values of system constructed by, 46-49, 61; philosophy, 61; power of present Ministry due to energy of, 62; sympathy with Véjar Vázquez's views, 69; use of all cultural agencies as means of education, 204, 205
Vázquez Vela, Gonzalo, 54, 70*n*
Véjar Vázquez, Octavio, quoted, 8, 21, 22, 33, 69, 97, 149; liberal philosophy: aims and objectives, 55f., 67ff.; why failed to remain in office, 69; hailed for his "school of love," 70*n*
Velasco, Luis de, 29
Veracruz, Alonso de la, 32*n*
Veracruz, University of, 199
Vera Estañol, Jorge, 45*n*
Veterinary School, 143
Viking Foundation, 191
Villa, Francisco, 43, 210
Villagrán Prado, Francisco, 130, 186
Villarrutia, artist, 214
Viniegra, Gustavo, 110
Virgin's feast day, 14
Visits and trips, educational, 103*n*, 120, 121
Vital statistics, 16
Vives, Juan, 28
Vocational and technical training, 98, 135-48; organization, 84, 85; history of: schools established, 137; provisions of organic law, 137; prevocational schools,

138ff.; types of training: careers prepared for, 140-48; purpose terminal or preparatory, 141; courses of study, *tabs.*, 141f.; values appraised, 148; three stages, 190; trend toward practical: financial aid given, 192; statistics re employment and training for it, 192*n*; three institutions at pinnacle of program, 193-97; music study and other arts, 208-12 *passim*
Vocational guidance, 53
Voltaire, 170
Voting representation, 76

War, resolve to combat, 120
Watson, Goodwin, 54
Wilson, Irma, 11; quoted, 219
Wolfe, Bertram, 46
Woman suffrage, 76
Women, higher education, 187; increased participation in public affairs: humanizing effect, 188; change in status of: increasing opportunities for education, 219f.
Women's University of Mexico, 96, 187f.
Workers' University, 188f.

Youth Army, 18
Yucatán, instruction in Maya folkways and traditions, 10
Yucatán, University of, 199

Zabre, Teja, 29
Zacatecas, Institute of Science and Arts, 199
Zapata, Emiliano, 43; *corrido* on, *text*, 210
Zapata, Rosaura, 93; quoted, 92
Zubirán, Salvador, 173
Zuloaga, President, 169*n*
Zumárraga, Juan de, 28, 164, 167